Kala Pani: Caste and Colour in South Africa

Rehana Ebr.-Vally

KWELA BOOKS
and SA History Online

This book forms part of the Social Identities South Africa Series, and has been produced with the financial assistance of the National Research Foundation, and of the Delegation of the European Commission through the CWCI Fund

Published jointly by Kwela Books and South African History Online

Kwela Books
28 Wale Street, Cape Town 8001;
P.O. Box 6525, Roggebaai 8012
Kwela@kwela.com

South African History Online
P.O. Box 11420, Maroelana 0161
Info@sahistory.org.za
www.sahistory.org.za

Cover design by Liam Lynch and Omar Badsha
Photograph on cover by Omar Badsha
Book design by Nazli Jacobs
Set in Plantin
Printed and bound by NBD, Drukkery Street, Cape Town, South Africa
First edition, first printing 2001

ISBN 0-7957-0135-7

Social Identities South Africa
General Editor: Abebe Zegeye

The identities of South Africa and its citizens have been undergoing crucial changes since 1994, when the first democratic elections resulted in the demise of statutory apartheid. This has led to an emerging ethos of democratic rule among all citizens of South Africa. But, although changes in South African society are clearly visible in increased social mobility, migration, access to jobs, training and educational and general reform in South Africa, the nature and influence of the identities being formed in response is as yet less clear. The SISA project aims to determine the nature of some of these new identities.

The project is shaped by research that indicates the South Africans, while going through flux and transformation in their personal and group identities, have a shared concern about the stability of their democracy and their economic future.

Titles in the SISA Series jointly published by Kwela Books and South African History Online:

Social Identities in the New South Africa
After Apartheid – Volume One
Edited by Abebe Zegeye

Culture in the New South Africa
After Apartheid – Volume Two
Edited by Robert Kriger and Abebe Zegeye

Kala Pani
Caste and Colour in South Africa
Rehana Ebr.-Vally

Coloured by History, Shaped by Place
New Perspectives on Coloured Identities in Cape Town
Edited by Zimitri Erasmus

The I of the Beholder
Identity formation in the art and writing of Breyten Breytenbach
Marilet Sienaert

Contents

1. MAJOR INDIAN STATES

India in 1860

2. DISTRICTS OF ORIGIN OF PASSENGER INDIANS

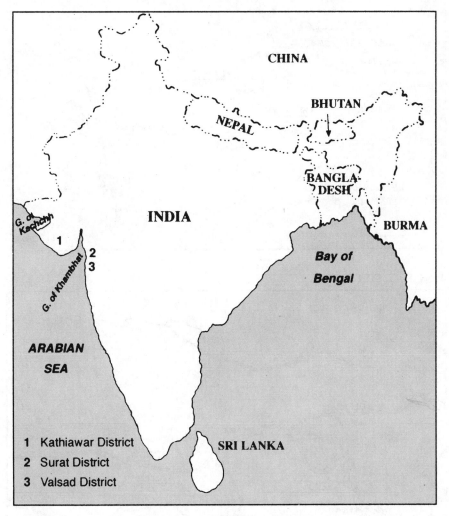

CHINA

BHUTAN

NEPAL

BANGLA-DESH

BURMA

G. of Kachchh

INDIA

G. of Khambhat

Bay of Bengal

1

2
3

ARABIAN SEA

SRI LANKA

1 Kathiawar District
2 Surat District
3 Valsad District

3. KATHIAWAR DISTRICT

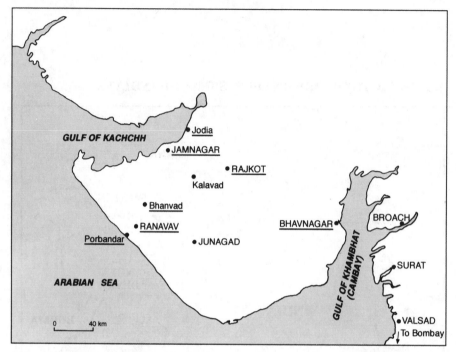

GULF OF KACHCHH

● Jodia

● JAMNAGAR

● RAJKOT

● Kalavad

● Bhanvad

● RANAVAV

Porbandar ●

● JUNAGAD

BHAVNAGAR ●

BROACH

GULF OF KHAMBHAT (CAMBAY)

● SURAT

ARABIAN SEA

0   40 km

● VALSAD

To Bombay

4. SURAT DISTRICT

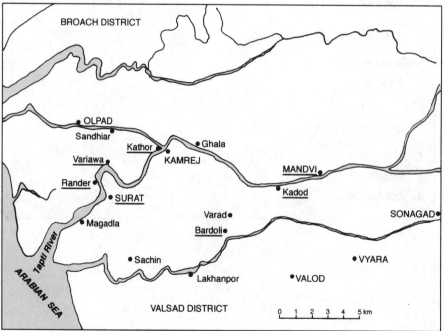

BROACH DISTRICT

● OLPAD

Sandhiar ●

Kathor ●

● Ghala

Variawa ●

KAMREJ

MANDVI ●

Rander ●

● Kadod

● SURAT

Varad ●

SONAGAD ●

Magadla ●

Bardoli ●

● Sachin

● VYARA

Tapti River

Lakhanpor

● VALOD

ARABIAN SEA

VALSAD DISTRICT

0 1 2 3 4 5 km

5. VALSAD DISTRICT

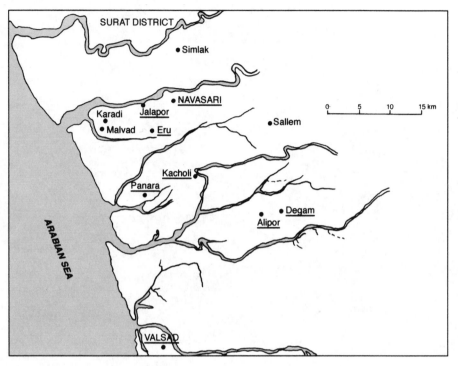

In Memoriam Prem Singh

Acknowledgements

I would like to thank the French Government for granting me a scholarship to further my studies at the Sorbonne University in Paris, and UNESCO for allowing me to complete my PhD in France.

My sincere gratitude to the National Research Foundation for facilitating the production and development of this book in English. In this regard I specially want to thank Lis Lange and Rachel Stewart for their patient editing of the manuscript.

I wish to thank the many friends in South Africa who took the time to find the documents pertinent to this research while I was abroad. To my friends and colleagues in France, and in particular to my supervisor, Dominique Colas, and to Denis-Constant Martin, I thank them for their patience in reading my French text and for encouraging me to publish.

Thanks also to Annari van der Merwe and her team at Kwela Books for their expert advice and kind assistance.

Last but not least, I wish to thank my mother, Zubeida Vally, and my friend Emmanuelle for their invaluable support all along.

Note on terminology

The noun *Indian* defines a range of concepts: it is the political identity of citizens of India, the country; it is used to attach people in the Indian diaspora to India; it is a distinct type of cuisine found alongside Chinese, Italian or French cuisine. It refers to people with distinct physical traits. In South Africa, where there is a recognisable community whose external features allow them to be attached to India, the designation and the self-appellation of 'Indian' applies.

Writing about people of Indian origin in South Africa requires a precision that allows one to understand the changes in their status in South Africa. The term 'Indian' is put between inverted commas to indicate a community in South Africa, as opposed to Indians from India. In this book they are considered an integral part of South Africa from the moment they declared their intention to remain in this country, despite the various governments' efforts to either repatriate or marginalise them.

Cover photograph: Mr Thakor Ravjee and his son Kamal at the Saptah Mandir, Prince Edward Street, Durban, circa 1985. The photograph was possibly taken at the celebrations of Krishnajayanti (Birth of Krishna) and is an excellent example of the importance of Indian tradition in the lives of some 'Indians'. Connecting with their perceived Indianness on auspicious occasions was, and is, one of the high lights in the quotidian for some 'Indians'.

Preface

Kala Pani ... Crossing the dark waters

> 'Then came the news that Mrs Tulsi had decided to send Owad abroad to study to become a doctor ... And at Arwacas some of Mrs Tulsi's retainers defected. Forgetting that they were in Trinidad, that they had crossed the *black water* from India and had thereby lost all caste, they said they could have nothing to do with a woman who was proposing to send her son across the *black water*. 'Water off a duck's back,' Mr Biswas said to Sharma. 'The number of times that mother of yours has made herself an outcaste!' There was talk about the suitability and adequacy of the food Owad would get in England. 'Every morning in England, you know', Mr Biswas said, 'the scavengers go around picking up corpses. And you know why? The food there is not cooked by orthodox Roman Catholic Hindus.'
>
> V.S. Naipaul, *A House for Mr Biswas*[1]

V.S. Naipaul's *A House for Mr Biswas* refers to two fundamental aspects of Hindu socio-cultural life: food and the belonging to a community. The importance of food and community can only be understood in the context of the caste system that regulates the life of all Hindu Indians. In the quote above, Mrs Tulsi's retainers react angrily to her sending Owad overseas to study. The focus of the anger is the voyage itself, the leaving the community and therefore *de facto* abandonment of a particular organisation of the world. The fear of the sea voyage is expressed in the metaphor of the crossing of the black waters, the *kala pani*. However, it is not just the decision to cross the sea that Mrs Tulsi's retainers are criticising. They are also aware of the perils involved in crossing the *kala pani*. Among these the most serious one was that at sea it would be difficult, if not impossible, to keep the dietary restrictions that accompany each caste. Breaking dietary prohibitions will cause contamination and impurity, which, in turn, will cause the individual to lose caste status. Thus, in *A House for Mr Biswas*, Naipaul captures the controversy that surrounded sea voyages among the Hindus. India is probably best known for its caste system. Generally accepted to be a social reality among Hindus, its influence on social organisation can to some extent be found among Muslims and Christians also. The caste system operates both at a social and at a spiritual level by defining the place that groups have in the world order. The social position of individuals is outlined within the caste system and it is only within the caste that the individual exists socially. This position in turn determines the limits of action by individuals and the boundaries of interaction between members of different castes. All individuals within this hierarchical system understand the position assigned to them. They generally marry within their caste and their social relations to a large extent are determined by the rules of the caste system. This general acceptance of the caste system as religiously ordained transforms it into a form of social control and surveillance that operates from the group to the individual.

The caste system can be regarded as a system of social function that is embedded in religion. It is, however, as will be seen in this book, far from static. In relation to the issue of the interdiction of sea voyages the 19th and 20th centuries represented a challenge to the interpretation of Hindu religious texts. The *Hindustani Review and Kayastha Samachar* in November 1903 discussed the dilemmas and controversies surrounding sea voyages; it grappled with the religious interdicts and approvals regarding sea travel in modern India:

> It is no doubt that in the comparatively modern Hindu Shastras there may be some condemnatory passages. But *slokas* from the Rigveda show that sea voyages were prevalent in ancient India. It should also be borne in mind that the only text against *samutra yatraswikaram* in the *Kali yug* has been interpreted by competent Pandits to mean the prohibition not of sea voyages as such, but the expiation of sins by drowning oneself in the sea [...] The text which interdicts *samudrayatra*, interdicts asceticism in the same breath. The authority of the text has long been disputed and never practically been obeyed, witness the long array of *sanyasis, sadhus* and *yogis*. Let the social leaders therefore judge practically and unfettered by consideration of authority and custom, utter the voice of abstract reason and say what will best conduce to the welfare of the *Kayastha* community.[2]

The controversy around sea travel in India sharpened during the British occupation. This tension was fuelled by the fact that the Indian Civil Service was more prone to employ persons with qualifications from abroad. In addition to this, to qualify as a barrister or to earn various specialised qualifications, study abroad, especially in the UK, was imperative. There was a strong incentive to leave the village in search of foreign qualifications. It meant improved social standing and the opportunity to become prosperous. The decision to educate a son abroad was normally taken by an individual family or by the student himself, who defied his family and travelled across the sea to England. While there was very little that the family could do once an individual had crossed the sea, leaving behind his community, religion found a way of readmitting those individuals who had lost their place in the community because of a voyage. A returnee could be readmitted to social privileges if he underwent a series of expiatory ceremonies. The decision to readmit the returnee was taken by the local *biradari* (fraternity). A feast, a contribution of money to local charitable purposes or an expiatory ceremony, the *praschhitya*, might be required.

The decision to leave the village and travel abroad was governed by the politics of the village and the caste system. Villagers understood their place and this was in many instances defined by the sharing and exchange of foods. The returnee, in conforming to the rules of reinsertion into the village, thereby accepted the local system of social control. This acceptance was expressed in the reinsertion ceremony by his declaration that he upheld the purity of the caste through the observance of food regulations.[3]

Indians who chose to come to South Africa during the latter part of the 19th century and the early 20th century probably experienced tensions around their crossing of the sea. The Hindus for whom caste represented the social and religious organisation of life undertook the journey to South Africa accepting that they could lose their caste status.

The immigrants' loss of caste status through the crossing of the *kala pani* represented only one part of the immigration process. Once in South Africa the second part of the process began, marked by the reconstruction of a world that reflected the structures they knew and with which they were comfortable. Indian immigrants to South Africa were probably regarded as outcaste in India, having chosen to seek a better life elsewhere, yet in South Africa the issue of caste did not disappear. Indians in South Africa regrouped themselves and reformulated the caste system to allow themselves to inhabit a world somewhat different to India yet similar enough to keep the memory of India alive.

---

1. Naipaul, V.S., 1978, *A House for Mr Biswas*, Penguin Books, England, pp. 349-350, emphasis added.
2. In *Selections from the Vernacular Newspapers Published in the Punjab, North Western Provinces, Oudh, Central Provinces and Berar*, 1881, pp. 160-1. Cited in Carroll, L., 1979, 'The Seavoyage Controversy and the Kayasthas of North India, 1901-1909', *Modern Asian Studies*, 13, 2, pp. 265-299.
3. For details on how food was an important during sea travel see Pearson, M.N., 1981, 'Indian Seafarers in the Sixteenth Century', in *Coastal Western India: Studies from the Portuguese Records*, Concept Publishing Company, New Delhi, pp.116-144.

Introduction

As a student in France in the 1980s and 1990s, I came into contact with people from all over the world. Some knew of Apartheid and had heard of Mandela but did not know of a country called South Africa. To them South Africa was a regional entity, not a country. South Africa was the equivalent of North Africa and my acquaintances, who were Moroccans or Tunisians or Algerians, would insist that I be more precise in situating my country of origin. Only the mention of Nelson Mandela would spark definite interest, even if in the end my mysterious land was 'Pretoria'.

Far from Apartheid South Africa and looking neither Black nor White, I was constantly required to substantiate, even justify, my origins. This was exacerbated in my encounters with Pakistanis, Sri Lankans and Indians living in France. In the streets of Paris, some chestnut and newspaper vendors would spontaneously greet me. They would try to establish contact by speaking to me in their mother tongue. My knowledge of Urdu and Hindi helped, but since I do not speak Tamil, I would proffer English or French. They saw me as a compatriot and would ask which part of *their* country I came from. My reply, that I did not come from their country, would elicit the enumeration of other possible homelands. If I was not from Pakistan or Sri Lanka, surely I was from Bangladesh or Mauritius. On telling them that I was from South Africa, they would try to find common ground between us and would see me as an *Africawalli*, a 'She from Africa'. They knew Africa as the land to which many of their compatriots emigrated a long time ago.

The common point in my encounters with people in France was that they saw me as Indian, Pakistani, Sri Lankan or Bangladeshi but not as African. This way of identifying people and placing them into a known and accepted context was disturbing. At first I was disheartened since, as a Black South African, I had chosen to distance myself from categorisations that recalled Apartheid policies of segregation based on culture and geographic origins. Soon, however, I understood that the mechanism of recognition to which I was subjected had no connection with any Apartheid policy. The way I look took precedence over the languages I could speak for the people I met.

My political identity of Black South African was a challenge to many people in France. The label 'black' that I insisted on using was to many synonymous with specific physical features that I do not have. My insistence on using 'black' introduced the register of colour into the conversation. Many people I met used the race and colour criteria to remind me that I was 'brown' rather than 'black'. The use of the racial label as a political choice within the South African context was too far removed to serve me as a definition in France.

In Apartheid South Africa, the segregationist regime used colour and later culture to ensure the supremacy of the White segment of the population. An effect of Apartheid legislation was that every South African acquired a precise political identity. The manner in which South Africans introduced themselves, among themselves or to people outside South Africa, reflected their attitude towards the politics of the country. Supporters of the Apartheid regime would comfortably use the categories imposed by the state. They would use them for themselves and to describe and define others. Opponents of the Apartheid regime refused to accept the imposed categories. They chose to use race, though in a different way, as the predominant criterion of identification. Thus, my use of Black South African was rooted in the realm of political identity.

Beyond an imposed political identity, ordinary South Africans were preoccupied with the travails of everyday life. The Group Areas Act and the Population Registration Act denied most South Africans the fundamental right of mobility. They were told where to live and how to live. Within these boundaries and despite being boxed into categories, ordinary South Africans found ways to express the socio-cultural aspects of their identity. They could name the communities they belonged to, their language, their religion, and where applicable and possible, their country of origin. It is within this context that I placed my research.

My encounters in Paris required that I explain the political situation in South Africa and, without realising it, I was explaining why I chose to be called a Black South African. My explanation was, albeit emotionally, an analysis of the politics of identity. I was, retrospectively speaking, expressing the different choices that the South African context and its politics allowed.

In 1990 I decided to visit India with friends from Paris and South Africa. This was to be my first trip to India, and I had already made up my mind that I was going as a tourist. I started from the premise that I knew nothing of the country. My friends and I visited the libraries, the Indian tourist bureau in Paris and bought travel guides to enable us to draw up a comprehensive itinerary. Going to India from Paris proved to be quite an adventure. My friends required entry visas and though I was aware of the politics between India and South Africa, I needed to be reassured. I therefore visited the Indian embassy in Paris where it was duly confirmed that as a South African of Indian origin I did not require a visa. I booked my air ticket to India but had first to convince the travel agent that the Indian authorities had waived any form of entry requirements for South Africans of Indian origin. This was the tacit state of affairs, though the Indian embassy refused to commit it to paper. As far they were concerned, I would not have any problems entering India. From others' experience I knew this to be a fact and decided that, despite the initial problems encountered at the travel agent, I should continue. My South African friends were travelling via Bombay and we were to meet in Delhi.

At the Paris airport, uncertainties about my entry into Indian territory began to emerge. The ground staff was reluctant to allow me to board the aircraft. According to their documentation South Africa did not feature in the list of countries whose citizens did not need visas. Finally, I was asked to sign an indemnity form absolving the Indian carrier of all responsibility should I be rejected at the port of entry.

Until the 1960s South Africans of Indian origin used to travel to India by ship. When India cut diplomatic ties with South Africa, 'Indians' had to find alternative routes and means of travel. Air travel was becoming acceptable and the majority of 'Indians' used to travel to India via Nairobi and later Mauritius. The net result was that every South African of Indian origin entered India through the port of Bombay. Since this was the case, the prospect of landing at the Indira Gandhi Airport in Delhi filled me with doubt.

At the airport, the customs official's first response was one of rejection. I calmly explained that I was probably an exception to the rule and that hardly any South Africans enter India through Delhi. Being able to talk Hindi helped. I was finally allowed to enter India with a visa stamped on a loose sheet of paper whilst my friends had theirs in their passports.

My visit to India raised a myriad questions. Why did the Indian government affix a detachable visa to South African passports? Did

the government in any way consider the South Africans of Indian origin as part of the Indian diaspora? Were South Africans of Indian origin the only segment of the South African population allowed into India? If so, were South Africans of Indian origin regarded as 'foreign
nationals' of India? During my stay in India, I hoped to find answers
and explanations to such questions. Proving that I was not Indian was
the burning desire that dogged me throughout the trip. From my accent and vocabulary in Hindi, Indians saw me as a 'foreign national'.
I looked like them but my behaviour, dress and language were different. My pleasure in being *different* was, nevertheless, seriously challenged in Pushkar.

We spent New Year 1991 in Pushkar and met two Rajastani gentlemen. Colonel was in his eighties. He was proud to tell us that he had
served in the Indian army during independence and after. His friend
was also a military official. At some point in our conversations, Colonel
brazenly pronounced a phrase that echoed in my mind for a long
time. 'You are a *Gujarati*.' I was taken aback. He was not wrong, but
how did he know? His response was curt: 'You look like one.' This baf-
fled me even more. For how was it possible that an Indian national
was able to correctly identify the area of origin of my ancestors, a
century after they emigrated to South Africa?

In India I was a tourist, yet being identified as Gujarati in the Rajas-
tan or the Maharashtra proved to be a frightening experience. I needed
answers. India could not provide them except by recognising me as a
'foreign national'. I accepted that my phenotype was akin to that of the
Indians but it was uncomfortable that an Indian could correctly locate
my origins. Despite my protestations of being a Black South African,
my Indian interlocutors saw me as a 'foreign' Gujarati. I had, despite
myself, become locked into the Indian diaspora. They would not acknowledge my Black South Africanness and saw me as an Africawalli:
she from Africa.

I understood the mechanisms of recognition used by my Indian interlocutors. As Indians they were used to recognising Indians from
the different regions of the country. Dress, language, accent, body
markings or, to a certain extent, physical traits are markers that an
expert eye could use to determine an individual's identity. My de-
portment, accent, dress and look in general were, however, different.

My interest in identity issues deepened. I began to ponder on the
mechanisms one uses to identify the other. Race, I realised, is one of

the obvious criteria in the process of othering. In Apartheid South Africa, the use of race as a classification generated the need to situate oneself in relation to the politics of the country. Closely tied to the race paradigm was the phenotype that – where possible – allows people to situate someone in a country. This was the case for me, constantly reminded of my Indian origins.

How are those people regarded as 'Indian' in South Africa perceived? Aside from their distinct physical features how do they see themselves and how are they perceived by others in the South African milieu? To try to answer these questions, I began researching 'Indian' identity in South Africa in the writings about this segment of South Africa's population. This was the origin of a doctoral thesis that constitutes the basis of this book.

The structure of the book reflects both the voyage of discovery that the search for the components of 'Indian' identity entailed and the methodological approach to the analysis of 'Indian' identity formation. Whilst the origin of the book is the question about the processes that took place after the crossing of the *kala pani*, the book itself starts off by placing Indians within Apartheid's racial classification. Part One deals with the legislative and ideological apparatus that justified and implemented Apartheid, tracing the genesis of Apartheid itself. Part Two proposes an exploration of the representation of 'Indians'. This section takes a close look at South African historiography on 'Indians'. It argues that most writing on Indians reinforced a view of the community as homogeneous, overlooking fundamental issues of social differentiation operating from within the 'Indian' community. In this section the narrative weaves the history of Indian immigrants to South Africa, who came as indentured labourers and passenger Indians, into the analysis of what historians have said about 'Indians' both before and after Apartheid.

The book starts its trip back in time and away from South Africa after first identifying the fundamental aspects of ethnic classification under Apartheid and the diverse voices that have narrated the history of the 'Indian' community and their perspectives. Part Three looks at the Indian origins of the 'Indians'. This section has multiple foci. The first is the examination of the caste structure and the role it has in guaranteeing Indian social structure and the order of the world as understood by Hindus. The second focus is on the ways in which Indian

immigrants to South Africa reorganised their worldview and their social behaviour in the new environment. What did they keep, what did
they lose, and how did they transform the caste system after having
crossed the *kala pani?* The third focus analyses the articulation between the social and spiritual axes of the caste system as re-created in
South Africa and explores its influence on religious rites and social
practices in the two largest Indian religious communities in South
Africa, the Hindus and the Muslims. The last part of this trip through
the constitutive layers of 'Indian' identity focuses on the present to
interrogate Indian identity in the context of the explosion, at least in
theory, of all ethnic identities after the demise of Apartheid.

Identity formation, it is argued throughout this book, is a two-way
dynamic process in which the presence of the other is an essential
component. Talking about 'Indian' identity implies also talking about
past and present stereotypes. The specific physical features of Indians
make them recognisable as such anywhere in the world. In South
Africa they also stand out as a distinct group. Yet, because of their history, South Africans have acquired some knowledge about what constitutes an Indian. This has led to the construction of stereotypes.
This stereotyping is necessary for it allows the non-'Indian' as well as
the 'Indian' to display their likes or dislikes of the other.

To the majority of non-'Indians' in South Africa, the 'Indian' is a
shopkeeper, likes gold, eats or sells samoosas, *kerriebols,* or curry and
rice. They eat spicy and hot foods. They have a distinctive ethnic dress
and their religions are also different. These basic identity parameters
have helped South Africans to create an image of the 'Indian' that allows them to articulate their otherness vis-à-vis the Indian.

Within the 'Indian' community differences are articulated to allow
subgroups to identify their members and to place other 'Indians' into
specific groups. These groups may be based on religious, linguistic, or
geographical criteria. These principles of differentiation were active
within the community during the colonial period and the Apartheid
era but, in general, the predominant image of 'Indians' was one of a
group defined through a supra-identity. The advent of democracy in
South Africa and the recognition of diversity became a reason for the
'Indians' to claim their specificity. Though the arguments of recognition are situated within the realm of religion, the effect is to consolidate the sub-communities as an integral part of South Africa's diverse
society.

'Indians' are South African; however, their experiences as South Africans have distanced them from India. For example, the men, as breadwinners who were in contact with other South Africans, opted to exchange their traditional dress for the acceptable Western style of dress. The difficulty in obtaining more than the basic Indian culinary ingredients imported from India influenced the 'Indians' to modify their cooking, to the extent that some Indians from the subcontinent are 'horrified' at the idea of calling South African 'Indian' cuisine Indian.

As regards cookery, Kumkum Bhasin, an Indian, came to South Africa in the middle of 1993. Her craving for homemade food was met by 'Indians' through invitations to their homes. After these experiences Bhasin decide to write the book *Simple and Easy Authentic Indian Cooking*,[1] which was presented as an 'attempt to reintroduce traditional Indian cuisine to the South African community'.[2] Kumkum Bhasin explores possible reasons for the absence of an *authentic* Indian cuisine in South Africa and emphasises the difference between 'Indian' cuisine and Indian cuisine.[3] Her disappointment with 'Indian' cuisine is captured in the following lines:

> Worried that we were missing out on home-food during our stay in the hotel, many South African Indians were very gracious and invited us to their homes for an Indian meal. True enough, we were very happy to be invited, *but somehow the food, which they claimed was Indian, turned out to be vastly different from the type to which we were accustomed in India.*[4]

It is within this context that the assertions of variety and similarity become fundamental. The process of 'Indian' identity formation is an example of how the contact between indigenous/settled and immigrant can influence changes and shifts within communities. Where necessary, members of the 'Indian' community refer to history to modify customs, rituals and other practices and habits of the present. Without the reality of the past, the malleability of the *now* cannot be explained. It is the ability to redefine the past in the present that has made the 'Indian' community so distinctly South African.

The advent of democracy in South Africa introduced political equality. The political identity as indicated in official documents is South African. But as citizens South Africans have also acquired the right to assert distinctiveness. Identity in South Africa as popularly expressed through the prism of culture needs to be examined. It is in this respect that a study of 'Indians' can raise questions about approaches to culture and identity in this country.

---

1. Bhasin, K., 1995, *Simple and Easy Authentic Indian Cooking*, Chris van Rensburg Publications, Johannesburg.
2. *Op. cit.*, p. 7
3. This she does through an injustice to Indian cuisine for she fails to recognise the regional diversity of cuisine, which is an expression of India's rich cultural mosaic. Furthermore her reliance on the pressure cooker leaves a bad aftertaste …
4. *Op. cit.*, p.7, emphasis added.

PART ONE

Tools for an ethnic divide

CHAPTER ONE

The social and political terminology of Apartheid

In South Africa, perhaps more so than elsewhere, concepts which normally are manipulated by an intellectual elite are being used by the majority of the people. What makes the South African case unique is the extent to which the formation and diffusion of concepts have been marked by Apartheid policies.

These concepts are expressed in a vocabulary that includes terms like 'race', 'population group', 'ethnic', '*Volk*', 'Bantu', and 'culture(s)'. These terms acquired a specific sense within the South African context and have often been used arbitrarily or vaguely, or are still used interchangeably, depending on the speaker's intention and the South African public's level of comprehension.

This chapter examines some general aspects of the social and political identity of South Africans by analysing the use made by South African rulers of a racial terminology, which, although being modified over the years, actually dates from the arrival of the Europeans to the Cape in the 17th century. In particular, the chapter focuses on the semantic divisions established in this terminology by successive governments. It is argued here that Apartheid South Africa's official sociopolitical terminology was instrumental in forging South Africans' self-perceptions, and that although not all South Africans have been influenced in their subjective identity by the objective identities imposed by the state, there is little doubt that the terminology has conditioned every South African's social and political representations.

Demographic data

Throughout South Africa's history there has been a mushrooming of specific terminology to describe demographic data. However, since 1948, Apartheid policy, largely based on this terminology, was not only given a 'scientific' dimension through anthropology but Afrikaner nationalism was also lent moral and scientific support by the *Volkekunde* (literally, 'the art of the people').

This analysis's point of departure will be the examination of the way in which official demographic data was presented in the *1988 South Africa Yearbook*, a propaganda document meant to depict a positive image of South Africa abroad. This particular breakdown of the demographic data was perpetuated in all official documents and speeches from 1948 – year of victory for the nationalist Afrikaners – until the release of Nelson Mandela in 1990.

Table 1: Major population groups and subgroups (estimates), 1985

GROUP	NUMBER
Zulu	6.4 million
Whites	4.5 million
Xhosa	2.9 million
Northern Sotho	2.9 million
Coloureds	2.8 million
Southern Sotho	1.9 million
Tswana	1.4 million
Shangaan-Tsonga	1.1 million
Swazi	1 million
Asians	820 000
Ndebele	440 000
Venda	180 000

Table 2: Composition by population groups (percent), 1985

YEAR	TOTAL	ASIANS	BLACKS	COLOUREDS	WHITES
1904	100.0	2.4	67.5	8.6	21.6
1911	100.0	2.6	67.3	8.8	21.4
1921	100.0	2.4	67.8	7.9	22.0
1936	100.0	2.3	68.8	8.0	20.9
1946	100.0	2.5	68.6	8.1	20.8
1951	100.0	2.9	67.6	8.7	20.9
1960	100.0	3.0	68.3	9.4	9.3
1970	100.0	2.9	70.4	9.4	17.3
1980**	100.0	3.3	68.0	10.5	18.2
1985***	100.0	3.1	68.8	10.3	17.8

Source: Central Statistic Service
** *Including self-governing Black states*
*** *Excluding the Republics of Transkei, Bophuthatswana, Venda and Ciskei*

In the 1985 census, the South African population was estimated at 6.4 million Zulu, 2.9 million Xhosa, 2.9 million North Sotho, 1.9 million South Sotho, 1.4 million Tswana, 1.1 million Tsonga, 1 million Swazi, 440 000 Ndebele, 180 000 Venda, 4.5 million Whites, 2.8 million Coloureds and 820 000 Asians. It is interesting to note that according to these official sources, this data did not include the population of the Transkei, Ciskei, Bophuthatswana and Venda Bantustans.[1] This population was however estimated at 3.3 million Xhosa in the Transkei and Ciskei, 1.5 million Tswana in Bophuthatswana and 340 000 Venda in Venda.

The aberrations of this demographic breakdown, of which the exclusion of the Bantustans – considered to be independent states – is only one, are in line with Apartheid propaganda and are also important indicators of the thinking behind the political and demographic breakdown which the founders of Apartheid created, used and vigorously promoted to serve their purposes.

By 1948 South Africa held the dubious distinction of having institutionalised racial differences within its population in order to achieve social discrimination. Later, in the 1970s, the South African government used 'cultural identity' and 'ethnic identity' as the criteria on which to base the cultural relativism that supported the segregation of specific cultural and ethnic identities. Thus justified, separate development – the formulation of Apartheid in the 1970s – was in some senses the culmination of the systematic racial segregation initiated in 1948. In order to understand the methodical division of the population as reflected in the above data it is necessary to have a closer look at the strategy of the different organs of the Apartheid state and the terminology they adopted, as this terminology was indeed one of the many vehicles of the state's ideology.

'Divide and rule': groups, subgroups and distinct people

The figures in Table 1 encompass a great variety of populations; each population group seems relatively small, with the largest one encompassing only 6.4 million people. The impression one gets here is a population divided and subdivided, of a mosaic of distinct people. 'Mosaic of people' has actually been one of the stereotyped expressions most commonly used to describe the South African population.

There seems to be some confusion about the use and understanding of the categories 'group' and 'subgroup'. Table 1, entitled 'Major population groups and subgroups', only presents one category, called 'group'. On the other hand, four groups are listed in Table 2 – 'Asians, Blacks, Coloureds and Whites' – suggesting that informed readers would be able to sort out the groups and subgroups by themselves. When examining this group/subgroup logic further, it becomes obvious that the only group that is subdivided into subgroups is the so-called 'Black group'. The twelve groups of Table 1 are down to four in Table 2. Three groups are to be found in both tables: 'Asians, Coloureds and Whites'. This misleading and blurred representation of the population in fact served to present a divided people and, above all, did not expose the White group as the minority it was, awarding it the second rank in size, immediately after the Zulu group. Despite all government efforts not even this carefully presented data could disguise the fact that Black people represented the vast majority of the population.

Population groups

How did Apartheid use the term 'population group'? Population group, a cornerstone of the official Apartheid terminology, forms part of an arsenal of social sciences concepts which, used in the particular South African context, assume a specific sense. However, the correct understanding of the concepts derives from the ways in which they were used in the official discourse. Here is an example:

> [...] its [South Africa's] population mix comprises substantive permanent communities [not random groups of individuals] representing the cultural identity of three continents – Europe (the Whites), Africa (nine distinctive Black peoples), and Asia (the Indians), as well as a large mixed race community.[2]

According to Martin West[3], 'population group' is a specifically South African term, invented by and for the Apartheid regime (1948-1990). It does not encompass a rigid reality and has allowed all sorts of abuses and transgressions. The interest of the legislators who wrote the Population Registration Act of 1950 resided in the preservation of the purity of the white race, threatened by a pre-1950s South African phenomenon: 'passing'[4]. One of many possible examples of 'passing' would be that of a person of mixed descent whose appearance was White and who decided to 'pass' to a White suburb in order to access the resources available to the Whites. The 'passing' could only be successful if the 'trespasser' was able to display compatible education, social habits and financial status. The 'passing' was done totally anonymously and in a solitary way, leaving behind family and friends darker in complexion. This practice, which has been traced back to the 19th century, would ensure that such a person's entire lineage acquired the status of a White person/family.

'Passing' prompted Apartheid legislators to establish strict frontiers between groups, in order to stop infiltrations. It was only natural that the National Party could not accept 'passing', fighting it through its legislative battery, first with the Population Registration Act, later reinforced by the Group Areas Act, the Prohibition of Mixed Marriages Act and the Amended Immorality Act.

Defining White

The Population Registration Act no 30 of 16 May 1950, according to which each South African was classified as belonging to a specific population group, was amended more than fifteen times between 1956 and 1986. This fine-tuning seems to prove the difficulty of classifying individuals within fixed groups. The law had to be adjusted to address a multiplicity of cases emerging from an unavoidable social mobility. Upon its creation, the Population Registration Act recognised three groups: the Whites, the Coloureds and the Blacks. Individuals belonging to these groups were supposed to have specific interests distinguishing them from the others.

It was not easy to legislate on racial and cultural segregation. Had it been simple to classify individuals according to groups, the state would not have had to modify, fine-tune and complete its definitions of the groups so many times. In fact, most of the Act is dedicated to the definition of what a White person is supposed to be, in order to prohibit access to the White group by any non-White person. More than an attempt to systematically define groups in general, the Population Registration Act was a monument of social engineering, erected to protect the purity of the White race and to guarantee its supremacy.

From 1950 onwards, each adult was listed on a central register and had to provide information such as name, gender, date and place of birth, population group, address, voting district and place of vote, date of registration or naturalisation as a South African citizen, date of arrival in South Africa if not born within the borders, family status, employment, language (linguistic group), and, for deceased persons, date and place of death. Blacks also had to specify their membership of a specific ethnic group and people neither Black nor White were classified as Coloured.

The first criterion used for classification was that of belonging to a race. On this criterion, Blacks and Asians obviously did not represent such a threat to the White group, being phenotypically immediately identifiable. Nevertheless, this criterion had to be refined and complemented by many others in order to cope with the difficult question of the classification of a Coloured person – and to avoid a White-looking Coloured person being classified as White. The Race Classification Board was created to ensure minimum infiltration.

Indeed, the only individuals who crossed the racial border between the Whites and the others were Coloureds. Only were they light in complexion and straight haired could they hope to cross the line. Other requirements for classification as a White included cultural criteria: fluency in Afrikaans, Afrikaans as a home language in most cases, level of education, religion, and an address in a White area. Those Coloureds who successfully managed their reclassification as Whites were in the majority schoolteachers, from well-to-do families, since being a schoolteacher presupposed access to higher education. Reclassification demanded very clever behaviour, both well thought-out and calculated. Indeed, those who wanted to be classified White had to break with their community and tacitly accept to live in anonymity. The belonging of each individual to a group had become the state's affair. Reclassification required the stamp of approval of the state.

State officials went as far as to implement extreme practices like the 'pencil test'. A state official would introduce a pencil vertically into the hair of the candidate for reclassification. Were the pencil to fall through, the conclusion would be that the candidate had a White person's hair. Were it to stay in the hair, the conclusion would be that the hair was too tight to belong to a White. The pencil test, with its role in determining the membership of a particular race group, was established thanks to the work of S.P. Cilliers, professor in sociology at the University of Stellenbosch, an Afrikaner university that produced most of the Afrikaner intelligentsia. Cilliers based his assertions on, among other things, his own observation on the behaviour of Coloured people:

> It was noticeable [...] that Coloureds attached more value to hair than to skin colour, since the Bushman and the Hottentot have also relatively light skins. A light skin did not necessarily indicate white ancestry, while a dark skin could be due to slave ancestry. Since the slaves were of a 'higher' cultural development than the aborigines, slave ancestry was not despised. Hair form, however, was a more accurate indication of 'primitive' or 'civilised' origin. Peppercorn or frizzy hair could only signify aboriginal ancestry, which came to be despised. Straight hair signified white or slave blood.[5]

Mistrust and suspicion were indeed the order of the day and the National Party was entirely aware of the fact that each light-skinned, straight-haired, White-looking Coloured could sooner or later be re-classified and so infiltrate the White group.

---

1. *South Africa 1987-1988,* 13th edition, new condensed edition, Official yearbook of the Republic of South Africa, edited by Ministry of Foreign Affairs, Pretoria, p.83.
2. In *South Africa 1987-1988, op.cit,* p. 83.
3. Martin West, 1988, 'Confusing categories: population groups, national states and citizenship' *in* Boonzaier E. and Sharp J. (eds), *South African Keywords, The Uses and Abuses of Political Concepts,* David Philip, Johannesburg, pp. 100-110.
4. On the 'passing', see G. Lewis, 1987, *Between the Wire and the Wall: A History of South African 'Coloured' Politics,* Citadel Press, Landsdowne, Cape Town.
5. S.P. Cilliers, *'The Coloureds' of South Africa: A Factual Survey,* Banier Publishers (Pty) Ltd, Cape Town, 1963, p. 27.

CHAPTER TWO

Apartheid, an empirically built fortress

The Population Registration Act of 1950 did not foresee the infiltration of Coloureds into the White group. This seems to indicate that the National Party did not take office with an Apartheid blueprint in hand. The various amendments and laws voted in between 1948 and 1961 indicate, rather, that the National Party worked empirically to build the monument of social engineering that was Apartheid. In other words, the National Party worked *a posteriori*, improving and fixing over the years what was to become the Apartheid system. Among anti-Apartheid circles it was indeed tempting – and is still so today – to assert that the National Party, taking power in 1948, had a blueprint ready for implementation. Brian Hunting, in *The Rise of the South African Reich*, wrote in 1969:

> [...] There has been nothing haphazard or laissez-faire about Nationalist rule, in striking contrast to previous regimes. Operating on the basis of a preconceived ideology, which has undergone very little change in the last fifteen years, the Nationalists have planned a strategy with care and worked step by step towards their goal. Nothing has been left to chance.[1]

The way in which laws were promulgated and amended over the years suggests instead that the National Party worked from the basic desire to maintain White supremacy and from the idea of large-scale segregation. The true social engineering of Apartheid could only have been built through the experiences of the party in office. Did Dr D. F. Malan not declare in Parliament on 2 September 1948 that 'the principle of Apartheid is that we have two separate spheres, not necessarily with an absolute dividing line, not separate territorial spheres'[2]?

Piet Cillié, editor of *Die Burger* newspaper from 1954 to 1978 and member of the *Broederbond*, supports this argument:

A system? An ideology? A coherent blueprint? No, rather a pragmatic and tortuous process aimed at consolidating the leadership of a nationalist movement in order to safeguard the self-determination of the Afrikaner.[3]

How is it possible to argue for a great Apartheid blueprint when the laws which were to give Apartheid's racial structure its very backbone were only promulgated two years after the National Party's victory, and when those same laws were to be amended again and again, each time more precisely, more systematically?

A particularly good example of the National Party's lack of a blueprint is the legislation around the Coloured population. This example is all the more eloquent as it does not fall within the Black/White paradigm. This intermediary category ended up encompassing ever-larger numbers of people, as the National Party's need to distinguish between White and non-White in order to protect its constituency grew. To understand the seven categories into which the Population Registration Act divided the Coloured group it is necessary to trace the terminology back to the early colonial period when the concern with miscegenation actually started.

The Coloured blur

Miscegenation in South Africa started with the arrival of Jan van Riebeeck in the Cape in 1652[4], and was to become an indisputable reality.[5] Europeans and the nomadic Khoisan people mixed. Europeans and slaves, whether local or imported, mixed. Miscegenation was so widespread that it produced a heterogeneous population of mixed blood people who were an integral part of the Colony. As J.S. Marais points out, 'In the first twenty years of its [the Cape's] existence, between 1652 and 1672, no less than 75% of children born at the Cape of slave mothers were half-breeds.'[6]

All these individuals would then be referred to as 'bastards'. The settlers soon started making distinctions between Europeans and non-Europeans and the terminology applied to the mixed population became more varied, including general notions like 'Kafir Proper', 'Baster', 'Coloured', *Kleurling* in Dutch – the latter applying equally to all non-Whites – and more specific denominations like 'Griqua'[7] or 'Malay'[8].

The Coloureds themselves used to differentiate between various possible combinations. A 'Baster' was the product of a relationship between Europeans and Khoisan. Only the 'Baster' could be considered a free person, not having any slave blood. The offspring of the slaves and the Europeans were 'Coloured' and remained in slavery.

Despite these nuances, until the beginning of the 20th century the term 'Coloured' referred to all 'non-Europeans'. The official Cape censuses of 1875 and 1891 did not make any distinction between 'Kafir Proper' and 'Coloured'.[9] The 1891 census indicated that the Cape population was comprised of two major categories: the Europeans or Whites and the Coloureds.

Thirteen years later, in 1904, the Cape census established an additional category, that of 'Bantu'. The novelty in the 1904 census was that Coloureds appeared for the first time as an intermediary group within which were placed all the individuals who did not belong to either the Black or White groups. Between 1891 and 1904, the urban Coloured population grew from 119 431 to 188 402 people. Over the same period, the rural Coloured population grew from 192 660 to 206 159 people.[10] The origins of a Coloured identity in the Cape are not only related to demographic growth but also to a series of events that made it necessary for the Coloured population to be differentiated from Black Africans. The first important event was the discovery of diamonds on Griqua land, on the banks of the Orange and Vaal Rivers, in 1867. The second event was the 1901 plague epidemic in the Cape.

In both cases Coloured people needed to distance themselves from the ill-fortune of the Black African population. In the second half of the nineteenth century African workers employed by the diamond diggers were treated appallingly. In this context the population of mixed origin were to organise themselves as Coloureds in order to defend their social and economic interests, which were perceived not to coincide with those of the Black population. The very first Coloured political organisation was formed in 1883 in Kimberley, and was called the Afrikaner League. In 1901, as the Cape Colony was ravaged by the plague, all non-Europeans were moved out of the Cape as a prophylactic measure. The Cape's Coloured population used the situation to introduce differentiation between themselves and the Blacks. This differentiation was probably based on colour and language. Coloureds spoke Afrikaans and were of a lighter complexion and were therefore different from Blacks. Whatever the colonial authorities thought of this distinction, the fact is that 7 000 Blacks were deported from the Cape Colony to the Uitvlugt Compound, as a way of managing the plague.

The aberrations of the classification system

The Afrikaner nationalists who prepared and amended the Population Registration Act in 1950 and beyond used categories or subgroups that already existed in the classification of Coloureds in the Western Cape. In 1959, the Population Registration Act specified that the Black and Coloured populations could by proclamation be subdivided into 'ethnic and other groups'. Six years later, in 1967, a Supreme Court judgment declared this 'void for vagueness', creating the need to specify subgroups. Section 5 (1) of the 1967 Population Registration Act was reworked and the Coloured group was from then on to be subdivided into Cape Coloured, Malay, Griqua, Chinese, Indian, Other Asiatic and Other Coloured. Individuals were declared as belonging to one of these subgroups according to either the classification of their natural father, or because they were members of that subgroup or because they were generally known as members of such a subgroup.

These groups were defined by 'race, class or tribe' and, in the case of the Indian, the Chinese[11] and the Other Asiatic, to a national home geographically located outside South Africa.[12] The open categories – Other Coloured and Other Asiatic – were used like a 'miscellaneous' file, under which all ill-defined persons could be given a label. A Coloured person from outside the Cape would be classified as Other Coloured. Other Asiatic would comprise all persons originating from Asia, other than from India and China.[13]

The Population Registration Act was an official attempt to classify systematically all individuals. The reality of this attempt to divide and enclose people into separate entities is well illustrated in the table below, which shows the requests for reclassification by South Africans during 1986:[14]

RECLASSIFICATION	REQUESTED	GRANTED	REFUSED
White to Cape Coloured	9	8	1
Cape Coloured to White	506	314	192
White to Malay	2	2	–
Malay to White	14	9	5
Indian to White	9	4	6
Chinese to White	7	7	–
Griqua to White	1	1	–
Cape Coloured to Black	40	35	5
Black to Cape Coloured	666	387	279
Cape Coloured to Indian	87	81	6
Indian to Cape Coloured	65	63	2
Cape Coloured to Malay	26	25	1
Malay to Cape Coloured	21	21	–
Malay to Indian	50	43	7
Indian to Malay	61	53	8
Cape Coloured to Griqua	4	4	–
Griqua to Cape Coloured	4	2	2
Griqua to Black	2	2	–
Black to Griqua	18	16	2
Cape Coloured to Chinese	12	10	2
Black to Indian	10	9	1
Black to Malay	2	2	–
Black to Other Asiatic	5	1	4
Indian to Other Coloured	2	2	–
Other Coloured to Indian	1	1	–
TOTAL	**1 624**	**1 102**	**522**

It is interesting to note that the largest number of requests emanate from Blacks wanting to be reclassified as Cape Coloureds (666) and from Cape Coloureds wanting to be reclassified as Whites (506). The

Coloured category represented a transitional step between Black and
White, the way to a better life, a life as a White, in a White area with
White privileges. In this sense being reclassified as Coloured marked
a sort of halfway stop in the upward movement to become White. The
high refusal rate for those upward-looking requests – 42% failure for
Blacks and 38% failure for Coloureds – suggests that the state was
particularly careful when it came to reclassifying upwards Black and
Coloured people.

Opposition critics towards classification

The constant classification and reclassification of people, which was
made all the more confusing and laborious through its empirical bases,
had as its ultimate goal the creation of the narrowest possible definition of 'White'. In other words, an entire bureaucratic apparatus was set
up to classify neatly the vast majority of the South African population
into groups and subgroups in order to keep 'White' separate and un-
soiled.

In 1950, when the National Party had the draft of the Population
Registration Act almost ready, the opposition, led by General Jan Smuts,
reminded the governing party of the delicate and difficult nature of the
task:

> [...] Don't let us trifle with this thing, for we are touching on
> things which go pretty deep in this land.[15]

The 'things' Smuts was referring to were in fact the classification of
Coloureds, and miscegenation. For the opposition party,[16] the Population Registration Act was an attempt to 'classify the unclassifiable'.
Moreover, they thought it impossible to implement. W.H. Stewart, MP
for the United Party, argued during the Parliamentary debates on the
act:

> He (the Minister) has taken care of all the particulars you could
> possibly want about the Europeans and all the particulars you
> could want about the Coloureds, mainly because he is going to
> attempt to solve the unsolvable problem, the absolutely unsolv-
> able problem as to what is actually a pure white person, what

is a pure Coloured person (if you can get a pure Coloured person) and what is the subtle mixture between the two, and which is which and which is the other. That is the problem he is trying to solve. God help him; he is up against the problem of the ages; it is unsolvable, and he knows it.[17]

The United Party was underlining the profound confusion around Coloured and White identity and how the implementation of the Population Registration Act, far from solving the problem, was going to worsen it. The opposition, unlike the National Party, knew only too well that 300 years of miscegenation had had an impact on all communities and that nobody, much less the Whites, could come out of the classification process unspoilt. The pain and suffering that would inevitably arise from the investigations required by the new act did not escape the legislators.[18] The opposition lambasted the text of the act, comparing it to Nazi racial laws:

I [Mr M. Kentridge] refer to clause 8 (2) of the Bill which provides that once the register has been drawn up and the Director has decided who is White and who is *Coloured*, it is open to the public at any time to go along and examine it, and it is open to members of the public to act as informers, to act as blackmailers, to act as snoopers. We can imagine what will happen. If my name appears on that register as a White person and they think for a moment that I have some Coloured blood in me, they could go and report me to the Director and they could have my name taken off that list. I take my own case as an illustration because Hon. friends opposite probably know that the Jewish race, to which I have the honour to belong, is probably one of the purest races, but I would like to tell Hon. members opposite that scientist Julian Huxley and other scientists in dealing with this matter, have declared repeatedly that there is no such thing as a pure race in the world, and particularly in a multiracial country such as South Africa. I say that Clause 8 may prove a boomerang to those people in South Africa who want this legislation because they believe they are White, because it may be possible for any member of the public to come along at any time and inspect the register and make a report to the Director, and then they will begin to worry whether they had any

Coloured blood in them some generations back, and if it is proved that they have Coloured blood in them, in spite of their associates, they will find themselves removed from the European list and placed on the Coloured list. I want to say to my Hon. friends over there that that has been the experience of Nazi Germany. It was found that no-one was safe in Nazi Germany. Not only did the ordinary blackmailer, the ordinary informer, the ordinary snooper, carry tales to the Nazi authorities, but even children were prepared to expose their parents.[19]

The act was passed by a mere seven votes, 63 against 56. The Nationalists certainly were hoping that they could contain the flux and change caused by social mobility which, if left uncontrolled, could mean the disappearance of the White race, or, at least in the short term, the loss of their political power.

The other apartheid laws: empiricism at work

Along with the semantic machinery provided by the Population Registration Act, the Nationalists armed themselves with a whole battery of laws that were to govern the minutest aspects of every South African's life, and, in the end, divide and shut South Africa away from the world. However, laws such as the Prohibition of Mixed Marriages Act (1949), the Group Areas Act and the Amended Immorality Act (1950 and 1957) were also empirical stepping stones that helped the development of Apartheid social engineering.

The Immorality Act

The fact that poor Whites used to live far away from their more fortunate brethren but close to the Africans (servants, farm labourers, or neighbours) facilitated interracial relations and the birth of illegitimate children.[20] This was a permanent concern of all governments since the beginning of the 20th century, since miscegenation was seen as one of the most serious threats to White supremacy. It was against this backdrop that the Jan Smuts-led government introduced the Immorality Act in 1927, which prohibited any form of sexual relations between Africans and Whites.

The intentionally strong religious and moral connotations in the choice of the term 'immorality' indicate that legislators were acutely aware that religious ministers, through their access to the illiterate population, were the most reliable transmitters of the Union's official policy. Legislators could rely on the fact that these zealous representatives of God's law, as well as the most ardent amongst their followers, would ensure respect for this law. The condemnation of sexual relations between Africans and Whites was in line with the position of the Dutch Reformed Church against any relations between Christians and Africans, these latter being 'pagans' and 'animists'.

That the Immorality Act was designed to reduce miscegenation should not obscure the fact that the choice of terms used in the law reflected strongly the Christian context within which relations between Whites and Africans took place. In the last analysis the purpose of the law was to prohibit relations between Christians and non-Christians. The limitations of this notion were soon to become evident since the vast majority of the Coloured population was Christian. Thus, despite law, religion and morality, miscegenation would continue under the noses of the lawmakers.

The Prohibition of Mixed Marriages Act and the Amended Immorality Act

When the Nationalists came to power in 1948 two more steps were taken to consolidate the Immorality Act of 1927, through a more thorough separation of all population groups: the Prohibition of Mixed Marriages Act in 1949 and the first amendment to the Immorality Act in 1950.

The Prohibition of Mixed Marriages Act banned marriages between Whites and non-Whites[21] and rendered null and void those mixed marriages of South Africans which took place abroad. In the meantime,

> Between 1930 and 1950, the number of mixed marriages actually declined from 9.5 for one thousand to 2.8 for one thousand and between 1943 and 1946, fewer than hundred mixed marriages per year took place against an annual total of almost 30 000 of white couples.[22]

The law simply accelerated an already existing tendency. On 12 May 1950 the 1927 Act was amended to also prohibit extra-marital relationships between Blacks and Whites. Offenders were sentenced to jail. Charles R. Swart, Minister of Justice, explained the aim of the act during his presentation of the law in Parliament on 1 March 1950:

> [...] The purpose of the Bill is to end the further mixing of blood between Whites and non-Whites so that the dimensions of the race problem would not be any more serious in the future than it is at present.[23]

The Group Areas Act

The Group Areas Act no 41 of 1950, adopted on 7 July, determined and controlled the space in which each population group – as defined by the Population Registration Act – was to be (re)located and live, and reinforced the effects of the Amended Immorality Act. This law, which guaranteed the physical separation of Blacks, Coloureds and Whites by confining each group to different geographic areas,[24] was meant, as its subtitle indicates, to 'provide the establishment of group areas, for the control of the acquisition of immovable property and the occupation of land and premises, and for matters incidental thereto'.

By the early 1950s the utilisation of the term 'group' in South African legislation was sufficiently well established for it to become part of the title of the new act. Since the 'groups' included in the new legislation were those defined in the Population Registration Act of 1950, Indians, still classified as Coloureds, did not appear as a separate group. In 1950, the National Party still hoped that Indians would eventually go back to India. They only became a permanent population, and therefore a population group, in 1961.

Lawmakers thought up the Group Areas Act out of the fear of racial conflict. As Dr T.E. Dönges, Minister of Home Affairs, put it at the presentation of the law to Parliament on 14 June 1950:

> Now, this, as I say, is designed to eliminate friction between the races in the Union, because we believe, and believe strongly, that points of contact – all unnecessary points of contact – between the races must be avoided. If you reduce the number of

the points of contacts to a minimum, you reduce the possibility
of friction [...] The result of putting people of different races together is to cause racial trouble.[25]

Dönges' speech reflects two different levels of White fear. On the one
hand is the fear of the loss of economic and political power and the
fear of seeing *their* race disappear through miscegenation. On the other
hand, there seems to be the fear of the unknown. It is the fear of the
Other which underlies the willingness to live in separate spheres. Thus,
through locking up each group in a geographically confined area, Whites
in general, and Afrikaners in particular, hoped to live hermetically and
become impenetrable to invasion by other groups. The Group Areas
Act locked and bolted South African society in such a tangible and
objective manner that communication between individuals from different groups became almost impossible.

One of the consequences of the law was the involuntary exodus of
the population. Up to the 1950s it had not been unusual to find people
of different races living together in poor urban neighbourhoods. With
the enacting of the law people were forced to leave their neighbourhoods and even those who owned their houses had them expropriated.
This was possible because the actual land rights belonged to the state,
which could repossess the land and then decide on its redistribution.
In order to implement the act the Apartheid government created new
structures in the state. The Land Tenure Board was followed by the
Group Areas Board, which had the power to recommend the allocation
of a certain area to a particular group and to decide on the portion of
an area to be sold to members of a group. White civil servants could
buy a piece of land at an official rate and then sell it at a higher price to
members of the group for whom the land was designated, should the
latter be able to afford it. This was the start of the forced removals.
Anyone who happened to live in an area targeted by the law had to
leave home and business to move to the Black or Coloured townships,
sometimes thirty or forty kilometres away from the urban centres. Township residents were allowed to work in the city, but had to go back at the
end of the working day. Special authorisations were, of course, given
to resident domestic servants who had to stay at their workplace either
because they worked full time or because they lived too far away.[26]

This spatial redistribution represented an incredible trauma for Black,
Coloured and Indian individuals. Although the National Party speci-

fied that everyone would have to make sacrifices, and insisted that it was not a segregationist measure, figures indicate that in 1976, 306 000 Coloureds (i.e. 1 out of 6) and 153 000 Indians (i.e. 1 out of 4) had been displaced, against 5 900 Whites (1 out of 666).[27]

The attempt at 'preserving interracial harmony', which was indeed the cornerstone of Apartheid, was based on the state's authoritarian and systematic control over individuals' private lives, guaranteed by the law. This caused the deepest trauma in South African society. As Prime Minister D. F. Malan put it in Parliament in 1950:

> What we have in this Bill before us, is Apartheid. It is the essence of the Apartheid policy, which is embodied in this Bill [...] most crucial for determining the future of race relations.[28]

Needless to say, the impact of the Group Areas Act was the most dramatic on the lives of 'non-Europeans'. In fact the act not only reinforced the effect of previous laws but it caused a mushrooming of legislation prescribing where people should live, conduct businesses, go to university and school, and even what friendships they should give up.[29]

In order to deal with the relations between races in South Africa the Nationalists chose to institutionalise the existing racial divisions. The enactment of the Population Registration Act law gave each South African an *objective* racial/ethnic identity; in other words, an imposed identity, like the identity given to an object through a name, or through a label stuck onto it depending on its shape and origin. The law determined the membership of a group through the apparent phenotype, and through a wide array of religious, linguistic and cultural criteria, which went as far as including clothing and social habits. By denying individuals the right to define who they were themselves the Apartheid state dispossessed them of their own identity, or at least managed to repress its expression.

---

1. B. Bunting, 1969, *The Rise of the South African Reich*, Hammondsworth, p.132.
2. W.K. Hancock, 1968, *Smuts – The Fields of Force 1919-1950*, Cambridge University Press, p.501.
3. Piet Cillie, Spring 1988, 'Bestek van apartheid: Wat is (was) Apartheid?', in *Die Suid-Afrikaan*, p.18.

4. Jan van Riebeeck was mandated by the Dutch East India Company to found the Cape Dutch Trading Post on the way to India.

5. However, historian Bernard Lugan – a lecturer at the French university of Lyons III – avoiding the issue of interbreeding, concludes: 'The vast majority of van Riebeeck's 80 companions were single men. This did not change much over time, with a ratio of one woman to ten men being the average amongst new arrivals in the Cape. This is how, from 1778 until 1807, out of 738 arrivals, there were only 64 women. If the Afrikaner population could grow so fast, it was thanks to the fecundity of their women, now legendary [sic].' Bernard Lugan, 1986, *Histoire de l'Afrique du Sud de l'Antiquité à nos jours*, Collection Vérités et Légendes, Perrin, Paris, p.60.

6. J.S. Marais, 1957, (1939), *The Cape Coloured People 1652-1937*, Wits University Press, Johannesburg.

7. The 'Griquas' are the offspring of Whites and Khoisans. This particular group was given this name when it joined the tribe of the *Grigriquas* on the banks of the Orange River in the 19th century, under the command of Adam Kok and later of Barend Barends. It is to be noted that the choice of a Griqua identity was a deliberate one by the individual; the Griqua denomination was not based on genetic criteria.

8. It is interesting to note that the Malays, who came from the Malay archipelago, arrived as Muslims. By extension, any person of the Muslim faith in the 19th century in the Cape was called Malay, regardless of their skin colour and their origins. This way, a Scot who converted to Islam automatically became a Malay and consequently was given the social and religious identity of a non-European. See G. Lewis, 1987, *op. cit.*

9. See I. Goldin, 1987, 'The Reconstitution of Coloured Identity in the Western Cape', in S. Marks and S. Trapido (eds), *The Politics of Race, Class and Nationalism in Twentieth Century South Africa*, Longman Group, United Kingdom, pp. 156-182.

10. G. Lewis, 1987, *op.cit.*, p.12.

11. After the 1899-1902 Anglo-Boer war, Chinese labour was imported and in 1906, 50 000 Chinese – most of them illiterate – from Canton were employed in the mines of the Witwatersrand. When Black labour started to be used more extensively, the Chinese workforce became redundant and the immigrant population was sent back to China between 1908 and 1910. The second wave of migrants from China took place in the 1920s. These were largely educated people, and were traders in diamond and gold. According to the 1985 census, there were approximately 11 000 Chinese in South Africa, all of them classified as Asians.

12. P.Q.R. Boberg, 1977, *The Laws of Persons and the Family*, Juta, Cape Town, p. 109.

13. Japanese people, very often business people and not permanently residing in South Africa, were given the status of 'Honorary Whites' [sic].

14. Table reproduced from M. West, 1988, *Confusing Categories*, *op. cit.*, p. 106.

15. Jan Smuts quoted in H. Giliomee and L. Schlemmer, 1989, *From Apartheid to Nation-Building*, Oxford University Press, Cape Town, p.82.

16. Opposition to the National Party was led in 1948 by General Jan Christiaan Smuts (1870-1950) from the United Party (the former South African Party). Smuts, an Afrikaner, was Prime Minister from 1919 to 1924 and liked to be referred to as a *Boer*. His genealogy in South Africa went back to 1692, and he was a fervent patriot. The opposition was opposed to the very idea of the Population Registration Act, as it argued that it was sheer utopianism and would be an extremely costly enterprise. The law, for instance, required that each person have a photograph taken, to be stuck onto his or her pass. The opposition argued that there was neither enough photographic equipment nor police resources in the country, and that Africans would provide unusable information to the police as far as residential addresses were concerned. The opposition also opposed the plan to make the pass compulsory for women. Smuts and his party considered it humiliating for a woman to be arrested on the street and interrogated by a policeman. (Women were to be exempted from carrying the pass but not from the compulsory possession of a pass. In 1952, the Native Co-ordination of Documents Act was to require African women to always carry a pass.)

17. H.A.D., 1950, cols. 6568-6569.

18. The unavoidable consequence of the promulgation of the Population Registration Act was that the state would be faced with a vast number of requests for reclassification from Coloureds. The Nationalists knew as early as 1950 that they would have to deal with an estimated 100 000 such requests from a Coloured and White population estimated at 6 million. However, in 1956, the Minister of Home Affairs declared that authorities had already processed 18 469 cases and that 90 000 requests still remained to be examined.

19. H.A.D. 1950, 6582-6583.

20. Everything separated poor Whites from educated upper class Whites, with language being one of the barriers. Educated Whites spoke High Dutch while poor Whites spoke various dialects, which were used among poor Whites, between them and their servants, and among servants if the servants did not speak the same vernacular. This White proletariat did not have access to the privileges reserved for the White upper classes. They lived in promiscuous proximity to non-Europeans, and were socially and economically excluded from White residential areas.

21. This term was used by the National Party to designate all individuals who did not belong to the White race. It was very widely used in segregated South Africa in shops, public places, buses, etc.

22. H. Giliomee and L. Schlemmer, 1989, *op.cit.*, p. 82-83.

23. E. Riley, 1991, 'Major Political Events in South Africa 1948-1990', in *Facts on File*, Oxford and New York, p. 20.

24. Black Africans, although covered by the 1950 Group Areas Act, were already the victims of several laws regarding domicile and property. The Land Areas Act of 1913 prohibited them from possessing and acquiring land. The places in which they were allowed to work but not live had been determined by the Native Areas

Act of 1920. In 1920, racial conflicts sparked by unemployment were spreading in the urban areas, and unskilled Whites found themselves competing with unskilled Africans. There also was a notion that cities were the Whites' reserved territory. Africans living in urban areas started to show a political consciousness and were immediately perceived as a threat. The 1920 law, amended in 1923 to become the Urban Areas Act no 21, allowed the state to control the entry of Blacks into White residential areas, especially in the urban ones, through the compulsory pass. Only Black Africans had to carry the pass. The Group Areas Act therefore refers to Blacks in all aspects of the law not relating to property, since they were already excluded from land ownership.

25. M. Western, 1984, 'Social Engineering through Spatial Manipulation: Apartheid in South African Cities', in C. Clarke *et al*, *Geography and Ethnic Pluralism*, Allen & Unwin, London, p. 115.

26. Group Areas Act no 41, 1950, section 4 (1): '[...] no disqualified person shall occupy and no person shall allow any disqualified person to occupy any land or premises in any group area to which the proclamation relates, except under the authority of a permit.' And section 4 (2) (a): '[A disqualified person could occupy a land or premises ...] as a bona fide servant of employee of the state, or a statutory body, or as a domestic servant of any person lawfully occupying the land or premises.'

27. Data extracted from H. Giliomee and L. Schlemmer, 1989, *From Apartheid to Nation-Building*, *op. cit.*, p.89.

28. H.A.D. 1950, Cols 7722, 7726.

29. The Immorality Act was amended in 1957 to prohibit any intimate relationship, whether sexual or not, between Black and Whites.

CHAPTER THREE

Social anthropology and *Volkekunde*

To turn Apartheid laws into a policy embodying the Nationalist Party's will 'to be fair' segregation had to be given a 'universal' character. Prime Minister D.F. Malan's speech in Parliament in 1950 contained all the ingredients that the government would use to justify Apartheid policy:

> [...] what justice is there for the non-European if he is in the position in which he is today? He will always have a sense of inferiority. He is unable to do justice to himself. On the basis of Apartheid, however, with his *own residential area*, he will be in a position to do justice to himself. There, he will be able to live his own life – there, he *can develop what is his own*, and only by the maintenance and the development of what is your own can you uplift yourself and uplift your people.[1]

The Nationalists came to power with the idea of an obligatory segregation. Over the years they amended and fine-tuned their first laws to respond to changed circumstances and new experiences. The different versions of these laws introduced the common usage of two different types of terms. On the one hand, there were very precise terms, such as 'classification', 'immorality', 'group', 'township', which, as we have seen, were used to impose an objective identity onto each individual. On the other hand, there were terms such as, 'race', 'tribe', 'ethnic group', 'culture', and 'class', the meanings of which were imprecise and which were used tentatively according to circumstances. All these terms became part of the day-to-day life of common South Africans as much as they penetrated the world of their beliefs and ideas. Due to the way in which terminology became part of the quotidian it is not enough simply to examine the creation of Apartheid terminology. Analysing the usage of this terminology is just as important.

The terminology

All Apartheid laws concerning population were based on the broad division of the population into three groups: Black, White and Coloured. The groups, as defined by the Nationalists, 'are deemed officially to have separate, identifiable interests and characteristics which distinguish them from other groups'.[2]

The categorisation of individuals into groups was done in two steps that involved first labelling people randomly according to mainly physical traits, and then classifying them according to language and religion. The development of categories implies more often than not a unilateral decision of those who create it and therefore classification is carried out without the consent of those being categorised.[3] In this sense, a category cannot be but an expression of its 'creator's subjectivity'.[4]

The categorisation of South African people was based on race for the Whites and the Blacks, on miscegenation for the Coloureds and on the criterion 'other race than White or Black' for the Chinese, Indians and Malays, none of which were criteria of their making.

The Nationalists raised the notion of group to that of a category. But were the groups created by Apartheid social groups from a sociological or anthropological perspective? Without dismissing the theoretical difficulty of defining a social group,[5] it is generally accepted that social groups have two main characteristics. On the one hand their members establish close and exclusive social relations. In other words, the members of a group can identify who belongs to the group and who does not. The second characteristic of a group is that it involves itself in social action by delegating authority to some of its members.

Taking this into account the 'groups' defined by the Nationalist government did not constitute social groups. In this sense what the Nationalist Party did was to give South African individuals an ascriptive identity.[6] How could the so-called Coloureds, as defined in 1950, have identified common characteristics for themselves? How could an Indian from Natal whose ancestors had immigrated at the end of the 19th century associate with a Cape Coloured? What could a Chinese and a Malay, of slave descent and Muslim faith, have in common?

It was not by chance that the Apartheid government divided people on the basis of ascriptive identities. It has been argued that the National Party divided and subdivided population groups to minimise the infiltration of 'foreign elements' into the White group. The more subdivisions within the other groups, the less chances of the White race being submerged under others. Moreover, the subdivision eventually allowed for a justification of segregation under the guise of separate development.

The promulgation of laws to guarantee segregation was, however, not enough. It was necessary to demonstrate to those very groups and to the world at large that Apartheid had laid its foundations in Western thought, and that Western thought did not contradict the Apartheid ideology. Disciplines such as philosophy, anthropology and the natural sciences were used by the architects of Apartheid to give credibility and assert the validity of the separation between mutating racial groups. As we will see, two periods are particularly important in the development of a scientific justification of Apartheid ideology: the 1920s – when social anthropology was introduced as a university subject – and the creation of the Bantustans during the 1970s.

A good example of the search for a justification of Apartheid in Western thought is the use of the concept of ethnicity. In Greek and Latin, the etymological sense of the substantive '*ethnos*" – people, nation – or the adjective '*ethnicus*' – pagans – has to do with exclusion. In both cases, they were used to distinguish the One from the Other and/or to exclude the Others.[7] According to Jean-Loup Amselle, the notion of '*ethnos*' amongst the Greeks designates a political category that embraces everyone who cannot fit into the '*polis*' category. Whilst '*polis*' is clearly defined, '*ethnos*', on the other end of the spectrum is rather blurred and derogative.[8]

In general terms, the quest for an identity implies the assertion of a difference and therefore of an opposition. From this opposition derives a hierarchy based on value criteria, and from there the step towards the exclusion of the Other or even segregation is easy to make. Once the separation between 'We' and the 'Other' has been effected the process of selection to establish who has the right to enter a given group starts to operate.

As Dominique Colas explains:

> One understands why, anchored into the imaginary structures as projections of bodily images, ideologies of ethnic identity produce metaphors of purity and animality. As soon as a group is supposed to assume a specific identity, modifications are perceived as alterations and threats. The logic of identity (of an

ethnic group as well as of a social class) is that of cleansing and segregation.[9]

The often proclaimed need for each ethnic group to develop separately and with a minimum of contacts with the other groups allowed the characterisation of Apartheid policy as the implementation of an ideology of ethnic identity, or, rather, of ethnic identities – since Apartheid's *leitmotiv* was always the diversity of peoples. Under Apartheid those ethnic groups were supposed not to have anything in common, not even the territory they shared.

The chapter 'Peoples and Languages' in the *Official Yearbook South Africa 1987-1988*, starts as follows:

> Throughout its history, South Africa has been a geographic designation rather than a reflection of a national reality. In fact, the country came into being not because of natural affinity between its people, but by artificial lines drawn on the map of Africa by imperial administration in Britain. Apart from the white community, of both Dutch and British descent, these lines arbitrarily incorporated in South Africa a number of disparate Black peoples, such as the Xhosa and Zulu, with their own clearly defined territories. And the result is that today South Africa has one of the most complex and diversified population mixes in the world, *a rich mosaic of distinctive minorities without any common cultural rallying point.*[10]

By emphasising the diversity and the resulting incompatibility of the peoples of South Africa, the narrator cites the official position of the Apartheid regime, dividing the population into separate and distinct minorities, without anything in common, and therefore having no option but to live separately. Behind the official rhetoric lurk the concepts of 'ethnic groups' and 'ethnic identity'. It is noteworthy that 'ethnic group', which was always strictly applied as a divider for the larger Black group, denotes the amalgamation of the ancient notion of 'tribe' and the more recent notion of 'ethnic group'. The criteria used to justify the denomination of 'ethnic group' were the existence of a social organisation, a religion, a conception of the economy, a conception of political systems, art, and language. The three groups defined in 1950 were therefore not subject to the same treatment. The White and Coloured groups were not subdivided into ethnic components. The Apartheid vision presupposed a particular interpretation of an 'ethnic group' and of '*ethnos*' in general. This ideology only came to fruition in the 1960s, under Verwoerd.

South African anthropology: social anthropology and Radcliffe-Brown

At South African universities the usage of the concepts 'ethnic identity' and 'ethnic group' followed the dynamics of the differences between Afrikaans-medium and English-medium institutions. In the early 20th century, universities reflected the cleavage between Afrikaner nationalists and liberal Whites. Afrikaans-medium universities were the bastions of Afrikaner nationalism whilst English-medium universities hosted more liberal Whites, Afrikaners or English people. As much as studies conducted by Afrikaans-speaking anthropologists from a *Volkekunde* perspective were going to differ from those conducted by their English-speaking colleagues, they had something in common, within an anthropology framework. Both used a scientific discourse to keep the Black man at bay.

In 1921 the University of Cape Town hired A. R. Radcliffe-Brown, one of the founding fathers of modern anthropology, to its chair of social anthropology, taking a definite step towards the establishment of a discipline that was still in its infancy. Jan Smuts was then the fifth Minister of Native Affairs, and he personally invited Radcliffe-Brown to this illustrious post.

Alfred Reginald Radcliffe-Brown (1881-1955), a British citizen, started his career as an anthropologist in the Andaman Islands and amongst the Western Australian tribes. His nomination triggered a chain reaction and soon all South African universities were to offer anthropology as a subject. The extent and importance of the reaction to the creation of the chair of social anthropology can only be understood against the backdrop of the constitution of the 'Native question' in South Africa.

The unification of South Africa in 1910 increased the size of the national territory, through the incorporation of the former British colonies of the Cape and Natal, the former Boer Republics of the Orange Free state and the Transvaal and the Zulu and Xhosa African kingdoms. The unification changed the balance of power between Blacks and Whites, thus turning the 'Native question' into a national priority.

Before unification each of the colonies and the Boer republics held differing views of 'the relation between the White man and the Natives'. In the liberal tradition of the Cape, it was generally admitted that Blacks could gradually be educated and could progressively be assimilated to the 'civilised' world; thus the acceptance of the franchise system as a criterion for a civilisation test for Coloureds. In the Boer Republic of the Transvaal, the Calvinist interpretation of the Bible, based on Abraham Kuyper, prevailed. In this interpretation God would have asked that the Black son of Cham be confined to servile chores. However, as much as these traditions differed regarding the possibilities of evolution for Blacks they agreed on one point: Blacks had inferior status. Lord A. Milner, British High Commissioner in South Africa, expressed the common view in a speech delivered in Johannesburg in 1903:

> The white man must rule because he is elevated by many, many steps above the black man [...] which it will take the latter centuries to climb and which it is quite possible that the vast bulk of the black population may never be able to climb at all [...] One of the strongest arguments why the white men must rule is because that is the only possible means of gradually raising the black man, not to our level of civilisation – which it is doubtful he would ever attain – but up to a much higher level than that which he at present occupies.[11]

Anthropology was to become the instrument justifying both the liberal and Calvinist traditions. During its formative years, anthropology was deeply imbued with scientific racism, social Darwinism and Eugenism. Radcliffe-Brown wanted the discipline to evolve towards a more pragmatic approach and conceived social anthropology as 'the comparative theory of the forms of social life among primitive people'.[12]

Anthropologists and experts from the Native Affairs Ministry needed anthropology to solve the Native question. Everyone seemed to agree that anthropological studies could help identify and implement social and political systems within which Natives and Whites could live without conflict.

Anthropology started to develop after the arrival of Radcliffe-Brown in the Cape: Bantu studies were offered to aspiring Native Affairs administrators, as well as African studies and later social anthropology. The schism between English and Afrikaans medium anthropology departments, which had been in the making since the 1920s when English universities started offering social anthropology while their Afrikaner counterparts advertised *Volkekunde* for the first time at the University of Pretoria in 1925, reached its peak in the 1940s. Social anthropologists used to take pride in their contacts with their American and British colleagues and criticised the adepts of the *Volkekunde*, literally 'the art of the peoples', for having withdrawn into the *laager*.

Applications and limitations of social anthropology

Saul Dubow[13] has shown how British liberal ideals in the second half of the 19th century influenced racist thinking in South Africa. He has demonstrated that the evolution of English thinking around the place of Blacks in civilisation was not taken into account in South Africa. On the contrary, in South Africa it was readily accepted that the White man was superior to the Black man and that therefore Whites had to exercise their superiority. The argument for the superiority of the White man was based on the alleged inferior intelligence of Black people who, having an inferior culture, were not familiar with the most rudimentary aspects of civilisation and therefore had to be kept at a distance. This separation increased the need to prevent any form of miscegenation that could be harmful to White civilisation.

Social anthropology did not oppose the policy of separation. Separation between Black and White people was judged necessary as a way to protect and keep the 'purity' of the White race at the same time that paternalistic attitudes were considered a duty of the civilised. In this sense White was always the yardstick in the hierarchy of colour. Radcliffe-Brown himself was in favour of segregation between Blacks and Whites for the sake of peaceful cohabitation.

The extent of the relation between scientific thought and politics was such that a politician such as Jan Smuts could use the one to explain the other. Smuts, who brought Radcliffe-Brown to South Africa, believed in two axioms: that there should not be any miscegenation between Black and White, and, forgetting the vast Coloured community, that Whites must model their behaviour on 'the granite bedrock of the Christian moral code'.[14] He, who was to oppose Apartheid's total segregation in 1948, spoke in those terms on 22 May 1917 in London, in front of members of the Imperial Institute and of various South African societies:

> We have realised that political ideas which apply to our white civilisation largely do not apply to the administration of Native Affairs [...] And so a practice has grown up in South Africa of creating parallel institutions – giving the Native their own separate institutions on parallel lines with institutions for Whites. It may be that on those parallel lines we may yet be able to solve a problem which may otherwise be insoluble [...] Instead of mixing up black and white in the old haphazard way, which instead of lifting up the black degraded the white, we are now trying to lay down a policy of keeping them apart as much as possible in our institutions [...] Thus in South Africa, you will have in the long run large areas cultivated by the blacks, where they will look after themselves in all their forms of living and development, while in suitable parts, you will have your white communities, which will govern themselves separately according to the accepted European principles. The blacks will, of course, be free to go and to work in the white areas, but as far as possible, the administration of white and black areas will be separate, and such that each community will be satisfied and develop according to its proper lines.[15]

In 1948, such a declaration would have come from an Afrikaner nationalist and would have been part of a plea for Apartheid. In 1917, when White superiority and colonial paternalism were alive and well, it was considered a plea for the separation of the races on the basis of different stages of civilisation.

Different understandings of anthropological concepts had an important role in creating the transition from White paternalistic superiority to Apartheid segregation. Radcliffe-Brown defined social anthropology as 'the theoretical natural science of human societies: it studies social phenomena through methods essentially similar to those used in physical and biological sciences'.[16] Influenced by both Herbert Spencer and social Darwinism, Radcliffe-Brown maintained that if there was natural selection, there was a natural hierarchy amongst humans. Social anthropology was an attempt to understand that hierarchy, to study practically the function of social entities. In this regard Radcliffe-Brown maintained that 'all social processes have a function which can only be interpreted in relation with the specific social structure within which it operates'.[17]

Social anthropology as the bastion of English-speaking South African academics, did not differ, however, that much from the *Volkekunde*. During its first fifty years, it limited itself to describing the Native peoples of South Africa. By embracing social Darwinism, biological racism and other liberal theories born in Victorian England, social anthropology did nothing but advocate the separation between White and Native people in order to prevent or at least circumvent the possibility of conflict. However, whatever the parallels that one can establish between social anthropology and *Volkekunde*, it was the latter that became the 'scientific' tool of Apartheid.

The South African Government's choice of *Volkekunde* as its scientific tool was not fortuitous. It was actually deeply rooted in the history of the rivalry first between the British colonies and the Boer republics and later between British liberals and Afrikaner nationalists. These tensions were partially expressed during the 19th century in the status of Afrikaans versus English. The recognition of Afrikaans along with English as South Africa's official languages in 1925 was not enough to appease a growing nationalist sense, which had been in the making for decades.[18]

The *'ethnos'* theory gave the Afrikaners the possibility of becoming a self-proclaimed ethnic entity, different from both other Whites and every other ethnic group. The expansion of *Volkekunde* as a discipline took place between 1920 and 1940. The Afrikaans universities – Stellenbosch, Pretoria and Potchefstroom – opened *Volkekunde* departments. Their aim was to disseminate the idea that racial segregation was the only viable solution to the Native question.

The *Volkekundiges* published very little, making it difficult to find examples of the kind of work they produced. What is left are the internal ethnological publications especially prepared for the Department of Native Affairs and a few doctoral theses and Masters dissertations from the Universities of Potchefstroom and Pretoria.

The first ethnology service was founded in 1925 under the auspices of the Department of Native Affairs. Its mission was to produce research that would help the Department in its task of administering

South African's Native populations. The ethnology service had to focus its research on the Natives' customs and habits, laws and inter-ethnic relations and bring any important results to the attention of the department.[19]

Volkekunde: theory and practice of the Afrikaner *Volk*

The theory of '*ethnos*' lies at the heart of the *Volkekunde*. According to them the world is naturally divided into *volke* (peoples). The natural existence of *volke* gives the division of the world into peoples its sacred character and explains why as a divine creation *volke* have to be respected. Despite the obvious similarities between the Afrikaans *volkekunde* and the German *Volkgeist*, the notion of '*ethnos*' used by the *Volkekundiges* derives from the Russian anthropologist Shirokogoroff. He defined '*ethnos*' as a process of ethnic awareness. For him any 'functional' group which differentiated itself from a given population would tend to develop a specialised language, a common cultural complex, to practice endogamy, and to become conscious of itself as a group.[20] The *Volkekundiges* mean by '*ethnos*' the *volk*, the ethnic group, a people with a certain number of common traits: language, culture, religion, tradition.

The concept of *volk* itself was not alien to the Afrikaans-speaking public. *Volk* in this context had to be read on a value scale. In upper case, *Volk* meant the *Heerenvolk*, the Race of the Lords, the Afrikaners. In lower case, *volk* referred to the peoples. The diminutive form of *volk* – *volkie* or little people – always referred to the other peoples. Jean Branford's *Dictionary of South African English* explains '*Volk*' as 'the Afrikaner *Volk* formed around its culture and then around politics'.[21]

Etymologically '*volk*' means 'nation' and is supposed to encompass all nations without exception. In South Africa, the term was manipulated to refer only to the Afrikaner *Volk*, which was itself defined as following the precepts of the Dutch Reformed Church, having European customs and habits, its symbology, and its historical and religious mythology.

The intention to forge an Afrikaans national identity appeared as early as 1875, when the Real Afrikaners Society (*Genootskap van Regte Afrikaners*) was founded in Paarl, in the Cape. The statutes of the society defined its objective as 'the defence of our Language, our *Volk*, and our Country.[22] From the moment the Afrikaans intelligentsia started to institutionalise its opposition to the British, the concept of *Volk* gained currency and eventually acquired a specifically South African meaning which in turn became the exclusive preserve of the Afrikaners.

The origins of the political use of the term *'volk'* can be traced back to the early 20th century, at the time of the Boer defeat in the Anglo-Boer War. The Boer national sentiment, which saw Boer identity threatened with the establishment of the Union of South Africa, started to concretise then in the form of a community identity specific to the descendants of the Dutch who had left the Cape in 1838. In the aftermath of the Anglo-Boer War the constitution of the Boer *Volk* was perceived as a means of survival against the British power.

During the early 20th century a whole range of new Afrikaner institutions made extensive use of *'Volk'* in their manifestos. The National Party in 1914, the Afrikaner *Broederbond* in 1918, the *Federasie van Afrikaanse Kultuurvereniginge* (Federation of Afrikaner Cultural Associations) in 1929, the *Reddingsdaadbond* (Salvation Action League), and the *Ossewabrandwag* (Ox-wagon Sentinel) in 1939 produced a wide array of documents in which *'Volk'* invariably referred to the Afrikaner nation. Each of these institutions meant to inculcate each targeted individual with their rights and duties as a member of the Afrikaner *Volk*.

Volkekunde's interpretation of the *'ethnos'* theory can be placed within a continuum started by the Afrikaner intelligentsia in the 19th century. By the 1950s the relation between ideology and politics was so direct that Dr T. E. Dönges, the Home Affairs Minister, could state without conceptual or political problems: 'The Party is the *Volk* and the *Volk* is the Party.'[23]

Given the way in which Afrikaner intelligentsia defined *'volk'* it is hardly surprising that culture and their use of 'cultures' in the plural constituted a central concept in their understanding of the world. For the proponents of *Volkekunde* human beings could only be true to their nature within an ethnic context. They argued that only through the ties to their *ethnos*, through language, religion, morality, could human beings be themselves in all their potential. The corollary of this was that the role of the state was to allow all human beings to live freely within their own cultural communities. [24]

Culture is the keyword of the *Volkekunde* anthropological theory. According to P. J. Coertze, a representative of this way of thinking, 'there are as many cultures as there are peoples'.[25] This conception of the world is concerned with the group as opposed to the individual. Only within the group can individuals define their identity and therefore it is only by belonging to an *ethnos* that they can express their national sentiment.

The assumption of the existence of various *volke* in South Africa, which needed to be studied as homogeneous identities, not only confirmed the theory of *ethnos* but allowed *Volkekundiges* to irreversibly lock individuals up into a group. When it came to studying those groups they did so, focusing on phenotypes, cultural practices, languages and customs, oblivious of any possible influence from external factors. This kind of anthropology was rigid and descriptive, more concerned with the phenomena than with their causes. Once an ethnic group was defined it was fixed in time and space, social dynamics being denied to it.

From Coertze's[26] *Volkekundige* perspective there are two types of cultures: free (*vrye kulture*) and closed (*gebonde kulture*), which are distinguished from each other by the degree of individual freedom showed by their members. Thus while closed cultures are primitive, composed of individuals lacking self-discipline, and are confined to a narrow social and organic entity,[27] free cultures contain individuals who are able to act independently from cultural norms. Belonging to a closed culture implies not only that neither individuals nor the collective can decide on their own progress but that fixity and obligation are features of the culture as such.

Considering that each culture is specific and unique, they advocated its preservation and defence by the culture's own representatives. The anthem of the *Genootskap van Regte Afrikaners* illustrates the political and religious implications of the *Volkekundiges'* understanding of the world:

> *Want al die nasies het een God,*
> *Hy reël ieder volk syn lot;*
> *Hy het ver ieder volk syn taal,*
> *Syn land, syn reg, syn tyd bepaal,*
> *Wie dit verag sal sy straf dra*
> *O God, beskerm Suid Afrika*

Since all nations have only one God
He forges the destiny of each nation;
He gave each nation its language,
Its land, its laws, its time divinely,
He who despises this will endure the punishment
O God, protect South Africa[28]

This advocacy for the defence and preservation of every culture, based on its uniqueness, however, did not preclude the White man from establishing his superiority in relation to the closed cultures of the African ethnic groups, and from accepting his role as a tutor of these inferior and immature groups.

Volkekunde's theoretical framework does not take into account any cultural interactions in its analysis and indeed warns against them as being the source of ethnic conflicts. The inexorability of ethnic conflicts is explained by the individual's and entire groups' inability to assimilate and understand exterior influences other than through conflict. The fear of conflict and ethnic fusion was at the very heart of South African politics and culturally based segregation was to rely on the praising of each *volk*'s intrinsic ethnic values. In this regard the *Volkekundiges* largely contributed to the creation of the Bantustans.

Volkekunde and Bantustans

When, during the 1950s, the National Party government decided to transform the African reservations into Bantustans it did so based on the work done by N. J. van Warmelo, who headed the ethnological service of the Native Affairs Department for forty years.[29]

In Van Warmelo's article 'The Classification of Cultural Groups', language is given primordial importance. Interestingly, the concept of language as a means of communication and cultural identification would be transformed into its opposite – language as a guarantee of absence of communication, and of separation – in the construction of the Bantustans.

The *Volkekundiges* described South African vernacular languages as carriers of an oral tradition that could also be understood as an obstacle to inter-ethnic group communication. In other words, while written culture is more permeable to other cultures through the writings, in a primitive culture with only an oral tradition, literacy remains the exception. Thus the oral character of a culture is a guarantee of its isolation. From the perspective of the Afrikaner *Volk* the maintenance of the oral and illiterate character of the African vernacular languages was a way of retaining its own supremacy and prerogative over civilisation. Under the guise of the preservation of cultures and of the necessity of separate development, the Bantustans were another attempt at preventing any form of communication amongst South Africans of different cultures, in order to preclude any access by others to the spheres of White power. By obstructing communication and learning about its culture by others, the Afrikaner *Volk* thought it would ensure the integrity of its own culture.

The separation, however, was far from only being a linguistic one. The creation of Bantustans was based on the allocation of fixed territories to the different African groups. The laws on these territories appeared in the early 1950s. In those territories Africans, now called Bantus, would then acquire so-called citizenship.

The term 'Bantu' appears at the same time in all official documents to designate all African populations. Once again, the term had a specific meaning in the South African context. The generally accepted definition of 'Bantu' is 'a name given to a large group of African languages and the peoples speaking them in South and Central Africa'.[30] The Apartheid state converted the meaning of 'Bantu' to 'African', and Bantustan was, by extension, to mean 'the country of the Bantu people'. Thus, Bantu became a substitute in the continuum of the political lexicon for the terms 'Kaffir' and 'Native'. For Vernon February, 'Bantu' became a derogative term in South Africa because of its political use:

> Bantu – a term of derogation, which in all innocence is a class two noun (plural) meaning 'people', but which in South African race terminology meant only and exclusively Black people.[31]

If there were any doubt as to the derogative character of the term 'Bantu' in South Africa the fact that the term disappeared from the *South Africa Official Yearbook*[32] in 1994 confirms the depreciative origin of the word.

The re-tribalisation of South Africa

The Bantu Authorities Act no 68 of 21 June 1951 abolished the Native Representative Council and replaced it by local, regional and territorial tribal authorities with executive, administrative and judicial responsibilities and powers. The Natives became Bantus, separated by their own vernacular languages. This marks the beginning of the re-tribalisation of South Africa. 'Independent' Bantustans would be governed by chiefs, nominated and supported by the Nationalist government. Explaining this new political orientation, the then Minister of Native Affairs said:

> The natives of this country do not all belong to the same tribe or race. They have different languages and customs. We are of the opinion that the solidarity of the tribes should be preserved and that they should develop along the lines of their own national character and tradition. For that purpose, we want to rehabilitate the deserving tribal chiefs as far as possible and we would like to see their authority maintained over the members of their tribes.[33]

The Bantu Authorities Act marks the beginning of the legislative implementation of separate government institutions. The notion of 'communal authority' is added at the local level, and for Africans living in urban areas, to the local, regional and territorial authorities. This law and the many that followed carried out to its full extent the Bantustan design:

- The Promotion of Self-Government Act no 46 of 1959, recognising eight 'Black national entities': North Sotho, South Sotho, Swazi, Tsonga, Tswana, Venda, Xhosa and Zulu.[34]
- The Bantu Homeland Citizenship Act no 26 of 1970, gave different citizenship criteria to the members of each Bantustan. The citizenship of all Africans was determined by their classification in virtue of the Population Registration Act which, as we have seen, proceeded more often than not on arbitrary criteria.
- Finally, the Bantu Homeland Constitution Act no 21 of 1971, foresaw the autonomy and later independence of the Bantus-

tans, stripping their so-called citizens of their South African citizenship.

The Department of Native Affairs and all the laws and documents relating to the Bantustans readily used all the notions conveyed by the *Volkekunde*. An ethnologist from the Bantu Administration Department actually expressed his satisfaction:

> From 1951 onwards, and according to the terms of the Bantu Authorities Act and its regulations, the traditional democratic forces within tribes were recognised and encouraged. The Bantu of South Africa's loyalty lies first of all with his tribal organisation, but with an improvement in educational possibilities for the Bantus, special development plans have allowed the tribes to modernise their councils and develop their political institutions.[35]

The creation of the Bantustans implacably follows the logic of the *Volkekunde*. Since the African ethnic groups were seen as closed and primitive, it was natural to give them their own territories. They could then develop within their territories while limiting the possibilities of interactions with others. Having placed the *ethnos* back into its historical and geographical reality, the different African ethnic groups would be able to thrive and flourish within their God-given vocation. As C.J. Maritz, who wrote his PhD thesis at the University of Potchefstroom in 1976,[36] put it, this God-given vocation can only be realised under historical and geographical circumstances. The Afrikaner *ethnos,* by giving the other *ethnos* a space in which to become a nation, was fulfilling its duty as a trustee. Maritz says that the duty of the Afrikaner *ethnos* is not to dominate, but to carry out its divine task, that of elevating other peoples. In this line of reasoning the creation of the Bantustans was additional evidence of the Afrikaners' magnanimity towards other *ethnoi*. This feeling of legitimate superiority was expressed in 1976:

> In this ethnic constellation, the White nation constitutes the most advanced group socio-culturally, economically, and politically. Measured by generally accepted economic and demographic criteria, this self-confident and virile people ranks among the top dozen most advanced nations in the world.[37]

Whether they are prepared to accept this or not,[38] the *Volkekundiges*
provided the National Party with the scientific and intellectual justification it needed to implement its vision of the ethnic divide and the
Apartheid policy on the Bantustans, among other things. Through
their definition of cultures, and especially by defining African cultures
as closed cultures, they placed the emphasis on the traditional aspects
of these societies and described all Africans as members of ethnic
groups devoted to the cult of their ancestors. By doing so, the *Volkekundiges* denied Africans the right to evolve and confined them to ancestral structures. They embedded ethnic groups in the past and deprived them of a future.

The contribution of the *Volkekunde* did not limit itself to advocating
ethnic divisions that degraded the vast majority of South Africa's population. They embraced an understanding of culture deeply influenced
by German romanticism, which had as its objective the recognition of
the Afrikaners as a nation in their own right. Alain Finkielkraut, commenting on Benda, offers the following definition of culture, which
sums up the *Volkekundiges'* conception of nation:

> Culture – the domain where man's spiritual and creative activi-
> ty operates. My culture: the spirit of the people I belong to and
> that impregnates both my highest aspirations and the most
> simple gestures of my everyday life.[39]

For this conception to be realised it was necessary to effect several op-
erations to separate Afrikaners from the 'Other'. Thus they isolated the
British on the basis of language and the Jews on the basis of religion.

While for the rest of the world the nation was considered to be a uni-
fying factor, Afrikaners in South Africa had a radically different interpretation of the concept. As the world was rebuilding itself into nations
after World War II, South Africa was placing the *ethnos* at the heart of
its concerns and the Apartheid state was making ethnic division its absolute priority in order to achieve total segregation.

---

1. H.A.D. 1950, Cols 7724-7725. Our emphasis.
2. E. Boonzaier & J. Sharp, 1988, *South African Keywords. The Uses and Abuses of Political Concepts, op. cit.*, p. 101.
3. G.Maré, 1993, *Ethnicity and Politics in South Africa*, Zed Books, London.

4. As an example, one could choose all people measuring more than 1,70m, blue eyed and shortsighted, Chinese and Arabic speaking, and make it a category. The people in question would not even know that they form a category and we actually would not need their agreement to place them in this category.

5. J. Rex,1989, *Race and Ethnicity*, Open University Press, Great Britain.

6. To this effect, the Census Director had the ultimate power to decide on the classification or reclassification of a person: 'If at any time it appears to the Director that the classification of a person... is incorrect, he may... after giving notice to that person and, if he is a minor, also to his guardian, specifying in which respect the classification is incorrect, and affording such person, and such guardian (if any), an opportunity of being heard, alter the classification of that person in the register.' Abstract of the Population Registration Act no 30 of 1950, Section 5 (3).

7. See A. D. Smith, 1996, *The Etnic Origins of Nations*, Blackwell, Oxford, p. 21 and J. L. Amselle, 1990, *Logiques Métisses. Anthropologie de l'Identité en Afrique et Ailleurs*, Payot, Paris, p. 16.

8. J.L. Amselle, *op. cit.*, p. 16.

9. 'On comprend pourquoi, ancrée dans les structures de l'imaginaire comme projections d'images du corps, les idéologies de l'identité ethnique produisent des métaphores de la pureté et de l'animalité. Dés lors qu'un groupe est supposé posséder une identité spécifique, les modifications sont des altérations et des menaces. La logique de l'identité (de l'ethnie comme de la classe sociale du reste) est celle de l'épuration et de la ségrégation', D. Colas, 1994, *Sociologie Politique*, Collection premier cycle/PUF, Paris, p. 465-466. Own translation.

10. *South Africa 1987-88, op. cit.*, p. 59. Own emphasis.

11. 'Watchtower Speech', 18 May 1903, in C. Headlam (ed.), 1931, *The Milner Papers 1899-1905*, Vol. 2, London, p. 466 quoted in S. Marks and S. Trapido, *op. cit.*, p.7.

12. A. R. Radcliffe-Brown, 1952, *Structure and Function in Primitive Society*, Cohen and West Ltd, London.

13. S. Dubow, 'Race, civilisation and culture: the elaboration of segregationist discourse in the inter-war years', in S. Marks and S. Trapido (eds), *op. cit.*, p. 71-95.

14. W. K. Hancock, *The Fields of Force, op. cit.*, p. 113.

15. W. K. Hancock, *The Fields of Force, op. cit.*, p. 113.

16. Quoted in K.M. van Meter, *La Sociologie, op. cit.*, p. 410.

17. J.P. Durand, A. Radcliffe-Brown, 'Structure et Fonction dans la Société Primitive', in K.M. van Meter (sous la direction de), 1992, *La Sociologie*, Textes Essentiels Larousse, Paris, p. 396. Own translation.

18. The antagonism between liberal Afrikaners – partisans of the United Party – and Afrikaner nationalists deepened at the dawn of World War II. The United Party went to war alongside England whilst Afrikaner nationalists wanted to side with Nazi Germany. Though the Smuts government supported the Allied forces, disgruntled Afrikaners formed ethnic associations modeled on the Nazi and Fascist examples of the Grey Shirts. The link of Afrikaner nationalism with Nazi Germany can be traced back to the creation of the Broederbond in 1918 and of the Ossewabrandwag in 1938. Both organisations, which worked hard at developing a sense

of belonging among Afrikaners, had close ties with Germany. Their leaders, who became state officials of the National Party in the 1950s and 1960s, studied in Germany during the 1930s. In this context the choice between Afrikaans *Volke-kunde* and social anthropology as an instrument for Apartheid was an obvious one.

19. 'The ethnological section was created [...] in order that the Department might have at its disposal the services of an academically trained anthropologist conversant with the ethnological and linguistic side of native affairs [...] Research [...] consti-tutes and must constitute the most important part of the ethnologist's work. His investigations are conducted primarily with a view to obtaining information of in-terest to the Department and its officers. It has been proved time and again that when a dispute has arisen, it is too late to obtain impartial evidence on the point as issue. Definite information on law and history previously collected, must [...] greatly facilitate an equitable settlement [...] The findings are made available for reference and study [...] in the series of 'Ethnological publications' of the Depart-ment [...] This series was started in 1930 [...] the Department is thus gradually building up a source of information for its own officers and at the same time contributing towards the scientific anthropological literature of South Africa.' H. Rogers, 1949, *Native Administration in the Union of South Africa*, Pretoria, Government Printer, p. 232-233.

20. J. Sharp, October 1991, 'Volkekunde: Roots and Developments in South Africa', in *Journal of Southern African Studies*, Vol. 8, No 1. Special issue on Anthropology and History, pp. 16-36.

21. The use of 'volkies' is cited as 'These volkies [...] work until dusk and still have energy to play the guitar and sing.' J. Branford, 1980, *Dictionary of South African English*, Oxford University Press, Cape Town, p. 319-320.

22. G. Dekker, 1947, *Afrikaanse Literraturgeskiedenis*, Nasionale Pers Beperk, Cape Town and Bloemfontein, p. 14. 'Die doel van ons Genootskap is om te staan vir ons Taal, ons Volk en ons Land'. Own translation.

23. T. E. Dönges in his article entitled 'Die Afrikaanse Gedagte en die Draers Daar-van' (The Afrikaner Philosophy and its representatives) in J. Degenaar, March 1978, 'Afrikaner Nationalism', occasional paper 1, Rondebosch, Centre for In-tergroup Studies, University of Cape Town, p. 23. 'Die Party is die Volk en die Volk is die Party'. Own translation.

24. V. February, 1991, *The Afrikaners of South Africa*, Monographs from the African Studies Centre Leiden, Kegan Paul International Ltd, London and New York, p. 100.

25. P. J. Coertze, 1973, *Inleiding tot die Algemene Volkekunde*, Voortrekker Pers, Johan-nesburg, p.61. '[...] soveel volke wat daar is, soveel kulture bestaan daar'. Own translation.

26. See P. J. Coertze, 'Akkulturasie', in G. Cronjé (ed.), *Kultuurbeïnvloeding tussen Blankes en Bantoe in Suid-Afrika*, Pretoria, 1968.

27. P. J. Coertze quoted in G.Maré, 1993, *op. cit.*, p. 26.

28. G. Dekker, *op. cit.*, p. 15. Own translation.

29. As Chief Ethnologist, Van Warmelo, who had obtained his PhD from the Uni-versity of Hamburg, published numerous articles in the Department's 'Ethno-logical Publications'.

30. *Chambers English Dictionary*, 1988, p. 110. In South Africa, the Bantu languages are subdivided into four major linguistic groups: Nguni, Sotho, Tsonga and Venda.

31. V. February, 1991, *op. cit.*, p.175.

32. *South Africa Official Yearbook 1994*, Directorate of Publications of the South African Communication Service, Pretoria, p. 95. The chapter on 'Peoples and Languages' is replaced by a chapter on 'The People' which, in the historical part, mentions 'South African cultural groups, less and less distinct'.

33. E. Riley, 1991, *Major Political Events in South Africa 1948-1990, op. cit.*, p. 27.

34. Quite important omissions were the Ndebele and the Shangaan.

35. J. Marchand, 1988, 'L'invention de dix patries africaines', in *Verrouillage Ethnique en Afrique du Sud*, Sous la direction de Claude Meillassoux, UNESCO/OUA, Paris, p. 24.

36. *Voogbestuur en Nasievorming by die Batswana van die RSA*.

37. *Yearbook South Africa 1976*, Pretoria, p. 78.

38. A.J. Bullier explains that he met Van Warmelo, who denied having been an instrument or agent of the Apartheid policy. He also refused the title of cultural anthropologist and considers himself a linguist *stricto sensu*. See A.J. Bullier, n.d., *Partition et Répartition: Afrique du Sud, Histoire d'une Stratégie Ethnique (1880-1980)*, Didier Erudition.

39. A. Finkielkraut, 1987, *La Défaite de la Pensée*, Gallimard, Paris, p. 16. Own translation.

PART TWO

Representations of Indians

CHAPTER FOUR

Representations of a South African minority

As we have seen in Part 1, Apartheid's legislation on ethnic identity impacted on every aspect of South Africa's social and political life. This chapter turns now to the study of one particular identity, the 'Indian' minority. The point of studying a South African minority in this context is to demonstrate – through one example – that all South African people have internalised the need to differentiate themselves from others in order to assert their specific identity. This identity was to allow them to have access to specific rights assigned to that particular group, and, often, to allow them to fight as a group for rights denied to them. Associating around identity is a normal human tendency, but in South Africa it was institutionalised by the Apartheid state, making all South Africans label-carrying individuals always able to define themselves inside and outside various designated identity strata.

For the sake of clarity during the course of this study, which covers 140 years, the South African population of Indian descent will be referred to as 'Indians', while the Indians from India will be referred to as Indians without inverted commas. This chapter looks at a series of questions around the development of an 'Indian' identity. How do 'Indians' perceive themselves in this country after 140 years of 'Indian' history in South Africa? What remains of the Indian identity transported to South Africa? How do they remember their Indianness? What have they retained of their collective memory? Why are so many 'Indians' conscious of their Indianness whilst clearly wishing to be fully considered South African citizens?

Demographic profile and historical overview

In 1996, South Africans were counted for the first time as citizens of a democracy. Out of a total of 40.6 million inhabitants, the 'Indian' population was estimated at 2.6% or 1 055 600 citizens.[1] Contrary to the examples of demographic descriptions analysed in the previous chapters, the 1996 census put the accent on Black Africans as the majority of the country's people and played down the role of cultural or ethnic differences among the South African population.[2] This image of identified yet integrated minorities in the South African population is in great contrast to the way in which 'Indians' were defined and treated for almost a century and a half – the Indian population of South Africa was not even considered as a minority, but as a 'problem' that, together with so many other similar 'problems', needed to be solved. In order to understand how 'Indians' became a problem it is necessary to retrace the origins of the 'Indian' population.

South Africa's first group of Indians – mainly Hindus from Madras – were imported in 1860 to work as indentured labourers on the sugar cane plantations in Natal. This was the outcome of a fierce debate around the need to import cheap labour to work for the Natal farmers. The intense work required in the production of sugar cane put off both White and Zulu workers, who were not prepared to leave other occupations or their land to take up hard work for very little pay – wages did not go beyond an average of 10 shillings a month. The resulting shortage of labour for the plantations left the Natal landowners with little option but to look for labour elsewhere.

The decision to import Indian labourers was backed by Act 14 of 1859 and triggered the first wave of migration of Indians as indentured labourers. Landowners negotiated with the Natal Government the contractual conditions to be imposed upon the Indian workforce, which, among other things, forced the indentured labourers to stay in Natal for a minimum of ten years.

In 1860, indenture contracts with one employer had a duration of three years at a 10 shilling a month wage. An increase of one shilling a month was granted for each year of work. The indentured labourer would be given accommodation and one meal a day, which would cost the planter about eight shillings a month. This indenture contract was, unsurprisingly, considered the cheapest in the world. After three years, the labourer had a choice between renewing his contract, accepting a plot of land from the British Crown the counter-value of which would be that of a return passage to India, or returning to India at the expense of the Natal government.

In 1865, the Indian government decided to put an end to emigration to South Africa because of the ill-treatment inflicted upon Indians in Natal. Moreover, most of the indentured labourers had reached the end of their contracts and had either opted for the piece of land or had gone back to freedom in India. Natal was therefore once again short of labour and the situation worsened when the discovery of diamonds in Kimberley and the prospect of wealth drove workers out of Natal. The Natal Government started fresh negotiations with India for new immigrants. It was agreed in 1874 that contracts would be for a period of five years. If after that period, the labourer decided to leave his employer, he did not have the right to leave Natal for another five years. After ten years, the conditions were the same as agreed to before.

The agreement reached in 1874 was tantamount to a conscious decision on the part of the Natal authorities to allow and even encourage the settlement of a genuine Indian community. The ten-year clause was created by the Natal government to have a cheap and available workforce at its disposal for the construction of harbours, railways and public buildings. More importantly, from the perspective of the development of an 'Indian' community in Natal, the government also asked that for each 100 men 40 women be imported.

Indentured labourers were not the only kind of Indian immigrants to arrive in South Africa. There were two other migratory waves of Indian traders. Soon after the arrival of the first indentured labourers, traders began to arrive. The first came from the island of Mauritius, mandated by established merchants to settle their trade in Natal. The second migration of traders originated in the state of Gujarat, India, around 1875. According to Fatima Meer, however, the first 'Indian' traders, or so-called passenger Indians, from Gujarat arrived in 1869.[3] By virtue of the agreement concluded with India on the immigration of indentured labour, the Natal government could not act to prevent further immigration of British Indian subjects to Natal. This posed a dilemma for the Natal authorities. If they wanted the much-needed workers for the plantations they had to accept the arrival of unwanted traders, who were soon viewed by their White counterparts as competition. The negative reaction to the Indian traders led to a series of anti-Indian laws, which will be analysed later.

The fact that 'Indians' were British subjects both complicated their dealings with the government of the British colony of Natal and acted as a protection against further abuse. The British Empire could not allow its Natal colonists to promulgate laws that would weaken the empire's position in India. Indians, on their part, knew that, in the case of difficulties or ill treatment, they could either appeal to the Indian government or invoke their rights as British subjects.

However, their British citizenship was a clear hindrance for those Indians who decided to try their luck in the independent Boer South African Republic. The first records of Indian presence in the Transvaal date from 1881. As Calpin explains, Indians were completely alien for the Boer population and as such they were soon rejected.[4] The independence of the South African Republic from British colonial power freed the Boer government from any restrictions when they passed anti-Indian legislation. Not only were 'Indians' banned from obtaining rights as *burgers* in the Transvaal but they also could only acquire property rights in allocated areas. Discrimination against 'Indians' in the Boer republic was, according to Calpin, one additional reason for Great Britain to declare war on the Boers in 1899.

Amongst the anti-Indian laws passed in the Transvaal the annual registration tax was the most offensive and all encompassing because it affected the entire Indian proletariat – in their majority freed indentured labourers. Transvaal law imposed an annual 3 pound registration tax for the renewal of each individual residence permit. This perpetuated the Indian population's immigrant status. Once freed from indenture, any Indian person who had arrived after 1895 and wanted to obtain the right to live in the Transvaal had to pay this tax for each family member. Indeed Gandhi himself became the spokesperson for the entire 'Indian' community after fighting against this iniquitous registration tax law.[5]

With the creation of the Union of South Africa in 1910 the old Indian problem of the colonies and the Boer republics became the thorny 'Indian question'. The Union government tried to address the problem on a national scale, but the two most affected provinces were Natal and the Transvaal.[6] Given the fact that the Union could not legislate directly against Indians because they were British subjects, a number of measures were adopted, aimed at discouraging Indians from competing with Whites in business and at eventually eliminating them altogether as competitors. Laws and regulations were officially directed at everyone, but their real target was the Indians. For example, business accounting had to be done in English, and not in any vernacular language, which was the Indian practice. Most 'Indian' traders only knew how to do regular bookkeeping in their own vernacular. They sometimes hired an English bookkeeper or learnt English bookkeeping themselves, but the representatives of the licensing bureau were merciless and sometimes used a few figures in Hindi on the margin of a book as a reason to cancel the shop's licence. Licences could also be withdrawn for lack of hygiene and cleanliness at the commercial premises. In fact, White shopkeepers had only to call upon the Licensing Bureau to have the 'Indian' shop that they wanted closed down immediately harassed by the licensing office.[7] A large number of 'Indian' businesses closed down as a consequence of this law.

The mounting tension around the presence of 'Indians' in South Africa reached its zenith in 1925 with the Asiatic Bill, tabled by Dr D. F. Malan, then Minister of Home Affairs of the Union of South Africa. The law, known as the Asiatic Bill because it was concerned with Indian immigrants, was portrayed as a tool to deal with the 'Indian question' but was in actual fact a major repatriation plan.

The 'Indian' historian P.S. Aiyar, writing at the time of discussion on the Asiatic Bill, explained that the object of the law was to ruin 'Indian' traders and farmers by declaring them aliens and by segregating them on grounds of unsanitary premises and unfair competition. The final aim of the legislation was to ruin the 'Indians' and pressure them to leave the country.[8]

Dr Malan himself put it very clearly in commenting on the interpretation of the Act:

> If you [the Indians] don't go back to your home gracefully, I will shoulder you out without your bag and baggage, but if you go like an obedient boy, sell up your goods and chattel on top of it, I will give you ten pounds and quietly go. Otherwise, I will make your life intolerable here but if you choose to remain here, do so as a pauper.[9]

The passing of the Asiatic Bill in 1925 flew in the face of the decisions reached on the treatment of British Indians at the Imperial Conferences of 1918, 1921 and 1923[10], and added to the growing tension between Indians, the Union Government and the Indian Government. By 1944, Dr N. B. Khare, a member of the Indian Government, declared to the National Assembly in New Delhi:

> I wish that India was in a position to declare war against South Africa here and now. [...] The whole of India will give enthusiastic support to the strongest measures that can be taken by means of economic and other sanctions, to make it plain to the

Union Government that this country regards the latest anti-
Indian legislation as intolerable and disgraceful.[11]

The independence of India in 1947 solved one part of the problem,
that of the relation between the Union of South Africa and the British
government around the treatment of British subjects. Between 1947
and 1961 'Indians' were considered as Indian citizens with the status of
foreign residents in South Africa. It was only in 1961 under the government of Prime Minister Hendrik Verwoerd, a century after the arrival
of the first immigrants and only after many repatriation plans had
failed, that 'Indians' were granted the status of a permanent population in South Africa. The decision was neither the sign of new-found
enlightenment nor a magnanimous gesture on the part of the South
African government. It was a way of stopping India's interference in
South African affairs.

Historiography and representations of the 'Indians' in South Africa

The task of sketching a profile of the 'Indian' community is extraordi-
narily complex. 'Indian' identity was shaped by a multitude of elements,
some of which are contradictory and difficult to analyse. The two most
accepted and widespread parameters to identify an 'Indian' identity,
and identities within it, are language and religion. This, however, is
deceptively simple because when opting to use language to look at the
differences between groups of 'Indians' the major obstacle is that, in
official documents, most 'Indians' declare English as their home language. Arriving at a synthetic definition of the 'Indian' community is
all the more difficult because most of the studies available point to its
homogeneity. Yet, the heterogeneity that we will demonstrate derives
from the many identity markers that the Indians brought with them
and that today's 'Indians' have inherited, diffused and transformed.

'Indian' identity markers derive from the heritage of the caste system, a large number of vernacular languages and dialects, various religions and different territorial origins. Not only does 'Indian' identity differ depending on how caste, language, religion and origin combine
but the way in which these parameters are used to define identity also
varies depending on the researcher's questions.

The weight that ethnic difference has had under Apartheid acted as

a deterrent to progressive writers against using ethnic analysis in social and political enquiry. The crime of Apartheid has been perpetrated
in the name of separate development, in the name of ethnic identity,
in the name of the group. The anti-Apartheid struggle – whether liberal
or Marxist – rallied around the rounding up of all excluded communities and around a homogeneous presentation of the struggle. Even
studies on specific groups presented them in terms of their opposition
to Apartheid and explained internal factions as the logical consequences
of the Apartheid policy. The state was held responsible for internal divisions as well as for the misery endured by those communities. Many
sociological studies were devoted to the demonstration of how the
state had manipulated history and attributed to groups of people an
identity that was not theirs. The view of ethnicity and identity as 'false
consciousness' went hand-in-hand with the type of social sciences that
privileged the analysis of the group over the focus on the individual.
Through this type of analysis anti-Apartheid social scientists wanted
to show how Apartheid, mainly through legislation such as the Population Registration and the Group Areas Act but also through the impo-
sition of racially-based education systems, was responsible for the crys-
tallisation of peoples' perceptions of the others.

The only representation that an Afrikaner child could have of a Zulu
child or that an 'Indian' child could have of a Xhosa child originated
in the image portrayed in school history books.[12] Separate development has closed off communities and the official Apartheid discourse,
very often the only link between communities, conditioned all perceptions of the others.

Historiography and sociography of 'Indian' representations
until the 1930s

The early historiography on the life of 'Indians' in South Africa until the
1930s is best represented by three authors: H.S.L. Polak, P.S. Aiyar
and P.S. Joshi, all of whom concentrated their writings on the experience and living conditions of the first Indian immigrants. All three focused on aspects of the political-economic and socio-cultural isolation experienced by the Indians in South Africa.

From a political-economic perspective the status of the 'Indians' as
British subjects was in conflict in South Africa with the treatment

they received both as indentured labourers and as traders. This historiography stressed how much 'Indian' dignity was offended by the colonial government's denial of their contribution to the development of South Africa and by the depiction of 'Indians' as usurpers of the Europeans' place in society. In relation to the latter these authors tried to prove through historical and statistical evidence that there was no intention on the part of the Indian population to usurp or infiltrate the White people of South Africa.

The 'Indian' historian Joshi, for example, in his *The Tyranny of Colour* (1937), reviewed more than sixty discriminatory laws against the Asians, from 1860 until 1937. He scrutinised legal documents, newspaper clippings, the committees in charge of preparing the texts of the laws, giving special attention to both the segregation of business areas and the prohibition of marriages between Indian and Whites. He then tried to demonstrate the absurdity of these laws in the eyes of the Indians, their aims being radically different from those that they were accused of. They did not want to marry outside their community, and could not understand the spirit of these relentless discriminatory measures. The South African Indian Congress declared to this effect that:

> [...] Over a period of ten years, one European in every 400
> 000 has married an Asiatic. Further, the annual variation is
> virtually nil, so that it can definitely be stated that marriages be-
> tween Europeans and Asiatics are not on the increase ... We
> object to legislation for the slur and stigma it will imply on us
> as a community and the insult it will cast on us as a race.[13]

All three authors concurred in pinpointing White prejudice and ignorance as the main reason for the discrimination and ill treatment experienced by Indians in South Africa.[14] Their writings looked at the devaluation of India's great civilisation by European civilisation and remarked on the incongruence of such an attitude, given that India was itself the cradle of Western civilisation. In this context Polak, Aiyar and Joshi[15] referred to racial segregation – which placed 'Indians' and Asians as inferiors to the White race – not only as an insult to the Indian people but also as a proof of the ignorance of those who preached this in the name of Christianity. This type of statement in the early historiography on 'Indians', however, was not devoid of an open acceptance of the existence of the racial and civilisational scale prevalent in

South Africa. According to British-born Jewish writer Henry Polak's *The Indians in South Africa* (1906),

> At the public lavatories, accommodation is made for Europeans, on the one hand, and 'Indians' and Kaffirs on the other. So is the civilisation of India confused, in that enlightened land, with the barbarism of the aboriginal natives.[16]

The acceptance of the hierarchy was particularly obvious in Aiyar's *The Indian Problem in South Africa* (1925) when he explained that not only did 'Indians' not consider themselves a threat to White civilisation but that they considered that they had a number of ethical principles in common with Western culture. Thus

> [The] Indian community is not in any way retarding the development of this country along the lines of Western civilisation and as a proof of our assertion we might say that the rising generation of Indians are practically assimilating European ideals and European culture [...] Give us a fair chance as the white man has, and then judge whether we adopt the white standard or not.[17]

The other focus of these authors' writings was White South Africa's lack of comprehension of the Indian social structure and the offences and misunderstandings which derived from that. This was a particularly sore point because 'Indians' acknowledged the *de facto* hierarchical relations with Europeans, but resented the treatment received from Whites, who disregarded the 'Indians'' social status. They were especially shocked to see a European labourer treating a *swami* – a Hindu priest – in the same way as an ordinary labourer.

Despite the fact that Polak, Aiyar and Joshi insisted on the role that European ignorance of Indian culture and social organisation had in the conflicts between South Africans and Indians, none of them actually explored social divisions and cultural differences within the 'Indian' population. They provided by omission a view of the 'Indian' population as a homogeneous community with no fractures and no divisions. What mattered to these authors was the actual status of 'Indians' within South Africa. Joshi concluded his book with a plea that could well have been shared by all three of them:

The Union Government should gradually repeal all anti-Indian measures. The Indians should be awarded the franchise, unrestricted rights of land ownership, and freedom of trade. The Union Government cannot keep cultured Indians without the right of vote. They cannot disallow the land ownership of Indians who are permanent residents of South Africa. The Indian trader is a blessing to poor people; the Union Government cannot refuse the licence to him. They likewise cannot deprive innocent Indian factory hands of their daily bread. South Africa will surely never have to rue its grant of equality to Indians. On the contrary, it will be a guiding light to the world in the matter of colour bar. It will not only enhance the strength and status of the British Empire, but will win the hearts of Indians and the co-operation of India. India will enrich its trade by consuming its gold, coal, fruit and sugar. It will stand beside it in its hour of need.[18]

Historiography and sociography of 'Indian' representations in the 1940s

During the 1940s, partially motivated by the Indian Government's attempts to interfere with the way in which 'Indian' people were treated in South Africa, there was a renewed interest in the 'Indian question'. This time, however, the 'Indian question' was seen and analysed through a White prism. This meant that, at least in some cases, the accounts were bluntly racist and anti-'Indian'.

Violet Wetherell's book, *The Indian Question in South Africa*, was intended as a topical account of 'Indian' life in the 1940s. Her main point, however, revolved around the political and socio-cultural identity of the 'Indians'. Particularly incensed by the Indian Government's declarations in 1944 she accused the 'Indians' of dishonesty and disloyalty when it came to discussing their national identity.[19]

Wetherell saw the roots of the 'Indian' question in both the ever-growing number of 'Indians' infiltrating South African society and in the low class origins of this population. According to Wetherell it was precisely the 'lowly-coolie class' character of the 'Indians' that constituted an obstacle to their integration in South Africa.[20]

As with the 1930s historiography the cultural otherness of the 'Indians' was seen as a major obstacle to their integration. Appalled descriptions of polygamy, lack of hygiene, dress sense, and cow worshipping, were found not only in Wetherell's analysis. The South African literature on 'Indians' during the 1940s offered a series of horrified details on these issues.

Wetherell's real focus was the wealthy 'Indians', those who had managed to enter polite European society. Her writings were particularly antagonistic towards the Natal Indian Congress and the South African Congress whom she saw as fighting an egoistic struggle in favour of an elite. She denounced what she thought was the real motivation behind any 'Indian' political stand: to obtain the right to do business anywhere. She accused 'Indian' traders of using Gandhi's stand on the anti-Indian laws to meet the ends of free enterprise.[21] According to Wetherell the 1940s demonstrated that the 'Indian' question did not have its origins in politics but in commercial ambition.

G. H. Calpin's *Indians in South Africa* (1949) constituted a far less partisan account of the 'Indian' question. He analysed the reasons behind the arrival of the first Indian immigrants to South Africa and explained how it was the fact that Indians were prohibited from taking up any other occupation that drove them into commerce.[22] In the 1940s, there was a shortage of schools and they had to create their own. However, when they were able to overcome all other social handicaps, 'Indian' schoolteachers were paid wages inferior to those of their European colleagues. Prohibited from enrolling at any South African university Indians had to go abroad to acquire higher education qualifications. All professional avenues being closed to the 'Indian' population the only option left was precisely commerce. Calpin explained both 'Indian' commercial success and the determination to stay in South Africa despite discriminatory measures through the traditional Indian belief that:

> The Indian sees himself not merely as the father of a family, but as the founder and head of succeeding generations bearing his name in honour and wealth. He will establish a family trust, make his pilgrimage to Mecca if he is a Moslem, and put his name in large letters on the properties he has built. He becomes a pillar of society during his lifetime and a benefactor of his family at his death.[23]

Calpin's interest in Indian beliefs and culture took him to the analysis of the political behaviour of 'Indians'. He concluded that the 'Indian' layman did not want to invest too much in the public sphere by militating for his political rights as a citizen. He saw a large gap between this ordinary and rather apolitical man and the politically committed leadership. Calpin saw the 'Indian' layman's main preoccupations as the right to free enterprise and to live where he chose, in harmony with his neighbours, even if they were Europeans.

Like all his contemporaries Calpin presented the 'Indian' community as homogeneous and self-contained. However, he showed greater insight in his investigation of the 'Indian' community's social and cultural practices. He was able to identify the cleavages between Hindus and Muslims but understandably – in his context – confined his study to the practices that manifested themselves in the public sphere.

The *Volkekunde* was not immune to the interest and concern that surrounded the 'Indian question' during the 1940s. The self-justificatory Afrikaner version of anthropological studies also interpreted and analysed the 'Indian' question. The fact that the *Volkekunde* analysis was published almost on the eve of the National Party electoral victory in 1948 makes it even more important because it was the *Volkekunde*'s view of the 'Indian' population that to a great extent shaped Apartheid's 'Indian' policy.

G. Cronjé, Professor of Sociology at the University of Pretoria, published his *Africa Without the Asians. The South African Final Solution to the Asiatic question*[24] in 1946. Cronjé's analysis of the Asian question had as its point of departure the fact that Asians were not indigenous to South Africa or the African continent. From this foreign status of the Asian people arose their 'threat to all indigenous racial groups, for the Whites and the non-Whites equally'.[25] Cronjé also derived from this formulation the methodology to deal with the Asian question: the solution was total repatriation or the creation of specific areas where 'Indians' could be confined.

Africa Without the Asians was constructed as a medical metaphor – articulated in five chapters: the origins of the question; the aggravation of the question; the attentive care given to the question; the danger of the question; the solution to the question[26] – that clearly identified the 'Indian' population as a disease in South Africa.

Cronjé's investigation into the origins of the 'Indian' question consisted mainly of the apportioning of blame for the first immigration of indentured Indians upon the Natal farmers who put their capitalist interests before the interest of the country. He condemned the effects of British interference with the Transvaal government's handling of the Indian immigrants. He placed the critical moment of the 'Indian problem' at the creation of the Union in 1910 when what he called the Indian 'invasion' was made possible through marriages between Indians and Malay and Coloured women. He blamed the South African government for having made the living conditions of 'Indians' in South Africa good enough for all repatriation plans to fail. Cronjé situated the 'nursing' period of the 'disease' between 1932 and 1945 when 'Indians' in complicity with Whites managed to defy all property laws. The 'Indians' constituted a danger, according to Cronjé, for two reasons. On the one hand they had a high population growth. On the other hand, they had great commercial ability and a tendency to expand. In this context Cronjé's solution was that Whites should stop buying anything at all from Indians. If government legislation did not have any effect, it was every White citizen's responsibility to cut the 'Indians' off from their means of subsistence by killing their business. Commercial exchanges, according to Cronjé's *Volkekunde* perspective, had to follow racial lines:

> The white Christians will rejoice at the following agreement according to which they will only purchase goods from white Christian businesses, Jews from Jewish businesses, Asians from Asian businesses, natives from native businesses and *Coloureds* from *Coloured* businesses.[27]

Cronjé explained that if this meant some degree of sacrifice on the part of some strata of the White Christian community, it was the only way of killing 'Indian' business. Such a sacrifice should be borne in the name and interest of the *Volk*. He called for an awakening of the national sentiment of the *Volk*, a regrouping of the organic entity as a way of ensuring its survival.

All these authors tended to present the picture of a homogeneous Indian community. Thus they argued that business was at the centre of the 'Indian' question. Even if they acknowledged that there were two different migratory waves (roughly, one from the North and one from the South); even if they acknowledged the fact that the 'Indians' of the Union in the first half of the 20th century were the descendants of two types of immigrants (indentured and passenger); even if they recognised that there were Hindus, Muslims and a few Christians: they still only referred to the rich 'Indian' shopkeeper. What these authors did not see was that the vast majority of 'Indians' was extremely poor and lived in the same appalling conditions as the Coloureds and Africans. By focusing on the stereotype of the rich 'Indian' shopkeeper and the laws affecting him, all authors, whether White or 'Indian', either offered the distorted perspective of a homogeneous community or gave the impression that all 'Indians' rallied around the 'Indian question', all being affected by the anti-Indian laws.

Historiography and sociography of 'Indians' – post-1961 representations

'Indians' became South Africans in 1961 at the height of Apartheid. Ceasing to be immigrants they became recognised as a permanent population of South Africa. This opened a new period of historical and sociological research and investigation into the manner in which the 'Indian' community related to the anti-Apartheid struggle. The results, as well as the focus, of this enquiry once again varied according to the theoretical and political perspectives of the authors.

One characteristic of South African liberal historiography, in general, is its focus from the perspective of the elites on historical processes within the political and economic sphere. Liberal historiography on 'Indians' fits within this trend. Authors focused their attention on the response of the 'Indian' elite, identified with the rich merchants, to the anti-Indian laws, simply assuming that the elite was actually representing the rest of the 'Indian' community. Underlying this sort of analysis was the assumption that dominant social groups are readily and *de facto* accepted by the masses and, conversely, that the masses were powerless and without political perception of their own.

Within this framework the works of B. Pachai (1971) and S. Bhana (1991) are excellent historical accounts. They were both based on archival work done in South Africa, India and Great Britain. Contrary to their predecessors, Pachai and Bhana were not exclusively interested in the hardships endured by the 'Indians'. They recounted a more complete history. They not only took a broad South African focus –

as opposed to the exclusive examination of the 'Indian' experiences in Natal and Transvaal – in studying 'Indian' history but they also looked into the reasons why Indians from Madras, Calcutta and Gurujat had come to South Africa in the second half of the 19th century.

Pachai and Bhana explained Indian emigration to South Africa in the context of social and economic upheavals combined with natural disasters in the subcontinent. Pachai and Bhana were not only concerned with a contextual explanation of the migration, but were also interested in the caste origins of the Indians who came to South Africa. In studying this they managed to challenge one of the popular myths about 'Indians' – that all Indian immigrants were of low caste extraction – and concluded that even if a majority of indentured workers were born to low castes, a number of them belonged to the *Brahman, Kshatriya* and *Vaishyia varna*s.[28] Bhana[29] argued that the focus on the supposed low-caste origin of all 'Indians' had occulted the real social and economic reasons behind the Indian migration to South Africa. He argued that by holding onto this notion of a homogeneous mass of uneducated workers, one tended to underestimate the complexity of the caste structure itself and the exaggerated schematisation that results, preventing one from understanding the rules of the caste structure and its possible evolution.

A second myth about Indian migration to South Africa with which these authors dealt was that Indians came to South Africa in search of an African eldorado, in order to get rich and send their gains back home. In this regard Bhana demonstrated that even if free Indians were harbouring great hopes about their life in South Africa, the interests of the Natal Government, the plantation owners and finally the British recruiting agents had a far larger role in promoting the emigration.

In *Setting down roots*[30] S. Bhana and J. Brain described the ways in which Indians settled in South Africa. They introduced the distinction between free and passenger Indians. According to the authors a free Indian was a freed indentured labourer, while a passenger was the Indian person who came to South Africa out of his/her own will.[31] Through the analysis of archival materials and interviews with descendants of passenger Indians the authors managed to produce a detailed historical reconstruction of Indians' settlement patterns.[32] This kind of work allowed Bhana and Brain to prove that family as . well as village links played a predominant role in the choice of South

Africa as an appealing emigration destination. In most cases the South African places in which immigrants settled were pre-determined by the people they knew. Either they had relatives in South Africa and had decided to leave India to join them or they had actually been called by established relatives to help in the latter's business.[33] The interviews with descendants of passenger Indians took place in 1982 and were a first attempt at reconstituting 'Indian' history through oral history. In his work Bhana managed to determine the existence of an Indian Diaspora through the memories of 'Indian' descendants in South Africa who could still cite their village of origin.[34]

Liberal historiography limits itself to the view from above. It confines the 'Indian' struggle to the tensions between 'Indian' and White power. However, despite its limitations, through the description of all initial hardships, the dissection of the anti-Indian laws and the digging in the archives, liberal historiography is an essential building block towards the compilation of data necessary to both analyse the process and to understand the 'South Africanisation' of the Indians.

From the 1970s onwards, as the anti-Apartheid struggle intensified, the writing of 'Indian' history was influenced by the activities of the Communist Party, the African National Congress and Marxist thought. This helped to contextualise the Indian struggle for political rights in the broader anti-Apartheid struggle. In the 1970s and 1980s, 'Indian' intellectuals as well as some sections of the 'Indian' population identified themselves as 'Black', that is to say as non-White South African victims of the same segregation as the rest of the non-White population of the country. Political radicalisation demanded a radicalisation of history writing. An entirely new historiography developed. It focused on the political mobilisation of oppressed communities, as opposed to the elites' struggle, and searched in the past for indications of solidarity between Apartheid victims.

As trade unionism, class-consciousness and mass conscientisation[35] were the order of the day within the anti-Apartheid movement, historians and sociologists felt the need for a different perspective on the 'Indian' experience. While the new historiography critiqued Apartheid's systematic attempts at isolating 'Indians' from other population groups, it simultaneously introduced the concept of social cohesion among all oppressed people. 'Indian' history was reworked and presented from below. This produced a profoundly new reading of the 'Indian' experience in South Africa. It acknowledged social and political differences within the 'Indian' community and made it possible to talk about a class structure. More importantly, it brought the suffering of the 'Indian' working class to the fore. History was not re-written. It was re-read.

The introduction of both the idea of difference within the community and of the history from below allowed for a new type of political analysis at the same time as it created the space to deal with historiographical myths.

The first of those myths was the homogeneity of the Indian political movement. Essop Pahad's[36] analysis of the history of the Indian political movements between 1924 and 1946 studied the 'Indian' communities' attempts to acquire the same rights as Whites and their rejection of anti-Indian legislation. Through an analysis of the schisms[37] and radicalisation that took place in Transvaal Indian politics in 1939 with the arrival of Yusuf Mohamed Dadoo, Pahad showed that 'Indian' political movements could not be depicted as homogeneously claiming specific rights for the community as a whole.[38]

At the origin of this myth was the perception of the 'Indian' community as non-differentiated. The work of Frene Ginwala[39] went a long way in providing a far more nuanced analysis of the 'Indian' community's social structure. Marxist analysis allowed Ginwala to identify a bourgeoisie, a petty bourgeoisie and a proletariat among the 'Indians'.[40] However, at the same time that she characterised the different 'Indian' social classes Ginwala considered 'Indians' as part of the oppressed Black majority of South Africa. Combining the analysis of the 'Indian' class structure and the racial and ethnic bases of Apartheid, Ginwala argued that the future did not lie in the claim for a specific ethnic status – inherently part of the Apartheid ideology – but in solidarity, in the merger of the vast Black majority. The price to be paid for this future was particularly high for the bourgeoisie but it was the only way of achieving freedom as South Africans.

The second historiographical myth was constructed around the figure of Gandhi. Liberal historiography presented any political organisation as the direct or indirect result of Gandhi's actions. This historiography contributed to the making of a myth that undermined the input of other actors in the struggle.

Maureen Swan's *Gandhi. The South African Experience,*[41] published in 1985, in a way 'killed the father figure' that was Gandhi in 'Indian' political mythology. Without taking away from him the merits of his actions for South Africa and for Indian nationalism in India, she situated him within the 'Indian' community in Natal and the Transvaal. She replaced him in his Indian context, an Indian from India, from Porbandar in Gujarat, a Hindu, from a merchant sub-caste, the Banians. Swan's analysis demonstrated how Gandhi's struggle was fundamentally constructed around the rights of the merchant class.[42]

Swan argued that Gandhi did not fight to suppress all statutory or caste inequalities, but for the interests and rights of 'Indians'. In this sense he was a reformer rather than a revolutionary. Gandhi conceived a struggle for each Indian social stratum.

> Gandhi was a social 'rebel' [...] [But] he was a revolutionary only to the extent that the technique of mass passive resistance implies elements of revolutionary style.[43]

Swan's analysis showed the limitations of the *satyagraha* in South Africa. Passive resistance, Gandhi's political weapon, requires moral autonomy and an acute philosophical consciousness on the part of the individual in order to be effective. These two ingredients failing, as happened in South Africa, passive resistance ceases to be a viable political methodology.

The demystification of Gandhi's role in 'Indian' politics, together with the far more sophisticated analysis of the 'Indian' class structure provided by Ginwala's work, contributed to a renewed interest in working class history.

Swan[44] herself brought together both issues in a study of Gandhi's role in the 1913 strike of 20 000 Indian workers in Natal. She asked many questions around the strike, ranging from its causes, its duration, its size and its impact.[45] She argued that liberal historiography has exaggerated Gandhi's role in the strike, giving a simplistic and reductionistic picture that denies the workers their own consciousness. Gandhi, Swan thought, would not have been able to mobilise 20 000 workers if they did not have serious grievances and motives for anger.

The desire to reaffirm the life and culture of the 'Indian' working class and its representatives was at the heart of some social scientists' preoccupations in the 1970s and 1980s. V. Padayachee, S. Vawda and P. Tichmann's article[46] on trade unions between 1930 and 1950 formed part of this renewal. They used the great economic crisis of 1929-33 as a background to their study of the emergence of 'Indian' trade unionism in Durban, Natal. The authors analysed the underlying forces that led to the growth of an 'Indian' proletariat and to the need for trade unions. Against the backdrop of the strikes they examined the relations between trade unions and political organisations to argue that far from being a given, working class-consciousness is fundamentally acquired.

Representations of 'Indians': conclusions

As has been seen in this chapter the state defined the 'Indian' problem and set the parameters for a characterisation of the 'Indian' community as a whole. The common denominator to all the works we have studied is that the 'Indians' are invariably represented within the ideological framework proposed by the political power.

Polak, Aiyar and Joshi considered 'Indians' as forming a social entity because, prisoners of their social and political circumstance, they cannot emphasise anything but the homogeneity of any oppressed community. Wetherell and Calpin asked the questions of their time – whether or not Indians belonged to the Union of South Africa and the consequences that either answer had for the political future of both the community itself and the Union government. Cronjé, as an Afrikaner influenced by the *Volk*, was only interested in the general threat that the presence of a foreign element posed to the Afrikaner nation. Bhana and Pachai confined their studies to the descriptions of events, to the search for the reasons for, and consequences of, the arrival of Indians on South African soil, and their migratory and settlement patterns. They described two distinct migratory waves and saw the birth of two distinct sets of social identities and economic conditions in South Africa while they acknowledged the existence of various linguistic and religious identities inherited from the Indian past.

The radical and Marxist intellectuals were no less trapped within the paradigm proposed by Apartheid. The Marxist analysis offered by Pahad, Ginwala, Swan and Padayachee *et al* linked the 'Indian' community, especially its working class, to the struggle of the South African Black majority. They placed 'Indian' class consciousness in opposition to the ethnicity-based ideology held by Apartheid. In the process, however, they erased all ethnic components of the 'Indian' identity, falling, albeit through the anti-Apartheid struggle, into Apartheid's ideological paradigm.

The first representations of 'Indians' in South Africa dealt with the issue of national identity. Were they or were they not South Africans? Were they Indians or not? Were they British subjects or not? Were they immigrants or not? Then questions were asked about who they really were and their history was examined and written. Once they became South Africans in 1961, they became known as Indian South Africans or South African Indians, even Asiatics under the Apartheid classification system. During the 1970s and 1980s, at the heart of Apartheid, they were associated with the Black majority through the prism of Marxism. The time was ripe for the negritude of 'Indians'. It was not the time for any acknowledgement of internal differences and divisions. It was the time to regroup against the common enemy, whose weapon was ethnicity.

Those who, like Wetherell and Cronjé among others, were totally opposed to cultural integration and were particularly fierce when it came to the assimilation of 'Indians' meticulously depicted some of the Indians' linguistic and religious practices in order to demonstrate how Indian culture was incompatible with European social practices.

Liberal and Marxist social analyses examined the history of 'Indians' in order to situate them in the South African context, excluding any socio-cultural approach that could have rendered visible any differences other than class. In this sense, both liberal and Marxist historians portrayed the 'Indian' community as culturally and ethnically homogeneous. Some religious and linguistic aspects of the community were of course evoked, but were considered irrelevant, and even radically opposed, to the aim: to show that 'Indians' were South Africans and to demonstrate the extent of their integration in South Africa. The emphasis on the homogeneity of the community was necessary to justify its rightful place within South Africa.

The liberal school concentrated on the laws directed against 'Indian' traders. Since these laws discriminated against these traders only, they helped to single out 'Indians' as a social entity, different from Africans and Coloureds. The liberals confined their study to the history of the 'Indian' merchants and their hardships. They only presented one aspect of the 'Indian' community. The Marxist school was concerned with the Indian workers. The descendants of the indentured labourers were given back a place in history. These workers formed the majority of 'Indians' and were the members of a class-divided community, engaged in the anti-Apartheid and the class struggles.

For almost a century of historical writing the representation of 'Indians' as a homogeneous group was firstly a necessary response to a political power that rejected them as foreign elements before 1961, and then became, after 1961, a necessary reaction against a political power that now rejected the 'Indians' as an ethnic group. By treating the 'Indians' as one block, the state could, before 1961, consider mass repatriation and the creation of separate residential areas. After 1961, the alleged homogeneity of the 'Indians' allowed the state to allocate a specific culture to the group and to recognise it as a nation. As a matter of fact an 'Indian' Bantustan – the Hindustan – was actually on the map at some stage, but never came to fruition.

In 1984, when the Nationalist Party government decided to set up a tri-cameral Parliament, the inclusion of 'Indian' representation was possible also thanks to this misrepresentation as a homogeneous group. The homogeneous character attributed to the 'Indians' resulted from their phenotype and their extra-territorial origins. If the Apartheid state had fully applied the principle of the *volk* (one language = one culture) 'Indians' would have been divided into many different nations. The state, however, was not concerned with the intrinsic divisions of the group as long as it could single out one entity, keep it away from the others and achieve the ethnic divide. It was not in the interest of the state to acknowledge diversity within the 'Indian' group. Whether to exclude them from power or to ensure their co-operation, it always was in the interest of the Apartheid state to single out 'Indians' as a homogeneous group.

Explaining away 'Indians' through their Indianness was not satisfactory either from a theoretical perspective or from a methodological one. From the early 1970s some sociologists[47] and historians have made some progress in dealing with the complexity of being 'Indian'. However, they did not place their studies in the larger social and political context of South Africa. While they acknowledged variables within 'Indian' identity, they restricted their exploration to the private sphere. Differences were presented as cultural facts, and as cultural facts their influence or repercussions needed no explanation. It was always assumed that once 'Indians' became South African they would adopt some Western values, and this once again helped to erase difference from the analytical framework. These researchers did not see that the differences defining social hierarchy inside the 'Indian' community also operated outside. In other words, what they did not see was that 'Indians' car-

ried their identity – with all that it implied, including social differentiation – into the public sphere.

---

1. The official census of 1996 used the inherited classification categories of African,
   Coloured, Indian and White. The 'Unspecified/Other' category of 0.9% or 365
   400 citizens could include persons who did not consider themselves as African,
   Coloured, Indian or White, but as South African.
2. *South Africa Official Yearbook 1994*, Pretoria, p.95.
3. F. Meer, 1969, *Portrait of Indian South Africans*, Avon House, Durban, p.15.
4. '[...] the "Indian" was an intruder from the mysterious East, with a centuries
   old tradition behind him, possessed a civilisation, a religion incomprehensible for
   the stolid *Burgher*'. G. H. Calpin, 1949, *Indians in South Africa*, Shuter and
   Shooter, Pietermaritzburg, p. 22
5. That was when Gandhi won his real representativity and legitimacy in the eyes
   of the 'Indian' masses. After arduous diplomatic and political negotiations with
   Jan Smuts, Minister of Home Affairs, Gandhi succeeded in having promulgated
   the 'Indian' Relief Act in 1914. The Mahatma did not gain his popularity and his
   status as a legitimate 'Indian' leader whilst campaigning against the so-called
   merchant laws. It was through the cancellation of the 3-pound individual tax
   that Gandhi's *satyagraha* – started in 1906 – obtained relative success.
6. The only province that was to fully resist Indian immigration, until 1990, was the
   Orange Free State. The following sentence was written into its 1890 Constitution: 'No Arab, Chinese, Coolie or other Asiatic Coloured will have the right to
   sojourn in this state for more than two months without prior agreement from
   the President.' Extract from *Wetboek van den Oranje Vrystaat, 1854-1891*. Chapter XXXIII quoted in G. Cronjé,1946, *'n Tuiste vir die Nageslag,* Publicité Handelsreklamediens (Edms. Bpk.), Johannesburg, p. 26. In Dutch in the text. Own
   translation.
7. L. E. Neame, in *The Asiatic Danger in the Colonies* is quoted by Polak on those
   measures that protected the Whites and aimed to maintain the 'Indians' in
   poverty: 'Outwardly, it [the Act] carefully avoids class-legislation, for, in theory,
   it applies equally to Europeans and Asiatics. But in practice, it operates against

the 'Indian' storekeepers. No white man is refused a licence; Asiatics often suffer what they regard as injustice. There is no appeal from the decision of the Licensing Officer, and they can only protest and submit. In Durban, the Act has been admittedly utilised in order to prevent 'Indian' merchants opening shops in the principal streets. The Licensing Officer is the servant of a body of white storekeepers. He knows their views, and whatever his personal opinion may be, he can hardly be expected to sacrifice his appointment by opposing those who employ him. As a protective measure to the white trader, the Act is valuable. From the standpoint of expediency, the system may find supporters. In reality, it is simply class legislation.' H.S.L. Polak, 1909, *The Indians of South Africa. Helots Within the Empire and How They are Treated*, G.A. Natesan & Co., Esplanade, Durban, Section I, pp. 8-9.

8. P. S. Aiyar, 1925, *The Indian Problem in South Africa*, African Chronicle Printing Works, Durban, pp. 16-17.

9. *The Indian Problem in South Africa, op. cit.*, p. 18.

10. The 1921 Imperial Conference recommended the treatment of British 'Indian' subjects legally residing in the British Empire in the following terms: 'The Imperial Conference, accordingly, is of the opinion that in the interest of the solidarity of the British Commonwealth, it is desirable that the rights of such 'Indians' to citizenship be recognised.' P. S. Aiyar, *The Indian Problem in South Africa, op. cit.*, p. 73.

11. V. Wetherell, 1946, *The Indian Question in South Africa*, Unie-Volkspers Bpk., Cape Town, p. 50.

12. Schoolteachers engaged in the struggle did clandestinely give parallel history classes. Official history books offered a historical perspective based on the history of the White man. Roy H. du Pre acknowledges in his work that 'it is a common complaint of Black people that South African History as recorded in the school textbooks and reference books is History by the White man, for the White man, about the White man. White-centred syllabi content depict South African history as a heroic epoch of the Afrikaner nation. Blacks are relegated to a subservient position of useless bystanders or at worst, marauding hordes of murderers and cattle thieves. The syllabi are also set out to make a conscious effort to coerce Blacks into accepting their status of second-class citizens.' Roy H. du Pre, 1990, *The Making of Racial Conflict in South Africa, A Historical Perspective*, History for the Layman Series-I, Skotaville Educational Division, Johannesburg, p. vii.

13. P.S. Joshi, 1942, *The Tyranny of Colour*, E.P. & Commercial Printing Co. Ltd., Durban, p. 228.

14. 'In regard to the 'Indian' question, the Afrikaners need to be informed that, from the points of view of civilisation and geographical position, India occupied a unique position in the world. They need to be educated in the fact that India is not, never was, a land of "coolies" but the motherland of such great men as Tagore, Gandhi and Bose. Afrikaners should personally acquaint themselves with India.' P.S. Joshi, *op. cit.*, p. 292.

15. 'The race prejudice of "Christian" peoples against Asiatics [...] is all the more reprehensible when we remember that Jesus Himself was an Asiatic, and that Chris-

tian saints like Augustine, Athanasius and Cyprian were Asiatics. It was an "Indian" Christian who, in his speech at the Church Congress held in England, said that "as an Asiatic, Jesus Christ in some of the British dominions would find the door of the Christian church slammed in his face".' P.S. Joshi, *op. cit.*, p. 288.

16. H.S.L. Polak, *op. cit.*, Section I, p. 6.

17. P.S. Aiyar, *op. cit.*, pp. 21-22.

18. P.S Joshi, *op. cit.*, p. 310.

19. 'The South African Indians themselves at the moment do not appear to have made up their minds whether they are the Union's Indians or nationals of India. If they wish to have fuller rights as South African citizens, they must learn to abide by the decision of the South African Government and not endeavour to appeal to India to bring pressure to bear on the Union Government when they are obstructed from getting their own way. South African 'Indians' are freely entitled to take all constitutional means to try to improve their status, but they must conduct any such campaign as Union nationals and not attempt to gain their objects by force in the form of intervention by an outside Government. As long as the South African Indians continue in this attitude, and appear to regard themselves as both nationals of India as well as South Africa, European public opinion in South Africa will not be encouraged to grant further rights to people whose allegiance to South Africa is patently divided.' V. Wetherell, *op. cit.*, p. 70.

20. V. Wetherell, *op. cit.*, pp. 24-25.

21. V. Wetherell, *op. cit.*, pp. 10-11.

22. 'They [the "Indians"] cannot become farmers without owning or leasing farmlands. They are denied employment in the three great state services – civil, railway, and with six exceptions, Posts and Telegraphs. The restrictions in the Liquor Act militate against them securing employment as wine stewards; the operation in the Apprentice Act practically closes the door to employment in skilled trades. The teaching service offers limited opportunities at inadequate wages. The solution is not to be found in segregation and repression, but in the creation of opportunities of employment in spheres other than trade, at a living wage.' G. H. Calpin, *op. cit.*, p. 161.

23. G. H. Calpin, *op. cit.*, p. 105.

24. G. Cronjé, 1946, *Afrika sonder die Asiaat. Die Blywende Oplossing van Suid-Afrika se Asiaat vraagstuk*, Publicité Handelsreklamediens (Edms. Bpk.), Johannesburg.

25. G. Cronjé, *op. cit.*, p. 7.

26. G. Cronjé, *op. cit.*, table of contents.

27. G. Cronjé, *op. cit.*, p. 142. Own translation.

28. Brahmin: *varna* of the priests; *Kshatriya*: varna of the warriors; *Vaishyia*: *varna* of the merchants. See Part 3.

29. S. Bhana, 1991, *Indentured 'Indian' Emigrants to Natal 1860-1902. A Study Based on Ships' Lists*, Promilla & Co. Publishers, New Delhi.

30. S. Bhana and J. Brain, 1990, *Setting Down Roots. 'Indian' Migrants in South Africa 1860-1911*, Witwatersrand University Press, Johannesburg.

31. S. Bhana and J. Brain, *op. cit.*, p. 43.

32. Bhana and Brain confined their study to the passenger Indians because of the

availability of data. The study is unfortunately limited to the passenger 'Indians' because they were the only ones who maintained some sort of contacts with their 'Indian' family and villages up to today. The descendants of indentured labourers do not have this kind of information to document their origins. No-one knows for sure why the free or ex-indentured 'Indians' did not maintain links with families and villages in India. It is suggested here that there was little incentive to keep a relationship with India for several reasons: illiteracy or very poor level of education, different stakes and goals, and the stigma of being indentured. Most of them probably voluntarily severed the link with India or could not maintain it.

33. The interesting settlement pattern in the case of the passenger Indians is that persons from a same village or area in India actually regrouped and settled together in South African towns or villages. Two very striking illustrations of this pattern are Potchefstroom and Pietersburg in the former Transvaal, where the 'Indian' community is a transposition of the Indian *zillah* (administrative district) of Kathiawar in Gujarat. Many passenger Indians came from towns and small villages from the Gujarati *zillahs* of Surat, Kathiawar and Valsad, North West of India. The importance of those towns and villages will be fully explained in Part 3. The migratory patterns of the passenger Indians are based on two major axes. Firstly, the family link, even if it is an extended link, since a clan is composed of an average of 50 to 100 people. Secondly, the village link. Bhana and Brain found out that there were two migratory waves of passenger Indians. The first passenger Indians arrived in South Africa to do business and sometimes establish subsidiaries of Indian and Mauritius-based companies. The second wave had the purpose of delivering services to the first settlers or to the entire community. They were salespeople, accountants, clerks, Hindu priests, Muslim Imams, and schoolteachers. The first ones, individually or collectively, brought the second ones.

34. Bhana used the ships' lists to trace information on the origin of indentured labourers. The analysis of the lists from the immigration offices revealed some important information on caste and village of origin. For the passenger Indians, migratory controls were not as thorough and there was very little documentary evidence to work on. It was Bhana and Brain's series of interviews with sometimes very old people that provided the actual evidence for the historical reconstruction.

35. In 1979, the Federation of South African Trade Unions (FOSATU) was formed, incorporating 12 trade unions with 22 000 members. Thirty six trade unions, among which were the powerful miners trade unions, formed a federation in 1985 around the Congress of South African Trade Unions (COSATU), representing 460 000 unionised workers. Mass conscientisation was done informally and clandestinely, with universities as starting points. Students would organise themselves in small groups under the auspices of the TIC, the NIC, AZASO or AZAPO (see annex on South African chronology) and would mobilise people in the townships during boycotts, mass actions, strikes.

36. E. Pahad, July 1972, *The Development of Indian Political Movements in South Africa, 1924-1946*, unpublished PhD thesis, University of Sussex.

37. Before 1933, the major 'Indian' political organisations were the Natal Indian Congress (NIC), the Transvaal Indian Congress (TIC) and the Cape Indian Council (CIC). The three organisations were represented by the South African Indian Congress at national level. They mainly represented the interests of the 'Indian' commercial elite. In 1933, a first schism broke within the ranks of the NIC, leading to the creation of the Colonial-Born and Settlers Indian Association (CBSIA). CBSIA was the first organisation set up to protect the interests of the 'Indian' masses. The NIC was marginalised by the CBSIA for a few years. The NIC was to make a come-back after a few years after having included the rights and concerns of the masses on its agenda. Despite this, the NIC was still very much an organisation fighting for 'Indians' like other organisations. After the arrival of Dr Dadoo in the TIC and Dr Naiker in the NIC in 1939, it was decided that the SAIC should not compromise with state power, and that the 'Indian' struggle was the fight of all non-Whites in South Africa.
38. The schism revealed two streams, one moderate and the other radical. The moderates were prepared to accept compromises with the White power whereas the radicals would not compromise on any matter, militate for equal rights for all and advocate for democracy.
39. F. Ginwala, October 1974, *Class, Consciousness and Control: 'Indian' South Africans 1860-1946*, unpublished PhD thesis, Oxford University.
40. F. Ginwala, 1977, 'Indian South Africans', *Minority Rights Group, MRG Report*, No. 34, London, p. 11.
41. M. Swan, 1985, *Gandhi. The South African Experience*, Ravan Press, Johannesburg.
42. She showed that he came for the merchants, and that even if he founded the Natal Indian Congress, led by the 'Indian' bourgeoisie that she called the commercial elite, members of the NIC were in their large majority passenger Indians. All meetings were held in Gujarati. This meant that all non-Gujarati-speaking 'Indians' were excluded, meaning for instance the Tamil and Telegu-speaking 'Indians', or the indentured or ex-indentured 'Indians', or the small bourgeoisie and the proletariat that Swan called the sub-classes.
43. M. Swan, *op. cit.*, p. xvi.
44. M. Swan, April 1984, 'The 1913 Natal Indian Strike', in *Journal of Southern African Studies*, Vol. 10 No. 2, pp. 239-258.
45. M. Swan, 1984, *op. cit.*, p. 240.
46. V. Padayachee, S. Vawda and P. Tichmann, August 1985, *Indian Workers and Trade Unions in Durban: 1930-1950*, Report no 20, Institute for Social and Economic Research, University of Durban-Westville.
47. F. Meer, *op. cit.*, A.J. Arkin, K.P. Magyar, G.J. Pillay (eds), 1989, *The Indian South Africans*, Owen Burgess Publishers, Pinetown, South Africa. C. Kuppusami, 1983, *Religions, Customs and Practices of South African Indians*, Sunray Publishers, Durban. These works offer a wealth of information.

PART THREE

Stratification of the Indian identity

Introduction

The process of mutual recognition

Who are the 'Indians' today? What distinguishes them from Indians, Sri Lankans, Pakistani and Bangladeshi, citizenship aside? How different are they socially and culturally? Which part of them is directly inherited from their Indian forefathers and which part of them derives directly from their South African experience? Why is it difficult for some 'Indians' to define themselves simply as South Africans? Why do some today still define themselves as South Africans of Indian origin, Indian South Africans, South African Indians, Indian Africans, African Indians, or even Indians of South African origin? What is the nature of the link with India today? Is it possible to systematise the link over several generations? What would be the criteria for such systematisation?

One is often defined through the eyes of the Other. The self-definition of an 'Indian' will differ depending on who the Other is in a conversation. The questions and answers in the conversation would depend on whether the interlocutor were a foreigner, another South African or another 'Indian'. Identity allows a person to establish difference and similitude, thus the process of recognition in a conversation varies according to one's self-definition in relation to the interlocutor's expectations and acquaintance with one's background. This is the reason why the nature, extent and expression of the recognition of an 'Indian' identity in South Africa will vary greatly depending on who is asking. Whilst living in Europe, I was often confronted with perplexity as far as my nationality was concerned. It often arose from ignorance about the 'Indian' population. Faced with a European interlocutor without much knowledge of South Africa, I would introduce myself as a South African and immediately find myself obliged to justify my citizenship because my phenotype told my interlocutor that I was from the Indian subcontinent. There I was, quickly running the person through 140 years of history, compelled to say, 'I am South African, of Indian origin, fourth generation.' Meanwhile, another person, South African, not of Indian descent, immediately identifies me as part of the 'Indian' community and my response is, 'I am South African. No hyphenation.'

Faced with another 'Indian', the situation is, contrary to expectation, far more complex. Being South African is of secondary importance. What matters here is what remains of my Indianness. Much information lies in the unsaid or in deductions made without my saying much. That information is extracted from me, willy-nilly, and derives from the acute knowledge that 'Indians' have of their fellow 'Indians'. The amount and kind of information required by my interlocutors varies according to their degree of communal consciousness and their self-perception in the South African context. For instance, I will not have to give the same amount of information to a first generation and to a seventh generation 'Indian'. The age of the interlocutor is also a deciding factor in the way the dialogue will turn out. Older persons will ask more questions because their set of 'Indian' identity markers is larger. In any case, my identity scan will have to include a certain number of markers which will help place me in a familiar context and will proceed to a full process of mutual recognition. This identity scan would look like this:

Name and surname	Rehana Ebrahim-Vally
Region of origin in South Africa	Transvaal (Gauteng)
Generation in South Africa	Third on paternal side
	Fourth on maternal side
Origin of my ancestors	Province of Gujarat
	District of Surat
	Villages of Mahuwa and Navsari
Languages	English, Afrikaans, Urdu, Gujarati
Dialects	Mehmon (Kachi)
Religion	Islam
Cooking	North Indian and Western
Clothing	Western
Music	Western and classical Indian

Some of this data is self-explanatory for any South African of Indian descent. My first name indicates that my family is of the Muslim faith; my surname, the first part of which is my father's first name[1], confirms this. Vally is a Muslim surname, of Arabic origin. No 'Indian' Hindu family could have such a surname and that is common knowledge. If Vallys converted to Hinduism, they would take a new Hindu first name and would be identified as 'converted Vallys'.

My informed interlocutor would probably identify my accent and place it in the province of Gauteng. The fact that I speak Afrikaans means that I am almost certainly not from Natal and the fact that it is not my first language means that I am not from the Western Cape.

Since it has been established that I am a Muslim, my interlocutor knows that I either speak Urdu, Gujarati, Mehmon or Kachi, or Konkani (Mehmon/Kachi or Konkani being dialects). The other Indian languages spoken in South Africa are Hindi, Tamil, and Telegu, spoken by Hindus. Older people will usually test me on my vernaculars because they still speak them, and some have a limited knowledge of English and Afrikaans. The question about my vernacular competence will be asked in English or Afrikaans and the conversation will carry on in one of the vernaculars I speak. If the person before me is originally from the south of India, s/he will speak either Tamil or Telegu and the process of mutual recognition will stop there. If s/he is originally from the north of India, the process of mutual recognition will intensify and go on to the next steps.

We will then, through my father's name and by a process of elimination, determine my *atak*. '*Atak*' literally means 'clan' or 'lineage'. The question in Gujarati will be, 'What is your father's name?' and then, 'Vally? Which Vally? The Canamia Vally?' The Canamia is a clan, to which most Vallys belong. I am not a Canamia Vally and I now have to explain that my *atak* is 'Chand'. The fact that my surname does not correspond to its supposed clan comes from the not unusual fact that my family carries the name of my paternal grandmother's *atak*. A change of name happened when the young man who was to become my grandfather wanted to emigrate to South Africa. The South African side of the family justified his entry into the territory by pretending that he was my grandmother's brother. This was a common practice in South Africa. Immigration became quasi-impossible with the 1911 law prohibiting any further importation of Indian workers and with the 1913 immigration law. Marriages used to be arranged between Indian families and their relatives in South Africa. The spouses-to-be arrived in South Africa under false identity, pretending to be members of the South African family. Immigrants who resorted to this method have usually retained their borrowed surname.

Now informed about my *atak*, my interlocutor is going to try to situate my village of origin, my *gam* or *tahsil*. This will follow from the *atak*. If I did not know my *atak*, we would go through the *gam* to identify the *atak*.

My family originated in Gujarat. Any 'Indian' can situate Gujarat
in the north of India. At this moment of the process, another step will
be made, provided I am from Gujarat. This information alone would
not be enough to determine whether I am Hindu or Muslim. The aim
here is to establish the degree of proximity between our respective villages. 'My' village is Surat. Surat is actually a district, a '*zillah*', a city. I
follow the ritual and narrow the research down to the actual villages
or '*tahsil*' or '*tahluk*': Navsari and Mahuwa. From thereon, the search
for connections is easy and my interlocutor is usually satisfied if any
common relative or even acquaintances have been identified. We become '*gamwalle*', village people. We could even become '*gamwalle*' if we
came from neighbouring villages.

My ways of cooking, my clothing choices and the music I prefer are
optional but complementary elements of information. They can also
provide information about who I am. The clothes I wear, if traditional,
can be an indication of my faith. The food I prepare can also be an indication of my faith or of my religious sub-group and of my linguistic
group and my village origins.

This itinerary through a personal example probably seems strangely
complex and incomprehensible to the uninitiated. I do not believe it
has been documented before. I call it the *process of mutual recognition*. It
is very commonly and systematically practised and aims to establish
the Indian dimension of an individual identity to determine at least
one common denominator between two people. This process of elimination enjoys an essential place in the social life of 'Indians' and allows people to feel closer through common or recognisable identity
markers. This systematic endeavour to research the Other's origins is
an attempt to situate them in their milieu and to give them back their
rightful rank in the extra-territorial and often mythical place that India
is now.

It is, however, important to note that such a conversation would
not take place between two more educated people, aware of the fact that
to dissect each other's origins is probably politically incorrect and irrelevant. Someone politically conscious would probably not go through
this process, which could be interpreted as a *faux pas* inherited from
Apartheid. It would be seen as a classical South African attempt to
automatically classify people. My first name, surname, phenotype and
complexion are anyway sufficient indications of my being an 'Indian'.
They are sufficient to situate me in a religious space and/or in this extra-
territorial space that is India.

For a younger person, fourth generation on average, the process of mutual recognition will go through phenotype and complexion, first name and surname. That which will be gauged of my Indianness is not established along the extra-territorial axis any more – now totally mythical or badly known – but around the religious sphere. We will come back later to the different perceptions that different generations have about 'Indian' identity.

CHAPTER FIVE

The caste system in India: tools for the comprehension of the Indian identity

This chapter is focused on another layer of the 'Indian' identity: caste. As much as caste as a social category is essential to Indian culture, the word itself is of European origin and can be traced back to the 16th century when Portuguese explorers used it to designate the Hindu castes.[2] 'Caste' or 'caste system' are at the heart of numerous erudite and sociological works trying to explain the complexity of Indian society. Any study on the question therefore runs the risk of being conditioned by a Western mind, influenced by specific representations of society inevitably based on Western notions and values. Accepting that this is the case, it is still important to attempt an analysis of the caste system so as to understand the extent to which being a member of a caste was fundamentally important in determining individuals' identities within the 'Indian' community.

In Hindi the word used to designate caste is *jat*. However, *jat* has many more meanings than caste. At a spiritual level, *jat* defines the self, the soul, the essence of the being. At the social level, it can be used to express divisions, gender, the nature of something, the race, the species or the breed. A *jat*, here meaning caste, can be subdivided into its constitutive elements. These are the *jatis* or sub-castes, which are themselves divided into fraternities called in Hindi *biradari* or *bhaiband*, which are actually a group of extended families. The best way of understanding the Indian caste system is to approach it from these extended families, the smallest unit.

The extended Indian family unit, the fraternity, or *biradari* or *bhaiband*, consists of an average of three to four generations. A *biradari* is a male-dominated structure in which the father is the head of the family. He rules his sons' lives, and is himself ruled by his elder brothers, his father and grandfather. The eldest son occupies the second most powerful position, and all other brothers are his subordinates. Hierarchy within a *biradari* is based on age in relation to the eldest brother, the father and the grandfather. Each son, when getting married, starts the construction of his own family, which will occupy a place within the fraternity/*biradari,* relative to his status within his family of origin.

The hierarchical organisation of the extended family is reflected in the terms of kinship that name each family member, both male and female. Although the female side of the family is dominated by the male side, all its members receive equivalent hierarchical kinship titles. Kinship terms often replace, and are sometimes added to the first name to indicate the individual's relative position within the family. In a family with three sons, for example, the elder son is called 'Elder brother X' ('*Bara Bhai* X'), the second one is called 'Middle brother X' ('*Gora Bhai* X') and the last one is 'Youngest brother X' ('*Chota Bhai* X'). There are terms for every kinship relation, like the elder maternal uncle or the elder paternal aunt's husband, etc.

The various extended families form the fraternity, and the fraternity in turn constitutes the smallest component of a *jati* or sub-caste. Fraternities, sub-castes and castes interact with each other in different ways. Thus individuals belonging to different fraternities of a sub-caste can intermarry. In other words, the fraternity is the exogamic section of a sub-caste. An individual would almost never marry outside his sub-caste and would never marry outside the caste. Thus the sub-caste is the endogamic section of the caste, which is itself, of course, endogamic.

Exogamic marriages between members of different sub-castes are possible because both sub-castes are part of the same caste. However, the most common and preferred practice is exogamic marriages within the same sub-caste

Caste, as mentioned at the beginning of this chapter, is a social category, but, contrary to the sub-caste, it does not determine the ways in which an individual will live, including who to marry; neither does caste determine what job a person can perform. That is the function of the sub-caste, often mistaken for the caste.

The determination of the status of a sub-caste, and by extension of an entire caste, is subject to very strict rules. Boundaries between sub-castes can only be overstepped according to certain criteria. The status of a sub-caste within a caste is determined by a purity/impurity continuum. For example, the Ahir sub-caste, whose trade is cattle and who lives in close proximity with animals, is closer to the impure end of the continuum than the Lohar sub-caste whose members are blacksmiths. Movement or transgressions from one level of the hierarchy to another – at whichever level of the structure – are only possible according to the subtle code of a purity/impurity continuum. In this sense it has to be stressed that the notion of purity is the backbone of the caste system. It regulates a social division that operates according to three principles: reciprocal repulsion, hierarchy and hereditary specialisation at the sub-caste level.

The Sanskrit terms *Suddha* and *Asuddha* are translated respectively as 'purity' and 'impurity'. '*Suddha*' cannot be used in everyday language to designate or qualify events. It evokes images of plenitude in the specific sense of perfection. The term evokes the most ardently desired condition of the human body and the most sought-after state. *Suddha* and *Asuddha*, the concepts of purity and impurity, apply to the animated beings, inanimate objects, places and situations which a human being encounters every day.

The rules that define the purity/impurity continuum and that therefore control marriages are of spiritual essence, and, in that sense, are abstract. However, the abstract spiritual essence is expressed concretely through the distance that one establishes between oneself, one's social position, one's practices, one's hygiene habits, and animality. Human impurity can be synthesised as animality because it is man's organic nature that is shown as pollution through blood, stain or death.

One's animal dimension as an impure phenomenon materialises at the individual level through bodily secretions (except for tears, considered pure because they are specifically human) and ingested foods (this creates the difference between being vegetarian, closer to pure in the continuum, and non-vegetarian, closer to impurity in the continuum). At the social level, animality manifests itself through occupations considered primitive (hunting, fishing), the relative distance to animals themselves (professions dealing with human or animal waste like barbers, laundrymen, tanners, drum-makers, etc.), and the temporary or continuous proximity to carnal expressions of life and death (professions dealing with women giving birth, midwives, or mourners). Professions or actions leading to a form of death are also seen as impure. Therefore oil pressers who crush the seeds of life, and butchers and barbers who castrate animals and circumcise boys, are considered impure.

The position of an individual along the purity/impurity continuum, and therefore the position of his/her sub-caste and caste, varies according to circumstances, external and internal conditions and their interpretations. It is noteworthy that purity/impurity truly operate as a continuum in which there is not a 'normal state' which constitutes the boundary between purity and impurity. As a matter of fact, as F. Apffel-Margin says, there is no term in any of the Indian languages for a 'normal condition' that we would call 'a neutral condition'.[3]

It is difficult to dissociate the pure from the impure, but the pure must be preserved from the impure whilst the opposite is not necessarily true. Marriages are made along this continuum. Marriages between a man of superior caste and an inferior-caste woman are thus qualified as '*anuloma*' marriages (Lit. to rub the right way), translated as hypergamic. Those marriages are actually possible and accepted, whilst their opposites – the '*pratiloma*' marriages (Lit. to rub the wrong way) or hypogamic marriages – are theoretically not recommended. Hypergamic marriages generate new sub-castes whereas hypogamic marriages are abhorred and their offspring become outcasts.

The distance that an individual must maintain towards impurity is precisely determined by the caste and sub-caste to which the individual belongs. The caste and sub-caste determine the extent and the circumstances under which an individual can navigate the purity/impurity continuum. Crossing of the boundaries established by the caste and sub-caste is regarded as a threat to the balance of the entire society, which each individual is supposed to be aware of.

The visible part of a caste-divided society is the sub-caste structure. The sub-caste is the social unit where hereditary specialisation takes place, where the fraternities are constituted. The sub-caste, moreover, is the social unit that operates in a given space and recognises a common, often mythical, ancestor.

Contrary to the sub-castes, castes are not very visible. The caste/*jat* is the group in which sub-castes and subgroups are found.[4] It would therefore in most cases coincide with a professional group consisting of various professional guilds made visible by sub-castes. Despite the fact that the larger size of castes makes them less visible, they function in the same way as the sub-castes and, by implication, operate among each other in the same way as the sub-castes. The belonging to a caste carries the same restrictions as far as marriages, diet and professions are concerned. A caste prescribes general rules of repulsion within itself and towards other castes in the same way that belonging to a sub-caste does. Castes occupy a hierarchical position in society at the same time that they support a social hierarchy.

The varna: expression of a spiritual axis

It might be useful to represent the social hierarchy along Y and X axes in order to understand the ways in which the caste system operates in society. The family, the fraternity, the sub-caste and the caste, from bottom to top, constitute the X axis. The ordinate axis (Y) represents the spiritual dimension of the caste system. It expresses a hierarchical representation of the human universe directly derived from the Hindu sacred scriptures.

According to the Hindu cosmogony, the universe is cyclically exhaled and reabsorbed by Vishnu, the guardian of the world. More than a sheer act of creation, the origin of the world lies in the organization of chaos into a universal order. Myths and canons of Hindu theology concur on this. Everything has its origin, place and function in a universal order. This cosmogony legitimizes the myth of origin of each sub-caste through the recognition of a real or mythical ancestor for each sub-caste.

The spiritual axis of the graphic representation has a social manifestation: four major social categories called *varna* in Sanskrit.[5] The four *varnas* are incarnated by the *Brahmins*, the *Kshatriya*, the *Vaishyia* and the *Shudra*. The *Dharmasastra*, or 'Treatise on the Natural Arrangement of Things', establishes the analytical division of humanity into these four hierarchically functional classes. This analytical division, which operates both in terms of social function and in terms of hierarchical distribution, is also based on the principles of reciprocal repulsion and complementarity.

Varnas attribute specific functions and responsibilities to four different segments of a social body divided into castes. In the *Dharmasastra*, Brahma, the Supreme creator, allocates responsibilities to the various social entities that form the Cosmic Man's body.[6] From top to bottom, one sees:

The *Brahmin* is the guardian of the Vedic traditions and rituals. He is responsible for the performance and supervision of sacrifices, and is in charge of the mystical power. He is the depository of the revealed world, the *Vedas*. He was created out of Brahma's mouth and reveals his power through the word. The *Brahmin* has authority over the cosmic order. He is the priest.

The *Kshatriya* is the holder of the secular power. He owes allegiance to the *Brahmin*, but supersedes him in the civil and political spheres.

Brahma has given him the strength (*Kshatra*). An emanation of Brahma's arms, he holds the power of the warrior. He has authority over the earth and the human beings. He is the king.

The *Vaishyia* is the keeper of the economy. Born out of the Creator's entrails, he has been endowed with *Vish*, the power of labour. He has authority over animals and the product of labour. He is a merchant.

The *Shudra* is the servant of the other three *varnas*, does not have any power and is of a servile nature. He has no authority. He is a serf.

Brahmins, *Kshatriya* and *Vaishyia* are 'twice-born'. They acquire the right to wear the sash that drapes their body from the left shoulder to the right hip during the ceremony of the Second Birth, which grants them the right to perform sacrifices. The *Vaishyia* depend on the *Kshatriya* and on the *Brahmin*. The *Kshatriya* depend on the *Brahmin* and the latter does not depend on anyone. Their *Dharma* – the responsibility of each of them and their common duty – is to maintain the spiritual, political and social order of the Cosmic Being for they are its axis.

Shudra are not twice-born. They are the servants of the twice-born and because of this they form part of the *varna*. There is nevertheless a fifth category that is totally dissociated from the *varna*: the untouchables. They are also called 'the primitive inhabitants' or *'tchandala'* (Lit.: 'Placed outside the village', Law of Manu X, 36, 51). Apparently they started being discriminated against during the Aryan conquests between 1600 and 1500 BC. The untouchables are outside the *varna*, as the *Shudra* are outside the twice-born society. They are *jat bahar*, or 'outside the caste' in Hindi, and therefore outcasts. Among the theories explaining the origins of the untouchables one suggests that they were the product of unfortunate alliances within the *varna*[7]. In other words, they constitute a population that violated the *Dharma* laws and that was expelled from the *varna* spiritual axis as it was guilty of sacrilege. Despite their untouchable nature this group is indispensable to the others because they perform temporal and social tasks such as those linked to blood, death and any form of serious pollution, which are abhorred by the others.

If one takes the purity/impurity continuum as the key in reading the suggested graphic representation of the caste system one sees that both axes measure scales of pollution. Thus the closer a *varna*/caste/sub-caste/fraternity/family is to the extreme right angle formed by both axes, the further it is from a state of total purity. Untouchables, being outcasts and outside the *varna*, are not included in the graph.

STRUCTURE OF CASTE SYSTEM

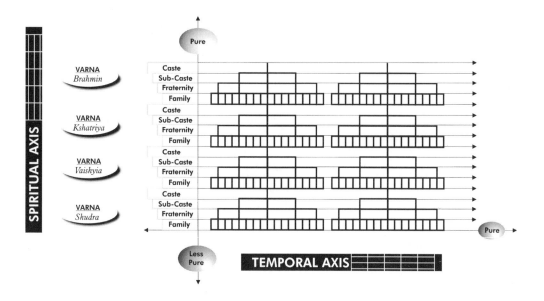

Mobility within the caste system: an essential factor

The sacred social order defined by the caste system is not, however, static. Actually, one of the paradoxes of the caste system is the existence of a mobility element that ensures both its stability and its continuity.

Mobility can be of both spiritual and social nature. Spiritual mobility is driven by the desire to attain the ideal state of *moksha* or *mukti*, meaning 'liberation'. *Moksha* can be attained through three paths: the *jnana* or path of knowledge, *karma* or path of labour or deeds, and *bhakti* or path of devotion. An individual's actions allow him to gradually come closer to *moksha* or *mukti*, by expelling him from the transmigration system (*samsara*) and by attaining the ideal state through the certainty of reincarnation. The promised liberation of the being aspired to by all believers is an important factor in the stability and continuity of the social system. Acceptance of the promise of liberation leads to the acceptance of the social system. The promise of liberation, however, is lived as an upward mobility factor.

A second form of spiritual mobility is the *Dharma*. Hinduism is not a religion but a *Dharma* – or conformity with the cosmic order. A *Dharma* has more to do with the nature and behaviours of mankind than with its beliefs. This is the reason why a theist, an atheist and an agnostic can all be Hindu. The *Dharma* allows freedom of thought but it requires strict obedience to the Hindu system of culture and life.[8] *Dharma*, however, differs according to the social position of the individual.[9] Each caste has a *Dharma* to follow, which confers upon it a certain number of tasks and responsibilities to perform, leading to the interdependence of all castes.

Social mobility operates in a more tangible way and manifests itself through the appearance of new sub-castes and the disappearance of others by absorption. Mobility, as mentioned earlier, can manifest itself upwardly or downwardly, through hypergamic or endogamic marriages and it remains extremely relative because it is confined to the closed sphere of the sub-caste. In some instances, however, an entire sub-caste can decide to move upwards and change the rules of its diet by becoming vegetarian. Such a move could be motivated for and allowed because of a sudden wealth gain.[10]

As a consequence of this upward movement the entire sub-caste can then change the rules that apply to its marriages, for example by preventing widows from re-marrying, a prerogative of high castes. The ascending sub-caste could also claim a mythical or real common ancestor, from the Hindu pantheon or from a higher caste. Once all these claims and rules have been implemented, the sub-caste can move upwards, one or more echelons, and change its name. It will nevertheless keep an attribute attached to its new name, a constant reminder of its previous status.

Indian identity: a group identity

The main observation from the study of the caste system is that the Indian individual exists not as an individual, but as a member of a group. The caste is an association of sub-castes and fraternities, which represents a value in the set of rules of the *Dharmasastra*. This status within the *Dharmasastra* confers upon the caste a social ranking and its accompanying set of duties and responsibilities. A caste is not a political association but a tangible representation of a group's – and therefore of an individual's – place in the cosmic order. Against this backdrop it is possible to imagine that individuals whose socialisation took place in a caste-driven society like India's would have internalised values pertaining to the caste system. These values would be at the very source of the individual's conception of the world and would be the origin of many of his/her conscious acts.

It is then conceivable that such individuals, once transplanted into a foreign environment, would immediately attempt to reproduce acquired and familiar social representations. Faced with the impossibility of reproducing the entire system, such individuals would transform some of their social practices and adjust them to new situations. How did the Indians who arrived in South Africa from 1860 onwards negotiate the drastic change of situation? Which parameters of their identity did they eradicate, which ones did they transform, and which ones disappeared?

---

1. This is not the norm. On the other hand, in many cases, not all the children bear the same surname.
2. Le Robert, 1984, *Dictionnaire Alphabétique et Analogique de la Langue Française*, Tome I, p. 659.
3. F. Apffel-Margin, 1985, 'Types of opposition in Hindu culture', in *Journal of Developing Societies*, Vol. 1, pp. 65-84.
4. 'We have only to think of the number of sub-groups of which each major occupational group is composed to appreciate this. Thus we may distinguish six merchant castes, three of scribe, forty of peasants, twenty-four of journeymen, nine of shepherds and hunters, fourteen of fishermen and sailors, twelve of various kinds of artisans, carpenters, blacksmiths, goldsmiths and potters, thirteen of weavers, thirteen of distillers, eleven of house servants.'
   Schlagintweit, *Zeitschrift der D.M.G.*, p. 578, quoted in C. Bouglé, 1971, *Essays on the Caste System*, Cambridge University Press, p. 17.
5. 'The term "*Varna*" has several definitions that correspond to different interpretations of the symbology of the system. These interpretations have consequences for the actual analysis of the system of *varna*. The most common meaning of *varna* in Sanskrit is 'colours'. Thus this interpretation would attribute different colours to each division: white for the *Brahmins*, red for the *Kshatriya*, yellow for the *Vaishyia* and black for the *Shudra*. This interpretation, however, oversimpli-

fies the concept of *varna* by only taking part of the meanings attributed to *varna* in the old Vedic texts. Colour is one of the multiple meanings of *varna* but its many etymologies vary according to its possible linguistic roots. They may derive from the term *varna* itself and signify "description", "praise", or "to colour an object". They may derive from the meaning of the term and therefore denote *"Jati"*. *Jati* here has three possible meanings: *"vrin"* or "selection" and "acceptance", *"varana"* or induction; and *varna* or the "quality specific to each *varna*".' K.N. Sharma, 1975, 'On the word "varna"', in *Contributions to Indian Sociology* (NS), Vol. 9 No. 2, pp. 293-297.

6. The first Vedic texts like the *Rig Veda* (X, 90, 12) explain *varna* as different parts of the Cosmic Man's body (*Purusa*): 'The *Brahmin* constitutes His mouth; the Royal (*Rajanya*, equivalent of *Kshatriya*) was made out of His arms; the *Vaishyia* makes His thighs; Out of His feet, the *Shudra* was born.' *Encyclopédie Universalis*, Paris, 1985, p. 330.

7. L. Dumont, 1966, *Homo Hierarchicus*, p. 98.

8. Radakrishnan, 1991 (1961), *The Hindu View of Life*, London, 1931, pp. 77-88, quoted in K.M. Sen, *Hinduism*, Penguin Books, p. 38.

9. M. Weber, 1958, *The Religion of India. The Sociology of Hinduism and Buddhism*, The Free Press, Glencoe, Illinois, p. 24.

10. 'At each end of the scale, there is peculiar rigidity in the system of caste [...] in between these two extremes, ritual rank tends to follow [...] economic rank in the village community.' F. G. Bailey, 1957, *Caste and the Economic Frontier*, Manchester University Press, p. 267.

CHAPTER SIX

Did caste disappear in South Africa?

Madrassi, Calcuttie and passenger: the origins of Indian immigration

On November 16, 1860, the SS Truro moored at the port of Durban. The ship was ending a trip started in Madras. On board were 342 British Indian men, women and children, who constituted the first Indian arrivals to the Colony of Natal. A few days later, another ship, the Belvedere, this time from Calcutta, landed its cargo of 351 British Indians. All new arrivals were indentured workers destined for the sugar cane plantations, recruited under a tripartite agreement between the Colony of Natal and the Indian and British governments. This was the beginning of a population movement between India and the port of Durban that between 1860 and 1911 brought to Natal 152 184 Indian people in 384 ships from the Indian ports of Calcutta and Madras. At the end of the 19th century, Madras and Calcutta were port cities respectively located in the presidencies of Madras and Bengal (see map 1 in Annex I); however, the Indian immigrants who arrived in South Africa, although embarked from Madras or Calcutta, did not necessarily originate from those cities.[1]

By 1911 the history and identity of the 149 791 Indians settled in South Africa, of whom two-thirds were Tamil and Telegu-speaking Hindus, had been unwittingly simplified by the equating of their ports of departure with their regional origin.[2] This mistake, which has been repeated by some historians too,[3] was not surprising given that the Indian immigrants referred to themselves as *Madrassi* and *Calcuttie*. Indians embarking from Calcutta were recruited in the Bihar and the United Provinces of Agra and Oudh, much further north than Calcutta, in the present states of Uttar Pradesh and Bihar. Those who embarked in Madras were recruited in the then Presidency of Madras, which included today's states of Tamil Nadu, Kerala, Karnataka, Andhra Pradesh and Orissa. This mistake about the immigrants' origins explains, among other things, why people from Calcutta spoke Hindi, whilst the majority of inhabitants of Bengal speak Bengali.

The vast majority of indentured immigrants were Hindus. According to the information in the ships' lists, 3% of the passengers embarking from Madras between 1860 and 1902 were Muslims, 1.3% were Christians and all others were Hindus. During the same period among those who embarked at Calcutta, 5.5% were Muslims.[4]

As mentioned earlier, not all Indian immigrants were indentured labourers. By 1870 there was a second wave of Indian immigrants who established themselves as merchants and small shop owners. These were the 'passenger Indians' who had bought their passage. Their presence in South Africa was not due to a recruitment agreement and because of this their entrance was not listed on the colony's registers.

Passenger Indians used several ports of entry: Durban, East London, Cape Town. When immigration to South Africa became difficult because of more stringent immigration laws, passenger Indians started using Delagoa Bay, in Mozambique, as the port of entry into South Africa. They would pursue their journey by land and settle in the Transvaal and the Cape.

By 1911 the number of passenger Indians was estimated at 30 000. Natal received 19 389. The Transvaal, the Cape and the Orange Free State received 16 760 passenger Indians between them, of whom only ten families were actually settled in the Free State. Outside Natal, two-thirds of the Indian population were passenger Indians.

Passenger Indians came from Northern India, from Gujarat and the Bombay Presidency. The first arrivals were Muslims, who spoke Urdu, Gujarati and the Mehmon and Konkani dialects. The Hindu passenger population arrived later, from 1890 onwards, and spoke Gujarati. A few members of minority religious groups, like Khoja and Parsi[5] from Gujarat, also emigrated to South Africa.

This chapter focuses on passenger and indentured Indian immigrants to South Africa, tracing their motives for emigration and their social origins in order to understand the type and extent of the social and cultural transformations they experienced once in the new society.

Social profile of passenger Indians

Passenger Indians were traders from Gujarat and the Bombay Presidency, followed by a few families from the south and north-west of India. Although their reasons for emigration were very different from those held by the indentured labourers, both population movements

were related. It was the presence of indentured labourers in the colonies
that, at least in part, motivated the subsequent migration waves of Indian traders. This pattern was also observed in East Africa, Fiji, Guyana
and the British Indies, for instance. The arrival of indentured labourers
would trigger the interest of Indian traders, who could foresee the potential for a commercial network. In the case of South Africa, passenger Indians established links with the Colony of Natal and settled
down thereafter.

Abubaker Jahvery is said to be the first who saw this commercial
potential in Natal in 1863, after the arrival of the first Indian labourers. There are no population figures available for 1863 but records from
1866 indicate that three years after the arrival of Jahvery the Indian
population in Natal amounted to around 6 445 people.[6]

Indian traders saw a commercial opportunity in the indentured population. Planters and farmers only supplied their workers with basic
foods like rice, lentils, dried fish and clarified butter. All the other goods
and utensils necessary for cooking and religious purposes, for example,
had to be supplied. This is precisely what Indian traders did. Jahvery's
success is believed to have triggered the interest of other merchants
from Gujarat and the Bombay Presidency, mainly Mehmons from
Kathiawar and Kutch and Sunnite Vohras from Surat. In fact, some
merchant communities from Gujarat are popularly known for their business skills and their ability to travel to commercially promising far-
away destinations. Some authors, like Fatima Meer, saw this entre-
preneurship as a characteristic of the whole Muslim Gujarati population
and attributed these skills of theirs and their ability to expatriate themselves to the fact that they were

> [...] emancipated from territorial and occupational restrictions
> of caste, [and] felt freer to pursue their ambitions over a wider
> field than their Hindu neighbours.[7]

Meer was probably referring to a text from the Law of Manu that for-
bids Hindus from crossing the seas under the threat of harsh expiation.
W. J. Argyle is of a different view.[8] He explains the predominance of
Muslims among Gujarati traders through the fact that their position
in Indian society was not a comfortable one. Regarded as impure, although not considered as untouchables, and disadvantaged because of
their faith, Muslim traders would have been readier to leave Gujarat
than their Hindu counterparts.

From a historical point of view the geographical location of Gujarat made it a commercial hub from as early as the 9th century, when Arab merchants made it their base for commerce.[9] More contemporaneously, their commercial importance did not shield the *Zillahs* of Kathiawar and Kutch from nature's caprice and towards the end of the 19th century they experienced repeated droughts and severe famines. Natural disasters together with the decline of craft activities in the villages displaced by industrialisation seem to have been at the origin of migratory waves from Gujarat.

Whatever the precise causes for their migration the traders and their families started arriving in large numbers in Natal around 1870. Steamboats were especially chartered to shuttle 400 passengers at a time between Indian and South African harbours. Most of the traders settled in Natal though some left for the Transvaal, lured by the mineral discoveries of the 1890s. The Natal government, however, did not welcome the immigration of Indian traders. The 1897 Immigration Law, although not directed explicitly at Indian immigrants, set a preliminary English skills test for immigration candidates that could not but curtail Indian immigration, restricting it to those individuals with a level of education such that they could be made part of the European culture. Given the formulation and timing of this law it is hardly surprising that it was interpreted as an anti-Indian law. The reasons to immigrate seem to have been stronger, however, than the deterrent of the law because Indian traders continued to pour into Natal through other ports.

The fact that passenger Indians were considered to be British subjects and that they emigrated as individuals conspired against more complete records of their provenance. However, given the relatively recent character of this emigration and that émigrés have kept in touch with their families back in India, historians have managed to reconstruct the village origins of many passenger Indians. Bhana conducted systematic interviews with 'Indians' born before 1911, or with their direct descendants.[10] The set of interviews conducted, on a smaller scale, for this research corroborate Bhana's data as a whole.

The youngest generation of descendants is able to quote their district and village of origin, because most families are still in one way or another in touch with their families in India. The following list shows the districts and villages in Gujarat from which the passenger Indians came:

ZILLAH/DISTRICT OF SURAT	ZILLAH OF KATHIAWAR	ZILLAH OF VALSAD
Surat	Kathiawar	Kacholi
Kholvad	Ratnagiri	Degam
Kathor	Porbandar	Alipor
Variawa	Ranavav	Eru
Rander	Bhanvad	Jalapor
Dhabel	Jamnagar	Navasari
Kadod	Rajkot	Panara
Navsari	Bavnagar	
Bardoli	Jodia	
Mandvi		
Bodhan		

By superimposing the list of villages upon the maps (see district maps 3, 4 and 5 in Annex I) it becomes apparent that passenger Indians' emigration followed the pattern of fraternity links and geographical proximity in India and that this same pattern influenced the way they grouped once in South Africa. This pattern conditioned the actual process of immigration, which went through two stages: inspection and settlement. Generally the son of an extended family was sent as a scout to gauge the opportunities *in situ*, to be followed afterwards by nuclear and extended family. The fact that the first passenger Indians were Muslim merchants introduces a variation in the reconnaissance stage – the young scout would be hired by an established merchant, or would set up his own business if he was wealthy enough. Once this first step was made, he would call for his wife and children and simultaneously encourage other members of his family, of his fraternity and co-villagers to follow.[11]

Muslim traders were not the only free Indians to arrive in South Africa. Hindu traders arrived in the early 1890s. They followed the same migratory pattern as their Muslim counterparts, although for some of them the reasons for the migration were different. Some left India, like the Muslims, to settle down as traders but some were actually contacted by established Muslim Gujarati traders to carry out specific tasks. They left their villages to work as skilled clerks or accountants for Muslim businessmen who knew of their abilities. Once settled, they would also call on their families, fraternities and entire communities to follow their example. A number of such Hindus later started their own businesses and used their hereditary specialisation as assets. They opened their own shops as tailors, jewellers, shoemakers, bakers, etc.

Social profile of the indentured labourers: caste distribution

During the 19th and early 20th centuries it was a widespread belief amongst Natal Europeans that only low-caste Indians or untouchables had immigrated to South Africa. This obviously served the racist purpose of discrimination against those referred to as 'coolies'. Whites lamented the social practices and lack of hygiene of the 'Indians' and attributed these to their supposedly low-caste origins.[12]

In her retelling of the famous train incident experienced by Gandhi, Wetherell approximated the notion of caste to that of social class and confused education and good manners with a superior caste. In a similarly reductionist fashion, she inferred that all Natal 'Indians', meaning the indentured labourers, had been driven from India by poverty. She suggested that poverty was the common denominator of the inferior social strata in India, excluding it from affecting superior castes.

It is probably true that the majority of indentured Indians emigrated for economic reasons. However, there is more to Indian emigration to South Africa than poverty. Shrewd and cunning recruiting agents convinced people to leave India. Agents or their sub-agents would lurk in temples, at weddings, community meetings, fairs and markets, and use snatches of conversation about an impossible marriage, a forced wedding, a bankruptcy, a bad crop, or a family feud to entice people to leave for greener pastures in a welcoming land of opportunity.

All ships' lists stated the surname and first name of individuals, their age, next of kin, and place of origin, distinguishing physical marks, and the sub-caste/*jati* or religion. Bhana worked through this information to reconstitute the origin and social profile of indentured labourers as well as to establish their reasons for emigration. He used the ships' lists, the Natal planters' and farmers' registers and the India Settlement Reports from 1872 to 1909.[13] Based on this information, he drew up a list of castes, which in fact are largely sub-castes as they specify hereditary professions. Through this research Bhana showed the presence amongst indentured labourers of sporadic superior and mid-level caste individuals – of the *Brahmin* and *Kshatriya varna* – among a majority of low caste individuals – *Shudra varna* – and untouchables. Unfortunately he did not give an indication of the correlation between caste hierarchy and belonging to a *varna*.[14]

The analysis presented here puts Bhana's work in the context of studies on the Indian caste system.[15] The analysis links territorial origin to the caste, completes the description of job specialisations (characteristic of a sub-caste), establishes the caste's most likely language, and adds the *varna* to which the castes in question belonged. This kind of analysis helps to explain why indentured labourers and passenger Indians were treated differently in South Africa and provides an insight into the continuity, modifications and overall evolution of the social stratification of indentured labourers in their new environment.

The lists show a wide variety of sub-castes. An accurate calculation of their number is not possible because they were named differently in different vernacular languages and each sub-caste might have therefore been counted more than once. In this regard it is also important to point out that even when a specialisation corresponding to a sub-caste in Telegu, for example, had its equivalent in Tamil, the distance between linguistic groups allowed for Telegu and Tamil-speaking people who were members of the same sub-caste, and therefore of an equivalent social extraction, not to relate to each other.[16] The following data is inspired by Bhana's tables.

TABLE 1

Majority castes and religions among passengers embarked at Madras, 1860-1902[17]

CASTES/RELIGIONS	AVERAGE IN PERCENTAGE
Agamudi	1.6
Balji (Balija)	3.3
Cavarai (Kavarai)	1.7
Ediya	2.0
Kapu	2.5
Mala	2.3

Malabar	3.5
Muslims	3.5
Odda (Oddai, Oddar, Wodda)	3.8
Pariah (Parayan)	14.6
Reddy (Reddi)	1.7
Vanniah (Vanniar)	14.3
Vellalah	4.4

Majority castes amongst Madrassi are Pareyar (14.6%) and Vanniya (14.3%):

- In Tamil-speaking regions, the Pareyar are outcastes who make and play the drum. The caste title arises from *Parei* or drum. The skin used to make the drum is impure and those who prepare it are therefore considered impure and are outcastes.
- In Tamil-speaking regions, the Vanniya are also outcastes. They are the oil-pressers from Orissa.

Then, in decreasing order:

SUB-CASTE	LANGUAGE	SPECIALISATION	VARNA
Vellalar	Tamil	Land labourer	*Shudra*
Vodde*	Telegu	Road worker	*Shudra*
Balija*	Telegu	Merchant	*Vaishyia*
Kapu*	Telegu	Farm labourer	*Shudra*
Mala	?	Fisherman or land labourers	Outcaste
Ediya*	Tamil	Shepherd. This specialisation is not certain but this is our interpretation	?
Kavarai*	Telegu	A subdivision of the Balija, therefore merchant	*Vaishyia*
Reddi	?	Farmer	*Kshatriya*
Agamudi*	?	Farmer	*Shudra*

The Malabar (3.5%) are also cited as a majority caste although they are not a sub-caste or a caste. Malabar actually refers to people's origin in the district of Malabar, today's Kerala. They supposedly declared themselves as Malabar to the agents who may have assumed that it was a caste.

This table is not exhaustive and there was a myriad of very small percentages attributed to castes from the *Vaishyia* and *Shudra varnas* and some percentages for outcastes.

TABLE 2

Majority castes and religions among passengers embarked at Calcutta, 1860-1902[18]

CASTES/RELIGIONS	AVERAGE IN PERCENTAGE
Ahir*	12.2
Bhur	1.6
Chamar	15.8
Chutree	2.8
Gararee	1.8
Kahar*	4.0
Koiree	5.6
Koormee (Kurmi)	5.9
Lodhe	1.8
Muslims	5.5
Pausee (Pasi, Pasee	1.7
Rajput*	2.7
Thakoor	3.4

Majority castes amongst *Calcuttie* are Camar (15.8%) and Ahir★ (12.2%):

- The Camar are by far the largest caste of untouchables in the valley of the Ganges, constituting the biggest portion of the land workforce. They are the 'leather people', the tanners.
- The Ahir★ are the herdsmen from today's Uttar Pradesh and Bihar, traditionally in charge of very large herds of oxen or cows, but are sometimes farmers, of the *Shudra varna*.

Then come in decreasing order:

SUB-CASTE	LANGUAGE	SPECIALISATION	VARNA
Kurmi		Farmer	Shudra
Kahar*	Hindi	Watercarrier fisherman, servant	Shudra
Thakoor		Land owner	Vaishyia
Khattri*	Hindi	Land owner	Vaishyia
Rajput*	Hindi	Land owner	Kshatriya
Lohde		Farmer	Shudra
Gararee		Farmer, cattle rearer	Shudra
Pausee		Palm wine maker	Outcaste
Bhur	Hindi	Farmer	

Any compilation of caste data can result in an oversimplification of a system that allows, as seen in the previous chapter, for spiritual and social mobility. The Kapu (see Table 1 – *Madrassi*) are South Indian peasants, who should be placed into the *Shudra varna*. However, in some regions, the Kapu enjoy a status close to that of the *Brahmins* and claim a Rajput origin. When this is the case, they use the title of Reddi, which Bhana cites as a farmers' caste. The *Reddi* would then be of superior caste, *Kshatriya*, which Bhana's labelling as farmers does not indicate. This could very well be one of several examples of successful caste upward mobility through the claim of a common *Kshatriya* ancestor.

The vast majority of indentured labourers, however, stemmed from the *Shudra varna* or was outcaste. It is possible to surmise, given the areas of specialisation declared by them, that their recruitment was based on skills. The majority of indentured labourers had land-related trades. They were farmers, land labourers, and herdsmen. The fact that indentured labour was a solution to the shortage of farm labour in the sugar cane plantation in the Colony of Natal[19] made the recruiting agents look among the lower Indian social strata, where farm-related specialisations could be found.

Unsurprisingly, agents tended to recruit mostly landless farmers. According to Bhana, *Shudra*s and outcastes formed the majority of the population in the regions from which the immigrants came. Ahir and Camar were the majority in the United Provinces of Agra and Oudh and in Bihar. To leave land that one did not own was most probably not that much of a dilemma for those who eventually decided to leave. As stressed by Bhana, most of these people, as *Shudra*s or outcastes, had subaltern functions in society:

> The total population of the United Provinces in 1901 was nearly 48 million. Just over 31 million people or 66% depended on agriculture of whom 75% were tenants, 14% field labourers, and 11% landlords.[20]

Those indentured labourers, from the small villages where the majority of the population of the Madras Presidency was concentrated, were also largely of peasant origin.[21] In the Madras Presidency 89% of the population lived in villages with an average population of 600 inhabitants.

The reason for the presence of a few *Kshatriya*, *Vaishyia* and *Brahmins* can then be examined, since we know that the Natal authorities had some kind of selection procedures. It appears that the *Kshatriya*, *Vaishyia* and *Brahmins* who emigrated to Natal were, in their majority, landowners. One should keep in mind that agents exploited material upheavals, family feuds and sentimental distress in order to convince people to leave. A caste of landowners like the Rajput, from the *Kshatriya varna*, could also host a number of individuals who were not *de facto* landowners. They could have left the land precisely because they did not own it anymore, and had simply been farming on other Rajputs' land. Bhana's statistics show that 25% of the Pariahs and Malas had switched from the status of servants to that of landowners or farmers. Among the *Brahmins* 60% had left their hereditary specialisation as priests to become farmers. The arrival of a small minority of immigrants whose specialisation had no relation to the land could be attributed to personal circumstances, misfortunes and cunning agents' tricks.

It is interesting that the Colony of Natal authorities kept a rather precise account of the caste origins of Indian immigrants. This certainly did not stem from a concern about the social profile of a cheap workforce, nor was it motivated by a desire to maintain social order amongst the immigrants. In fact, the notion of caste and the duties and treatment derived from it were only respected until the emigrants boarded the ships. People were treated according to their caste rank throughout the recruitment process and up until they were in the depots where they waited for departure; they were accommodated separately, and appropriately fed, according to their caste requirements. During the several subsequent weeks on board, and once past the limits of Indian territory, once in the Black Waters, the *Kala Pani*, there was no room for relations based on the caste code. The exiguousness of this new environment momentarily swept aside the caste stratification and levels of promiscuity never experienced before led to unheard of changes in the travellers' habits.

People probably assumed that this was a temporary situation, though some only believed in caste in the social and geographical context of India. One passenger, a Pariah, is reported to have told a *Brahmin* fellow passenger:

> I have taken off my caste and left it with the Port officer. I won't put it on again till I come back.[22]

The long journey towards the unknown resulted in unprecedented friendships between people who could not have been seen together in their villages. The emigrants developed fellow traveller friendships or links to become *jehajibhais* or ship brothers, equivalent to *Bhaiyacharaya* or fraternal links, transgressing caste and religious frontiers. On board the packed ships there was simply not enough space to keep the necessary physical distance between castes. The fact that this situation was presumed to be temporary made the contacts acceptable to most passengers.

Adrian Meyer relates a legendary story of an elderly woman who had boarded a ship in Calcutta en route to the Fiji sugar plantations:

> [...] each caste cooking food at a separate hearth. Suddenly, a wave rocked the boat, the pots fell over, and the food was mixed. The passengers had the choice of going hungry or of eating the polluted food and they chose to eat. After that, food restrictions ended.[23]

A new identity structure might have been in the making. However, upon arrival in Natal, once the journey and the anomalous behaviour it had engendered were over, the passengers expected caste to naturally reassert itself. This was not the case. The reality of indentured labour in the colonies was far from allowing the reinstatement of a caste hierarchy. Indian indentured labourers were indiscriminately dispatched by the

Coolie agents to various farm estates and plantations. They had to share shacks and eat the same food regardless of their caste status.[24] Demography also played a role in upsetting the caste structure. There were approximately 40 women to 100 men, without any caste quotas being respected. The unequal ratio between men and women further contributed in destabilising the social observance of the caste hierarchy. It was also not uncommon that families who had boarded together in Madras or Calcutta were forcibly separated by the Coolie agents upon arrival in Natal. The promiscuity that had started during the sea voyage was aggravated on farms and plantations.[25]

The archives of the Natal administration contained numerous accounts of complaints by 'Indians' about unacceptable living conditions with regards to caste. Among these there are two examples representative of the trauma experienced by immigrants, which relate the shock that enforced cohabitation between castes meant for some of them.

The first example relates to the pollution of Hindus by Pariahs. The complaint was recorded in 1909, approximately forty years after the first arrivals. It was lodged by about 30 Hindus against two Pariahs, outcaste police constables. The grievances were based on notions of purity and pollution and stemmed from the imperative to separate the pure from the impure. Here are some extracts from the complaint:

> There are two Indians here of the Pariah caste named Anjuru and Munsamy, brothers, who are appointed as constables. [...] what we wish to point out is that if a pariah touches our things or makes arrests we are polluted. [...] We have six other Indian constables here but they are not a pariah caste and do not harass us at all. [...] As nine-tenth of the Indians in this division are above the pariah caste, we hope that you will take such steps on our behalf as to procure immediate dismissal of these two constables.[26]

Some Hindus could not stand the reality of being searched by outcaste police constables. The mere fact of their homes being searched and of having their belongings touched by the Pariahs was polluting. It is possible also that the Pariah constables used their official status to 'harass' higher caste Hindus, quite aware of the shock that this would provoke. This attitude probably did not result from a sentiment of liberation from the caste system but, most probably, from the sense of impunity derived from the actual fact of being in South African territory.

Tensions that originated in the proximity between castes could have far more dramatic consequences than letters of complaint. Bhana and Pachai mentioned isolated reports of quite a number of suicides among the Indian immigrants.[27] These suicides were attributed to harsh living conditions and ill treatment, the inability of Indian immigrants to adjust to the new environment, and, finally, to enforced promiscuity with lower castes or outcastes, which was experienced as ignominious.

The losses of the voyage

The process of immigration brought about three fundamental losses for the Indian indentured labourers: the loss of the sub-caste, the loss of the *Brahmin*, and the loss of elders. All three of them had fundamental consequences for the way in which 'Indians' reconstituted themselves in South Africa.

As explained in the previous chapter, the sub-caste (*jati*) is the most visible component of the hierarchical system within which the caste system operates. The caste system is not only a component of the daily life of Indian individuals to which it is necessary to refer so as to situate oneself in one's social environment. The caste system is also a representation of a conception of the cosmic world and the world in general. Indian persons identify themselves through and within their sub-caste. Within a caste structure, one recognises the other through the prism of the sub-caste. The process of mutual recognition starts there. In India the sub-caste is the criteria of identification, the starting point of the process of mutual recognition and othering, the most fundamental identity marker at the village level. In South Africa, reduced numbers of people, isolation and promiscuity separated 'Indians'' conception of the world from the sub-caste they knew they belonged to. Despite this radical subversion of the caste system, the importance of belonging to a group was so internalised among Indian immigrants to South Africa that they started situating themselves within a group in order to relate to those outside the group.

Some researchers point to this phenomenon as the early sign of a 'demise' of the caste system during the first decades of Indian immigration to South Africa. Their theory is that the linguistic group supplanted the caste system. The need to survive in an unknown and inhospitable land would have driven the indentured labourers to consciously rid themselves of identity markers acquired within a caste system and to transform them into linguistic terms.

What some researchers see as the simple and straightforward disappearance of caste is a far more complex process defined by mutations rather than by a vanishing of the caste system *per se*. The seeming disappearance of the sub-caste did not mean the necessary disappearance of the caste system as such. The sub-caste is not a static category. As shown in the previous chapter, it could be changed, absorbed into other sub-castes, adjusted. Consensus could lead all the members of an entire sub-caste to acquire a new status on the purity/impurity continuum and to climb several echelons up the spiritual axis. This did not mean that Indian newcomers did not need or want to live in groups. As a matter of fact the Indian identity as inherited from India is structured by the group. The individual does not have intrinsic value outside a group. The Indians in South Africa needed to reconstitute some sense of the social stratification that the crossing of the Black Waters had upset.

The forced 'disappearance' of the sub-caste was not the only major change among the 'Indian' community The other major sign of change was the disappearance of the *Brahmin*. As explained in the previous chapter, the *Brahmin* or priest holds the sacrificial power and is the purest of all human beings. He is situated right at the top of the caste edifice and represents an indispensable pillar for the balance of the whole structure.

The anthropologist Gina Buijs sees in the absence of the *Brahmin* the absence of the notion of power, which is, according to her, the cement of the caste system. The absence of the *Brahmin* is the central argument of her justification of the disappearance of caste in South Africa.[28]

This type of analysis has two main shortcomings. On the one hand it reduces caste hierarchy to the notion of power. On the other hand, by implication, the analysis negates the spiritual dimension of the *varna* hierarchy. Hierarchy, although fundamental to the maintenance of the caste system, is not based on power relations between one caste and the other. The balance of the entire structure is based on caste interdependence. Caste hierarchy is set by the distance a caste maintains between itself and the notion of impurity.

Within this framework the absence of the *Brahmin* marks the disappearance of a spiritual dimension that is the very basis of the caste structure. This fact emphasises the importance of the spiritual axis on the graphic representation of the caste system and therefore its importance in the actual functioning of the system. The very small number of members of the twice-born, which stemmed from the absence of the *Brahmins*, left the vast majority of *Shudra* and outcastes without spiritual landmarks and guidance. This fundamental lack of spiritual sense had concrete social expression in the loss of meaning of the spatial dimension of the classification, the *jati*, the sub-caste, and the hereditary specialisation became meaningless.

The other element absent during the first decades of the Indian immigration to South Africa was the elders. Most social scientists seem to have overlooked the importance of the elders in the Indian social structure. As explained before, Indian fraternities consist of extended families where the ultimate authority rests with the eldest man, be it father or grandfather. The very process of recruitment of indentured labourers left out the elders. The recruiting agents preferred to pick young men between the ages of eighteen and thirty. This category represented 64% of the *Madrassi* and 72% of the *Calcuttie*. Only 0.85% of the *Madrassi* and 0.32% of the *Calcuttie* were older than forty. Among the families that actually emigrated to South Africa, 18.3% of the immigrants, most of them were either nuclear families or single parent families accompanied by children younger than fifteen years old. The fact that only 18.3% of the indentured labourers came to South Africa with their families and that in all cases these families were nuclear families confirms the absence of elders in the community.

The unequal ratio between men and women, the small number of nuclear families, and the fact that the families were usually separated upon arrival, together with the predominance of people under the age of thirty among the immigrants, made it impossible to reproduce the structure of the Indian extended family in South Africa.

Fraternities could not be perpetuated or reproduced and neither could they be maintained through a relation with the fraternity members left behind. Indentured labourers, contrary to passenger Indians, cut all links with their families in India from the moment of their arrival in Natal. There is no information available to explain why the majority of indentured labourers severed their family and village links. A possible explanation, however, can be constructed through the combination of two sets of circumstances. On the one hand the majority of indentured immigrants was illiterate and therefore epistolary exchange with relatives was out of the question. On the other hand, it was the disturbing experience of crossing the *Kala Pani*, and its long-lasting

effects. Frene Ginwala's research supports the plausibility of this explanation. She notes that an annual average of only 345 letters and 600
pounds sterling were sent to India from Natal between 1883 and 1890.[29]

The promiscuity experienced from the day of departure led to the
transgression of many of the caste system's elementary laws. Once over
the *Kala Pani*, guilty feelings were added to the sense of being polluted,
making it impossible for the indentured labourers to maintain any links
with their villages. They were polluted and would have polluted family
and sub-caste members who stayed behind. Moreover, many indentured labourers were deeply disappointed by the reality in South Africa.
In their search for their fortune they had not only found themselves
indentured but they had transgressed fundamental cultural and social
codes. Shame, disappointment and dishonour weighed too heavily on
the immigrants to allow them to keep in touch with their families, fraternities and villages.

Elements of a reconfiguration: the birth of the 'Indian' community

On their own in an unknown land, deprived of the fundamental markers mentioned before, the indentured Indians, however, did not re-
nounce their need to be identified through a group. The characteristic
dynamic of the caste system that organises the Indian world provided
the newcomers with the tools to create three distinct categories of Indians upon arrival in South Africa: the *Madrassi*, the *Calcuttie* and the
passenger Indians. The first two categories only functioned in Natal
and obviously referred to the port of departure from India. Indenture
was the common denominator of both these categories, which distinguished them from the third one. A hierarchy based on the degree of
freedom enjoyed by each individual was starting to operate. The passenger Indians were not indentured, had the power to set up their own
businesses and to decide on their departure from India and eventually
on their return.

Linguistic differences operated within each of the three categories.
Language barriers inside the *Madrassi*, the *Calcuttie* and passenger
groups allowed the Indians to deepen social stratification through the
creation of smaller groups. These linguistically constituted groups, which
are still to be found within the 'Indian' community, were the Tamil-
speaking, the Telegu-speaking, the Gujarati-speaking, the Mehmon-

speaking and the Konkani-speaking people. The linguistic groups were formed on the basis of Indian majority languages and dialects but did not necessarily correspond to the majority languages and dialects spoken in the provinces from which they came.

Caste-based practices such as endogamy, which was sought to maintain caste purity, were rapidly transposed to these linguistic groups. The indentured labourers who embarked at Calcutta came from the United Provinces and Bihar. They spoke Hindi in their majority, but also Bihari and Bengali. In South Africa, the *Calcuttie* became the Hindi-speaking group and absorbed the Bihari and Bengali-speaking minority groups. Bengali and Bihari are closer to Hindi than to Tamil or Telegu and the first common denominator was the belonging to the *Calcuttie* category. This group is still known today as the Hindustanis.

There is no direct link between the constitution of the Tamil and Telegu-speaking groups and the regional linguistic distribution in the Madras Presidency. Tamil and Telegu-speaking people respectively represented 39% and 36% of the population of the Madras Presidency at the beginning of the 20th century. This proportion was radically different from that observed amongst the immigrants who embarked at Madras: 56% spoke Tamil and 39% spoke Telegu. This different linguistic representation stems from the zillahs and tahsils of origin. A predominance of Tamil-speaking people was observed amongst the *Madrassi*, and Tamil is still the predominant linguistic group amongst the descendants of indentured labourers in South Africa.

The passenger Indians arrived in a scattered fashion and out of their own will, which explains why it is so difficult to trace them in the colonial records. Nevertheless, we know that they came from India and Mauritius. The linguistic groups formed by the passenger Indians also depended largely on their districts and villages of origin. Those originating from Gujarat spoke Gujarati, Mehmon and, for a smaller minority, Urdu. Those who came from the Bombay Presidency spoke the Konkani dialect. Passenger Indians did not have to endure the promiscuity of the barracks and did not as a whole suffer the same constraints as the indentured labourers. They were largely Muslims, who came with their families and/or had the possibility of inviting their relatives and fellow villagers to join them after a while. These factors made them members of a specific group. Hindi-speaking passenger Indians followed a different trajectory from that of the Hindi-speaking indentured labourers and they did not regroup under one Hindi-speaking linguistic group.

They belonged to two radically different categories: indentured and free.

The radical differences between indentured and free Indians determine that the focus of any investigation into the evolution of 'Indian' identity has to follow the path of both: the descendants of the indentured Indians and the descendants of the passenger Indians. This distinction is actually the origin of many prejudices still observed in some sections of the 'Indian' community today.

The formation and existence in South Africa of seven functioning linguistic groups of which three – Tamil, Telegu and Hindi – could have constituted a substitute to caste, at the very least allowed indentured labourers to regroup and find some comfort in the absence of an operating caste system.

The caste system, however, did not disappear in South Africa. Pollution and dietary rules had been transgressed, upsetting fundamental codes of the caste system, but this did not mean that 'Indians' did away with the caste system. Indentured labourers who decided to stay in South Africa started reconstructing a social reality with the means at their disposal, paramount amongst these being their experience of the caste system.

'Indians' started the reconstruction of their relational networks from values internalised in India. Their identity and the intrinsic structures of the 'Indian' community reflect the caste structures, are rooted in the necessity to exclude and regroup, and are governed by the notions of purity and impurity. Values and practices inherited from the caste system started operating inside the linguistic groups that constituted the *Madrassi* the *Calcuttie* and the passenger Indians. These practices – endogamy within the linguistic groups, the reconstitution of fraternities, the reinstatement of dietary rules and the perpetuation of dress codes – constitute the focus of the next layer of this exploration of 'Indian' identity.

---

1. 'One of the restrictions initially imposed was that the labourers recruited for Natal would be shipped from Madras. This restriction was later modified to allow recruitment through Calcutta, as well as Madras. These limitations meant that most recruits, including any Muslims, would be likely to come from the general areas of these ports and their hinterlands. W. J. Argyle, 1986, 'Migration of Indian Muslims to east and South Africa', in *Islam et Société en Asie du Sud, Etudes Réunies par Marc Gaboriau, Collection Purusartha, Editions de l'Ecole des Hautes Etudes en Sciences Sociales*, Paris, p. 141.

2. S. Bhana and J. Brain, 1990, *Setting Down Roots: Indian Migrants in South Africa 1860-1911,* Witwatersrand University Press, Johannesburg, p. 36.

3. F. Meer, 1969, *Portrait of Indian South Africans,* Avon House, Durban, pp. 20-21.

4. The Muslim minority amongst the indentured was referred to in South Africa as 'Hyderabadees' from the district/*zillah* of Hyderabad, but there is no evidence that they actually came from Hyderabad. One can only infer that this appellation emerged upon their arrival in Natal in order either to establish a distinction between Muslims and others or to express the fact that Muslims, having embarked at Madras, were actually from today's Andra Pradesh, from villages from the district of Hyderabad.

5. Khojas are the disciples of the Aga Khan, a sect of Shia Islam. The name apparently derives from an Arabic word meaning 'Honourable Disciple' or 'The Respected'. Parsi are Zoroastrians, adorers of Fire. They are called Parsi in India because of their Persian origins. They are the Guebres expelled from ancient Persia by the Muslims who took refuge in northern India.

6. S. Bhana, 1991, *Indentured Indian Emigrants to Natal, 1860-1902. A Study Based on Ships' Lists,* Promilla & Co, New Delhi, p. 3.

7. F. Meer, *op. cit.,* p. 16.

8. W. J. Argyle, *op. cit.,* p. 137.

9. S. C. Misra, 1964, *Muslim Communities in Gujarat: Preliminary Studies in their History and Social Organisation*, Asia Publishing House, London.

10. Between 1986 and 1990 Bhana interviewed 631 individuals. He also collected information with an analysis of the *1936-1937* and *1938-1940 South African Indian Who's Who and Commercial Directory* and the *1960 South African Who's Who.*

11. Passenger Indians from other regions are in the minority in South Africa and it is therefore difficult to apply this or any particular migratory pattern to them. One could think of some kind of emulation triggered by the success of the first passenger Indians that would be relayed to others by word of mouth in the villages. They probably migrated via kinship and village links as well.

12. 'In 1893, Mr Gandhi was having some unpleasant and most regrettable experiences. South African custom had become, and still is, conditioned by the fact that the bulk of its Indian population is derived from very low strata in India. Indian gentlemen in India even today – unless they are exceptionally broadminded – do not wish to travel nor associate in any way with untouchables. The European must not be too severely blamed if he had and still has separate railway coaches for Europeans and non-Europeans. The restrictions imposed upon Indians were naturally galling to one of Mr Gandhi's aristocratic connections and expensive English education. Had Natal's early Indian immigrants been high caste Indians, the whole complexion of the South African Indian situation would have been entirely different.'
V. Wetherell, 1946, *The Indian Question in South Africa,* Unie-Volkspers Bpk., Cape Town, pp. 7-8.

13. The India Settlement Reports gathered information on British-ruled Indian districts and provinces.

14. S. Bhana, *op. cit.,* p.71.

15. L. Dumont, 1992, *Une Sous-Caste de l'Inde du Sud: Organisation Sociale et Religion des Pramalai Kallar*, EHESS, Paris, and 1996, *Homo Hierarchicus*, Gallimard, Paris; J.H. Hutton, 1963, *Caste in India: Its Nature, Function and Origin*, Oxford University Press, Bombay ; M.N. Srinivas, 1962, *Caste in Modern India and Other Essays*, Asia Publishing House, Bombay.

16. Bhana collected all religions and castes and grouped them under the headings of 'majority castes and religions'. There are numerous transcriptions for each sub-caste or caste, as for each term transcribed from Indian languages and dialects. We have opted for Louis Dumont's transcriptions, since he is regarded as an authority in this field. Where a caste appearing on the ships' list is not to be found in Dumont's works, we will use Bhana's transcription and highlight it with an asterisk.

17. S. Bhana, *op. cit.*, p.74.

18. S. Bhana, *op. cit.*, p.81.

19. In 1885, an economic recession affected the sugar industry and the Natal authorities repatriated 85 indentured labourers who did not have any training in farming. They were barbers, beggars, scribes and weavers. In the same year, the Natal authorities indicated that the people from Bellary, on the West coast of India, as well as the *Madrassi* Muslims, were not suitable for sugar plantation work. The Natal colony thus did operate some kind of skills selection. For more on this, read S. Bhana and J. Brain, *op.cit.*, p. 32.

20. S. Bhana, *op.cit.*, p.39.

21. In 1901, 71% of the Madras Presidency province lived off the land.

22. S. Bhana, *op. cit.*, p.16.

23. Adrian Mayer, 1973, *Peasants in the Pacific*, University of California Press, Berkeley, p. 158 in Gina Buijs, September 1992, 'The Influence of Migration on Ethnic Identity; A Historical Analysis of the Disappearance of Caste Among Indian South Africans', paper delivered at a conference on *Ethnicity, Society and Conflict in Natal*, University of Natal-Pietermaritzburg, p. 7.

24. The only concession made by planters regarding Indian culture was the provision for basic foods to be imported from India, like rice, lentils and desiccated fish.

25. The work of B. Pachai and S. Bhana, 1984, *A Documentary History of Indian South Africans*, David Philip Publishers, Cape Town and Johannesburg, and Hoover Institution Press, Stanford, California, contains authentic documents accounting for all sorts of complaints by Indian labourers about their living conditions and the resulting promiscuity. All accounts were recorded by the colonial administration. For more information on this, consult the section on the social situation, pp. 2-30.

26. B. Pachai and S. Bhana, *op.cit.*, p. 26.

27. B. Pachai and S Bhana, *op. cit.*, pp. 17-20.

28. G. Buijs, *op. cit.*, preface.

29. Reports of Protector 1883-1890, quoted in F. Ginwala, 1974, *Class, Consciousness and Control: Indian South Africans 1860-1946*, unpublished PhD thesis, Oxford University, p. 24.

CHAPTER SEVEN

Migration of an Indian identity

Layers of identity

Differences in motive as well as in the immigration process itself constituted the backdrop against which an 'Indian' identity was developed in South Africa. The formation of groups around common experiences and identities started in the late 19th century. The first group classifications emerged upon arrival: *Calcuttie*, *Madrassi* and Passengers were groups that, although established by the circumstances of the voyage, were accepted as an initial identity by the immigrants themselves. Soon afterwards two more fundamental identity layers formed the basis for distinction between groups: language and fraternities. Linguistic categories operated along the divisions between seven different languages and dialects while the fraternities operated along the lines of village links. To understand today's 'Indian' community it is necessary to analyse the different ways in which these identity markers combined and operated in each group within the community.

Identity markers have different functions: they create distance, enhance differences and similarities, and also establish degrees of compatibility. Every member of the 'Indian' community is familiar with these forms of defining identity; however, particularly in the case of the new generation, which might be as far removed from their immigrant ancestors as seventh generation, not everybody knows what the underlying reasons and criteria for these markers are.

From the perspective of the process of development of an 'Indian' identity these markers evolved from the stratified social identity characteristic of the Indian caste system into an 'Indian' identity mostly confined within religious parameters. This overarching process determines the approach to diversity within the 'Indian' community. In other words, given the importance attached to religious identity the analysis of the different groups within the 'Indian' community should be done through the lens of the two major religious communities in South Africa: Hindu and Muslim. Thus the rest of this chapter will focus on the analysis of how language, village and caste intersect with a broader religious identity in defining various degrees of distance, similarity, difference, and compatibility between members of the 'Indian' community.

The Hindu community

The Hindu community represented 68% of the South African population of Indian origin in 1980, of whom 91.5% lived in Natal.[1] Within the Hindu community, the first level of identification is linguistic. Hindu people can be Gujarati-speaking, originally from the north of India, Tamil or Telegu-speaking southerners, or Hindi-speaking from central and northern India.

Linguistic differences speak of the social hierarchy developed historically between the Gujarati-speaking descendants of the passenger Indians and the Tamil, Telegu and Hindi-speaking people, descendants of the indentured Indians. The Tamil and Telegu speakers and the so-called Hindustanis are still often regarded as of inferior social extraction. The notion that descent from free ancestors is a signal of social superiority, although unsaid, operates as a first marker within the process of mutual recognition.

Both the history of Indian immigration to South Africa and the caste system combine to establish distance between Gujarati on one hand, and Tamil, Telegu and Hindustani on the other. The latter are regarded as low caste because, as explained in the previous chapter, during the sea voyage they had to give up some of the restrictions pertaining to their caste position.

This perception of Tamil, Telegu and Hindustani is reinforced by the practice of a strictly endogamous behaviour among the Gujarati, descendants of free passenger Indians, and in their rejection of any alliance with these other Hindu groups.

The Gujarati community was able to transpose its caste structures to South Africa because its members emigrated as entire fraternities and as members of sub-castes from the same villages – although the sub-caste did not operate in South Africa at the social level of the hereditary specialisation. This transposition of the caste structure implied, among other things, that Gujarati-speaking immigrants were not exposed to the social mixing across castes that other groups experienced. In terms of the caste system this has kept the Gujarati pure and unpolluted. The strict endogamic practices of the Gujarati fraternities and the links with today's India are an expression of the importance of caste in the life of this group.

Religious orthodoxy, and the notions of purity and impurity attached to it, are also important elements of differentiation among the Hindus in South Africa. However, in this case the lines of purity are defined along a historical paradox.

In India southern Hindus consider themselves more orthodox than their northern counterparts. They claim not to have mixed with the various groups who invaded the country and consider themselves as a pure people compared to the northern Hindus, who mixed with the Aryan invaders and received various other spiritual influences. By implication, the strain of Hinduism practised in the south of India is posited as closer to the original precepts and therefore purer.

In South Africa the north/south axis of purity has been reversed. Hindu indentured labourers who came from the south were 'soiled' during the sea trip and they and their descendants are considered by their counterparts of northern origin less pure because of this. A new implicit social hierarchy thereby developed in South Africa, which, in placing north before the south on religious matters, ran counter to Indian orthodoxy. The contest for superiority amongst the Hindu members of the 'Indian' community extends to the race issue. Tamil and Telegu-speaking Hindus claim superiority in racial terms: they consider themselves Dravidians as opposed to Aryans. The term Dravidian usually applies to a group of languages spoken in the south of India. In South Africa, the term is used by the descendants of indentured labourers to identify themselves as a racial group that was preserved from miscegenation. Being Dravidian in South Africa means to have a darker complexion than the Aryan northern Indians. A dark complexion here is therefore a subtle indication of an Indian racial purity that could help to redress the sins committed as regards caste duties in the immigration process. Here the north/south axis not only defines a continuum of purity/impurity based on race, which runs opposite to the continuum of purity/impurity defined through caste, but it also creates differences in actual Hindu religious practices.

The Festival of Lights, for example – *Deepawali* for most Hindus and *Diwali* for the Gujarati – does not take place on the same day for all Hindus in South Africa. It takes place on one day for the Tamil speakers and on the following day for all other Hindus. This difference, which reflects a hierarchy, was imported from India and has to do with the actual chronology of the festival. Popular beliefs have it that the god Râm went home northwards from today's Sri Lanka. He would therefore have gone through the south before crossing all other regions. Votive lamps are lit in front of every home in order to guide Râm through his journey home. The symbolic interval between the celebrations by southerners and northerners still prevails. In South Africa, where they might be neighbours, southern and northern Hindus still celebrate the Festival of Lights on two different days.

Telegu-speaking Hindus, whilst they originate in the south, celebrate *Diwali* on the same day as the northern Hindus. This apparent contradiction has to do with the way in which they wish to celebrate. Tamil-speaking Hindus in South Africa are the only community that does not consider *Diwali* as a vegetarian festival. All other communities celebrate *Diwali* as a strictly vegetarian event. Everyone agrees that *Diwali* is a celebration of Râm's and Sita's victory over the demon Ravana. Nevertheless, whether *Diwali* is a vegetarian occasion or not depends on the focus of the celebration. The Tamil speakers celebrate the destruction of the demon that had imprisoned Sita, whilst the others celebrate the triumphal return of Râm and Sita, symbol of the victory of light over darkness.[2]

Whether temples are Tamil and Telegu or Gujarati also marks a difference in liturgical objects. The former are in their vast majority dedicated to Siva, one of three gods who, together with Vishnu and Brahma, form the Trimurti, the three figures representing the Supreme. Siva's cult dates back to the non-Aryan pre-Vedic civilisation of southern India, which explains the predominance of his cult in south India and, by extension, amongst Tamil and Telegu-speaking Hindus of South Africa.

The rites and liturgy of the most important religious ceremonies also differ. Marriage is by far the most important occasion in an 'Indian' family, regardless of its faith. Marriage represents the union of two families and two fraternities. It also celebrates the couple's entry into adulthood and accompanying responsibilities. 'Indian' marriages are celebrated with splendour and usually mean exorbitant expenses for one of the families.

Marriages take place within each Hindu community between fraternities who belong in the same endogamous and linguistic sphere. They are arranged according to very precise sets of rules. 'Indians' who get married do not act in isolation and on their own, but on behalf, and to the benefit, of the family and the fraternity. Apart from a few exceptions, the family, and not the individual, chooses the spouse. Parents or relatives identify a potential partner for their child. The services of a matchmaker are still called upon sometimes in order to guide a family in its choice and to approach the targeted family on its behalf. Traditionally, the boy's family ventures out to look for a suitable family into which the son can marry.

A Hindu marriage is more than a sacrament. It is considered as an act of God, a creation of God. Both spouses are the actors in this creation; they symbolise the mythical parents of creation. They re-enact the parts of Siva and Shakti or Vishnu and Lakshmi. Marriages are divine creations and therefore cannot be dissolved. Before a marriage arrangement is concluded, a priest consults each person's astral chart in order to ensure compatibility. Marriage is also a rite of passage or *Samskara*. The importance of the occasion is marked by the length of the festivities. Weddings usually last more than a week. Various festivities and exchanges of gifts between families take place during the week in the run up to the wedding and are all meant to bring both families together. The wedding meal is invariably vegetarian as a sign of purity. Purifying rituals are also performed on both spouses.[3] The variations in the rituals are of a regional nature in India and do not have any impact on the common spiritual meaning of all Hindu marriages.

In South Africa, Hindu marriages and related practices differ from one community to another. Even if marriage has the same significance for all Hindus, preparations and rules differ. The common denominator in all Hindu weddings is a concluding ceremony during which the ties between the bride and her mother are irreversibly severed, whether symbolically or verbally. The bride enters a male clan, her husband's clan. She must leave her family and deny it any influence, for she now has to follow her new clan's rules. These rites of rupture during which the bride separates from her mother and extended family are meant to celebrate the awakening of new ties with the new clan. The ceremony is called *imli gotai* in Hindi, *thare vako* in Tamil and Telegu and *kanyadhan* in Gujarati. The woman is given to the man as a gift from one family to the other.

Contrary to what happens in India, the Tamil and Telegu communities of South Africa have developed close links. They probably forged these ties through their common experiences in South Africa and by the fact that they form the former *Madrassi* category. Their practices are therefore quite similar and marriages between Tamil and Telegu are a common occurrence. They can marry their first cousins in order to bring two fraternities closer and to further and definitively link the mother's clan to the father's. In the male dominated system of the fraternities the mother's clan has an inferior status. By concluding a marriage between her son and the daughter of a maternal uncle, the mother brings her clan closer to her husband's and at the same time consolidates the fraternity. Through this procedure the maternal clan acquires a higher status. It is to be noted that this ascension can only take place through the maternal uncle, not through an aunt. The maternal clan can only benefit through a male. Marriages are thus also a way of adjusting and fine-tuning the status of each family when the need arises. Except for the marriage between cousins, Tamil- and Telegu-speaking Hindus are endogamic.

All Tamil and Telegu weddings take place at the groom's home. The groom's family considers the bride as a gift and celebrates her arrival by taking on all expenses. Nevertheless there are some variations between Tamil and Telegu marriage rituals particularly about the *Tâli*, the nuptial sash, a symbol to be found in every Hindu marriage. The Tamil priest presents the sash to the groom who brandishes it about with both hands and ties it around the bride's neck. The groom's sister or cousin stands behind the bride, holding a votive lamp. The groom ties three knots to the sash and symbolically ties the bride to himself forever. Among Telegu Hindus, the sash is not tied in the same manner. The groom and bride stand facing one another and two adult relatives hang a white sheet between them. The groom has to lean over the sheet to tie the sash around the bride's neck. He then puts a handful of rice on his wife's head. The screen formed by the sheet represents the time when the spouses did not know each other, before God brought them together. The rice is in memory of Râma, who is believed to have done the same on his wedding day. On that day, the rice then turned into red coral, the sign of a virtuous wife.

Marriage among the Hindustanis shows the long-lasting importance of the north/south axis that marked Indian immigration. Hindustanis are Hindi-speaking descendants of Indian indentured labourers. Their ancestors came to South Africa as part of the *Calcuttie* group of first arrivals. Their experiences in Natal did not differ greatly from those of the Tamil and Telegu; however, Hindustanis are endogamous and their marriage rituals and practices are very different from those of the Tamil and Telegu groups, descendants of the *Madrassi*.

Except for a few minor details Hindustani weddings are comparable to the Gujarati ones, all of which reinforces the already mentioned importance of the transposition of the north/south axis. The only particularity of Hindustani marriages is that it is the girl's family who initiates the search for a spouse and it is also her family who pays for the wedding.

Hindustani and Gujarati communities are endogamous within the linguistic and religious spheres. Both communities usually avoid marriage arrangements between families who already have been united through marriage less than four generations previously.[4]

The close relationship between the characteristics of the immigration process of the Gujarati-speaking Hindus and their endogamic practices has already been touched upon. They tend to privilege marriages within the territorial community, revealing strong village ties even today. The vestiges of the caste system amongst Gujaratis are strong enough for them to be able to cite the name of their sub-caste (*jati*) and describe its job specialisation. It is often the case that Gujarati-speaking Hindus have retained the name of their sub-caste, or of one of the fraternities or even of their village of origin, as their surname. A great number of family surnames were originally names of sub-castes, now Anglicised. A few examples are Reddy (Telegu farmers), Chetty (Tamil and Telegu traders and usurers), Padayachee (farmers from south India), Thakor (landowners from northern India), Naidoo and Naik (a sub-caste of the Boyas, Telegu farmers), Patel for Hindus and Muslims (village counsellors or village leaders in Gujarat).[5]

The Gujarati, and among them particularly the Surtis and Kathiawaris, still have an acute sense of caste values and this shows in the manner in which they follow certain rules regarding marriages. The small size of the Gujarati communities, however, does not make the practice of endogamy within South African territory possible. It is the permanent link with their Indian relatives that still allows the elders to arrange marriages between Indian and South African Surtis and Kathiawaris. Endogamic exchanges with the village of origin and other settlements of the Indian diaspora that permit the maintenance of purity within a sub-caste, are, however, a privilege of wealthy families. Less well-off Gujarati families have to content themselves with the more limited opportunities for marriage exchanges available within South Africa.[6]

Gujarati and Hindustani marriage rituals only differ in the timing and the way in which the marriage is concluded. For the Hindustani, a marriage is concluded when the groom applies red powder to the forehead and eyebrows of the bride. The groom's sister extends the red dot along the bride's hair parting. Among the Gujarati, the marriage is concluded a few days before the official celebration during a ceremony called *chundni adwhai* (lit. 'the draping of the sari'). During the *chundni adwhai*, the bride is presented with gifts and her mother-in-law puts ivory bangles on her wrists.

For Hindus marriage is the union of two families and fraternities. It is a tangible manifestation of the importance of belonging to a group. The definition of the group emerges from the superimposition of linguistic differences, the north/south divisions, and the distinction between indentured and passenger Indians. Whilst the definition of the group in India would operate quite unequivocally along caste lines, in South Africa Hindu identity has become almost entirely a religious issue.

The predominance of religion as an identity marker notwithstanding, there are vestiges of the caste system still operating among the Hindu community. They are particularly evident in the observance of dietary rules that express degrees of purity and impurity.

Vegetarianism is still considered as a primordial value from the religious perspective. Through vegetarianism, families and fraternities attain a higher degree of purity on the purity/impurity continuum. Vegetarianism, the prerogative of the higher castes in India, has become in South Africa an often deliberate move to reach a higher rank within the social and religious Hindu hierarchy. When a Hindu marriage is concluded outside the agreement of the families because it does not correspond to their endogamous purity requirements, it is often labelled as a 'love marriage' as opposed to an arranged marriage, which is the traditional way. In these instances, it sometimes happens that spouses do not follow the same dietary habits. As a general rule, the wife adopts her husband's lifestyle. The only exception to the rule is that of a vegetarian woman who enters a meat-eating family. She then has the prerogative of either remaining vegetarian or converting her home to vegetarianism. It is therefore possible to find meat-eating families becoming vegetarian whilst the opposite is quite rare. In any event, one's vegetarianism is always a source of respect for it means greater purity, always interpreted in the religious sense.

In India, a vegetarian status must be acquired by the entire sub-caste and directly depends on the sub-caste's spiritual and social status within the caste system. Neither a family nor an individual can decide to become vegetarian. Changing dietary rules means a change of status, which can only be achieved through the caste itself. In South Africa, on the contrary, both Hindu families and individuals can decide to become vegetarian because there is no strong caste system to regulate the social and spiritual hierarchy of groups. In this case vegetarianism itself is the manifestation of South African Hindus' caste awareness.

Stratification and diversity are two fundamental characteristics of the Hindu sub-community. While the stratification finds expression through different aspects of their religious practices and beliefs, diversity is realised through the many institutions that promote the specific cultural identity of each sub-group.

Most of these associations were founded during the early 20th century; among them are the Tamil Vedic Society, The Surat Hindu Association, The Kathiawari Hindu, The Telegu Association and The Hindi Association. All of them have the aim of promoting the cultural and religious specificity of each community and of providing for the well-being of their members. The South African Hindu Maha Saba was founded in 1912 and brought together approximately 40 Hindu associations.[7] This association promotes the spread and practice of vernacular languages as well as of Hindu cultural studies. Maha Saba actually acquired the status of an official representative body of the entire Hindu community, and is consulted by Parliament and other national institutions on issues of import to the Hindu community.

The Muslim community

The 'Indian' Muslim community represented in 1980 approximately 20% of the 'Indian' population. Out of the total 'Indian' Muslim population 40% lived in the Transvaal and about 55% in Natal.[8]

Contrary to their Hindu counterparts the Muslim community appears homogeneous. This is consistent with the Islam egalitarian precept according to which there is no social stratification within the Umma. The South African government's perception of the Muslim and Hindu Indian communities, which tacitly posited the division among Hindus against the unity among Muslims, contributed to strengthen cultural stereotypes:[9]

> Hinduism has adherents among the Tamil, Telegu, Hindi and Gujarati-speaking Indians.

The Muslims are generally devout and affluent. They adhere to the Sunni strain of Islam.

Nevertheless, the *South Africa Year Book*'s description of the Muslims corresponds with the image that this community wants to give of itself, based on the fact that Islam does not separate the social from the religious sphere of life. Within the Umma, the community of the faithful, there are no differences. Linguistic differences, for example, are considered instruments of communication without any dividing power. Similarly, territorial origins, in principle, are not seen as identity markers capable of asserting distance and difference. Finally, the practice of Islam in Arabic is designed to homogenise practices and unite the faithful.

'Indian' Muslims do not escape the rule and present themselves as followers of the universal principles of Islam, obedient to its duties and requirements. The actual practice of these precepts within the 'Indian' Muslim community does not necessarily follow theological orthodoxy. On the contrary, very powerful linguistic, territorial and traditional distinctions prevail within this Muslim community. Behind the appearance of cohesion there are quite deep linguistic and territorial divisions. It seems possible that this sense of hierarchy and difference is the outcome of the influence of the stratified Indian social system that Muslims must have experienced before migrating to South Africa.

Whether the ancestors of the 'Indian' Muslims were converts, *ajlaf*,[10] or not, *ashraf*,[11] the experience of the Indian social environment could not have left them untouched. As a matter of fact certain characteristics of the 'Indian' Muslims indicate a far more complex relation between social context and group and personal faith than is apparent. The endogamic practices within each group of the Muslim community, for example, seem to have been a result of the influence of the caste system.

Muslims within the 'Indian' community are the descendants of passenger Indians from Gujarat, the Bombay Presidency and north-west India (today's Pakistan), and of indentured labourers from Hyderabad and Madras. Muslims from Gujarat belonged to various linguistic groups: the Gujarati, Urdu, Mehmon and Konkani speakers. In this case linguistic divisions are also associated with territory and religious differentiation between the followers of Shia and Sunni practices of Islam.

The Gujarati- and Urdu-speaking Muslims came from the districts of Surat, Kathiawar and Valsad in Gujarat. From Surat, they came from the villages of Surat, Kholvad, Rander, Kadod, Kacholi, Variawa, Kathor, Bodhan, Vadod, Navsari, Dhabel and Bardoli. From Kathiawar, they came from the villages of Kathiawar, Ratnagiri, Rajkot, Jamnagar, Bhanvad, Ranavav and Porbandar. From Valsad, they came from Valsad, Jalalpor, and Alipor. Their common denominator, apart from being Muslim, was that all of them spoke Gujarati. Those from Rander and Surat also spoke Urdu. A small percentage of Urdu-speaking people who came from those villages and spoke Urdu as well as Gujarati seem to have declared Urdu as their only language.

Originally Gujarati was spoken by Muslims as well as Hindus from Gujarat. However, because of its Sanskrit origin and its Hindu connotation, Gujarati has become the language *par excellence* of the Gujarati Hindus. The teaching of Gujarati and the teaching in Gujarati is today confined to the University of Durban-Westville in KwaZulu-Natal and to schools and institutions like the Surat Hindu Association, managed by Gujarati Hindus and with a strong religious connotation, even though the schools themselves are 90% secular.

Gujarati and Urdu have acquired very specific religious connotations in South Africa. Gujarati became the linguistic preserve of the Hindus of Gujarati origin, whilst Urdu became the preserve of the Muslims of Gujarati origin. This transformation took place relatively recently and can be attributed to the awakening of religious consciousness among 'Indians' and the assertion of different faiths through distinct linguistic identities.

Both Hindu and Muslim passengers were schooled in Gujarati in India and they perpetuated this tradition in South Africa by sending their children to Gujarati-medium schools. Their children received parallel and complementary schooling in Gujarati in order that they learn to speak, read and write Gujarati. This was considered essential for the maintenance of links with families in India and for their own culture.

Gujarati Muslim women, the first generation of 'Indians' born in South Africa, remember attending Gujarati school in Durban and Johannesburg until the 1950s. Their parents as much as the girls themselves regarded this complementary schooling as an asset in terms of marriage prospects. It would facilitate their integration into Gujarati-speaking families in South Africa. It was indeed regarded as a great asset for a new daughter-in-law to be able to correspond with her new family in India. In fact, most Muslim families also saw Gujarati school as an alternative to Islamic schooling after puberty. After puberty, a girl cannot attend Madressah, the Islamic school, any more and Gujarati schooling was then a good preparation for endogamous marriages. Gujarati schools were and still are managed by Gujarati-speaking Hindus while Gujarati-speaking Muslims introduced and headed most of the Madressahs.

By the 1960s, the third generation of 'Indians' born in South Africa seem to have been less interested in keeping in touch with their family and village connections in India. The need to adjust to South Africa; the growing importance of English as a medium of communication at schools and in family businesses; the decline of the practice of vernacular languages outside the strictly family ambit; and the growing distance with India, all contributed to a decline in the frequency of contacts with their villages of origin. Contrary to their ancestors' experience, the survival of the third generation of 'Indians' in South Africa no longer depended upon their knowledge of a vernacular language, but rather upon their command of English and Afrikaans.

Upon their arrival in South Africa, the passenger Indians started founding their own schools, secular and religious, with the major vernacular languages as the media of instruction. Gujarati schools were primarily secular, where traditional arithmetic, Gujarati, history and geography of India were taught. Those schools were an effective medium for the maintenance of links with India. The Indian national anthem and folk songs were often sung there.

Gujarati Muslims introduced Islamic schools. In these religious schools, Muslim children were taught Islam and Urdu as a medium to understand Islam. Muslim children used to – and still do – attend Madressah every weekday afternoon for about three hours, after school. They start at the age of five and the entire curriculum can last ten years. Children learn to read the Quran in Arabic. Today explanations are given in English or Afrikaans, whereas previously it was in Urdu. Urdu was previously the preferred medium of instruction since all primary sources and translations of the Quran were imported from India. They chose Urdu rather than English because they were more fluent in Urdu.

Elderly 'Indians' recall the manner in which Madressahs were introduced in South Africa. In the early days of arrival, the teaching would be entrusted to the person considered most apt in the absence of an Imam. Some Madressah teachers did not have the required status of

Hafez-ul-Quran[12], but were nominated by the community. Families used to remunerate the teachers whereas today they receive their wages from the Muslim communities' representative bodies.

With the establishment of the Madressahs, Urdu gradually lost its primary function as the vernacular language for Urdu-speaking Gujarati people and became the medium of the Islamic precepts for Gujarati Muslims in South Africa. The identification of Urdu with Islam was reinforced by the Urdu script, of Arabic-Persian origin, which conferred upon the Urdu language some kind of imagined proximity with the original language of the Quran. The compulsory Urdu-medium Madressahs meant that non-Urdu-speaking Gujarati Muslims, Mehmon and Konkani for instance, had to learn Urdu either at Madressah or by themselves. These developments actually reinforced the popular perception that associated Gujarati and Hindu. The evolution of these perceptions means that in South Africa today, a 'Gujarati' is a Hindu Gujarati whilst a Muslim Gujarati is referred to as a 'Muslim'.

During the past twenty years, there has been a growing decline of the vernacular languages, replaced by English. This is particularly evident in most Madressahs. Third and fourth generation 'Indians' speak English outside the home. Within homes, vernacular languages are now confined to communication with the elders. In this regard, learning Urdu at Madressahs actually meant learning a second language. The Madressah teachers currently trained in India or Pakistan comment on the Quran in English and teach children Arabic for the reading of the Quran itself. Arabic now replaces Urdu as a second language for the interpretation of the Quran. This evolution has its origins in the Arabisation of 'Indian' Islam.

Amongst Urdu-speaking Muslim passenger Indians there were three groups based on territorial origins. The first group, known as Miabhais, came from the districts of Surat and Rander in Gujarat.[13] The second group is a tiny minority known as the Pathans. They originally came from the north-western border of India. This small group's ancestors came to South Africa as part of a British army contingent sent to fight during the Anglo-Boer War (1899-1902), under the command of Lord Roberts.[14] The Pathans are *Ashrafis*, who claim Afghan origins in India. This means a higher status in India, as opposed to local converts. They do not enjoy superior status in South Africa, but are popularly considered brave and physically strong. The third subgroup consists of the Hyderabadees. They are the Muslim counterparts of the

Hindustanis. They descend from the indentured labourers who came to South Africa from the south of India. The old hierarchy between indentured and passenger Indians also operates among the Muslims. The Miabhais and the Pathans, both of passenger descent, think themselves superior to the Hyderabadees, descendants of indentured labourers.

This historical hierarchy influences the status of Urdu as a language outside the religious sphere. While Urdu enjoys respect and a relatively high status within the space of the mosques and Madressahs, as a home language its status is doubtful. This is so because Urdu-speaking Muslims may originate from Gujarat or be Hyderabadees and therefore descendants of indentured labourers. This is the reason why people whose home language is Urdu will emphasise their territorial origin during the now familiar process of mutual recognition.

Territorial and linguistic differences do not only operate among Urdu-speaking Muslims; they are also used as identity markers for Muslims who speak different dialects.

Mehmon is a dialect that derives from Gujarati. Mehmon-speaking people are known as the Mehmons. They descend from some passenger Indians who came from Gujarat. They belong to a merchant community found particularly in the north of Gujarat. They were locally converted to Sunni Islam and, prior to their conversion, most of them belonged to the Lohana sub-caste of Sindh. The Lohana sub-caste is one of the *Kshatriya varna*. Legend has it that a Muslim saint, Yusuf Din, the descendant of a famous Persian saint, Abdul Qadir Jilani, managed, after ten years spent in Sindh, to convert two Lohana notables, Sunderjee and Hansraj. This triggered the conversion of the 700 Lohana families placed under their authority. These 700 families started calling themselves Mehmons. The newly-converted Lohana left the province of Sindh for the district of Kathiawar because of tensions with their Hindu co-villagers.[15] The Mehmons of South Africa are subdivided into five distinct endogamic groups formed around their village origins, which are Ranavav, Bhanvad, Porbandar, Jamnagar and Ratnagiri in the district of Kathiawar.

The Vohras are Gujarati-speaking Sunni Muslims.[16] The Vohras from India were small-scale farmers who gradually became traders. Large numbers of Sunni Vohras emigrated from Gujarat to South Africa, Zambia, Zimbabwe and East Africa. In South Africa, Vohra signifies a Gujarati-speaking community of Muslim traders. Their only difference with the Mehmons is their language. It is possible that there were some links between Mehmon and Vohra communities. It seems that originally Mehmons might have been part of the Vohra communities that separated because of their language specificity. Through a process of mutual exclusion, Vohras and Mehmons could have grown apart on South African soil.

The Konkani form a small linguistic group based on their speaking Konkani, a dialect derived from Marathi. This small and close Muslim endogamic community came from the Bombay Presidency. They practice Sunni Islam, but follow the precepts of Imam Shafei whilst the other Indian Sunni Muslims follow Imam Hanifa. Most Konkani live in the Cape.

Apart from the seven linguistic groups already mentioned there are other communities who did not group around linguistic and territorial origins. These are the Khojas and the Bhoras. Both extremely small, closed and strictly endogamous, they literally transplanted themselves into South Africa and did not join any other group. Both Khoja and Bhora communities are Ismaeli Shiite Muslims, followers of Ali. Ismaeli are adepts of a Shiite group that broke away from the main Shiite community because of the succession of the seventh Imam Isma'il, deceased in 762. Khojas and Bhoras were converted to Islam in India in the 15th century by missionaries from the Shiite nizari and mustali sects. The Khojas joined the nizari and the Bhoras the mustali.

Originally from northern Gujarat, the Khojas, like the Mehmons before conversion, used to belong to the Lohana sub-caste from Sindh and withdrew to the districts of Kathiawar and Kutch following disagreements with their Hindu neighbours. They came as passenger Indians from 1890 onwards and established themselves as traders in South Africa. They form a discrete community that does not encourage interaction with other Muslims or Indians, a situation which is reinforced by their Ismaeli Islam. The Pretoria Khoja community is probably one of the largest in the country, since they have the only Khoja mosque in South Africa, and their own local religious community, the *jammat*.

A few Muslim families declare themselves as Shiite Bhoras in Durban. They say their ancestors came from Gujarat. South African researchers are divided on the social and religious profile of this small community. Fatima Meer says they were regarded as heterodox by the Muslim orthodoxy, whilst W.J. Argyle says that, like the Khojas, Bhoras are Ismaeli Shiite.

Caste-like structures among Muslims

Belonging to the Umma is determined by the mere fact of being Muslim. From this perspective, linguistic differences are very much a peripheral notion that should not alter the fundamental sense of belonging to the Umma that all Muslims have. Within this framework linguistic differences within the Muslim community do not represent a threat to the basic unity of the Muslim identity and are thus acknowledged *de facto*. Despite these principles, in South Africa strong emphasis seems to be placed on language and the village origin from which group sub-divisions and distinct communities emerged. These groups favour matrimonial unions along endogamic lines defined by both village and language. Larger Gujarati and Urdu-speaking groups tend to favour village origin over language for marriages.

Caste cannot be acknowledged or even thought of within the Muslim community, as it runs completely counter to the egalitarian principle of Islam. Yet the social stratification of the Muslim community as well as some practices within each group do present analogies with the stratification and behaviours pertaining to a caste system. The ancestors of today's 'Indian' Muslims were converted to Islam. However unthinkable it is for most Muslims, the fact that their ancestors were Hindu prior to conversion and that after conversion they still lived in close proximity with Hindus, suggests that Hindu social structures must have influenced Muslim ones even after conversion.

The groups based on linguistic and territorial origin are peripheral to the Umma, but have retained their validity and sense for most 'Indian' Muslims, at least until the most recent generation. It is possible to propose the hypothesis that there is a Hindu collective memory subtly operating among 'Indian' Muslims that is enacted through the situating of people in a social and spiritual hierarchy. The conversion to Islam has facilitated the eradication of a spiritual hierarchy consciousness. The social position that converted Muslims used to occupy in the Hindu social structure was directly linked to the place in the hierarchy of their spiritual position. Islam gave the converts an equal status with all other Muslims. For equality to become a reality in India, the converts would have had to make *tabula rasa* of the Hindu social structure in order to start anew. In this regard what is interesting about Hindu conversion to Islam is that it took place at the sub-caste level, that is to say that, with a few exceptions, entire sub-castes and fraternities were converted, and not individuals.

The Muslim converts proceeded with the elimination of the Hindu cult and all its attributes, which immediately gave them a new status. They became impure for Hindus because they had extracted themselves from Hinduism. Unlike untouchables, however, they could live side by side with Hindus because they were not a source of pollution.

Interestingly, conversion to Islam did not wipe out the cohesive subcaste structure but rather modified it in order to welcome a new faith. All converted Muslim Indian communities in India and elsewhere have at least retained the family and fraternity structure through endogamy. Interviewed in 1983, E. A. Timol, from the Durban Islamic Centre, said the following about the general strong feeling about the maintenance of endogamy:

> We feel strongly about intermarriage. Yes, we, Muslims, generally want to marry within our religious and specifically cultural and linguistic group. We prefer a Gujarati to marry a Gujarati, and a Urdu to marry an Urdu and so on. We want this to happen because we want good marriages, a good family, and this is a very strong feeling.[17]

The subtle influence of a Hindu past does not stop at the practice of endogamy. It can also be observed in certain ritual practices. The presence of Islamised sacrificial and liturgical Hindu rituals, for example, is particularly obvious in the marriage ceremonies.

The meaning of Muslim marriages is very similar to that of the Hindu marriages described earlier. Marriage seals the union of two families and consolidates fraternities. Celebrated with great pomp, they are of pivotal social and religious significance. The average number of guests is about 400, like at Hindu weddings. One clan alone can easily comprise 100 people, and in most towns and villages, the custom is for each family to be represented by at least one person. Whereas Hindu marriage is a sacrament, Muslim marriage is a contractual commitment that assures the social continuity of a family. According to the Prophet's Hadith,[18] Muslims who get married accomplish half their faith. Marriage in this sense is socially as well as religiously meaningful.

Each spouse's commitment is registered separately. The bride is married by proxy in the presence of witnesses. Three of her paternal and maternal uncles are the witnesses, or *wakil*. They come to her home to ask her whether she agrees to marry the groom. After registering her agreement to the marriage, the *wakil* go to the mosque at an agreed time. They meet with the groom and all the male guests for a ceremony called the *Nikah*. The *wakil* inform the Imam that the woman has agreed to the marriage, and once the consent has been obtained from the groom, the marriage is declared valid by the Imam and recorded in the *jammat*'s marriage register. These are the only prescribed steps for a Muslim marriage. A meal and a gathering can happen, but a marriage should not last more than a day.

In South Africa, among the 'Indian' Muslim communities, a certain number of rituals and practices are added to these brief required steps. These additional rituals were originally Hindu and therefore represent the vestiges of Hindu influence in the 'Indian' Muslim community. Among Muslims from Gujarat, some traditional ceremonies and events happen one to two weeks before the *Nikah* and are very similar to those observed among Hindus.

One of the gift-awarding ceremonies is called the *peramni* in Urdu and *peramri* in Gujarati. It is a very joyful, although serious, ceremony during which the woman's clan presents gifts to the most important members of the man's clan. The future husband also receives gifts. Some women from the man's clan sit in a row and the female representatives of the woman's clan file past them, offering presents. The gifts are sometimes trivial. They can be potato and onion necklaces, crowns made of socks or stockings, etc. The two future mothers-in-law are tied to the same chair, then freed and asked to hug. Men also receive presents but are usually not the objects of the farce. This first step is meant to break the ice and trigger the beginnings of a friendly and intimate relationship between both clans. This is followed by the presentation of gifts that need to suit each clan representative's rank. The groom's mother, for example, is given gold or intricate fabrics, aunts receive fabrics, and the younger sister would receive a piece of costume jewellery or a fashionable garment. Men, who traditionally receive shawls in India, are given shirts in South Africa. This *peramri* takes place several days before the *Nikah*.

Another gift-awarding ceremony takes place approximately at the same time in another home. During the *moharoo* (for Gujarati-speaking Muslims) or *mameroo* (for Gujarati-speaking Hindus), the bride's mother is presented with gifts from her clan.

The future husband gives most presents to his betrothed during a ceremony called the awarding of the *Khooncha* (lit. 'trays' in Gujarati and Urdu). This time, the man's clan goes to the woman's home. Little girls carry decorated trays on which gifts are displayed for everyone to admire. Friends and neighbours are also invited. Everything is organised for the exchanged *Khoonchas* to give an impression of opulence because the honour of both clans is at stake. The *Khoonchas* given to the groom by the bride's side are equally ostentatious and both sides proceed with the gradual exchange of *Khoonchas* with the support of a great many expressions of admiration.

The Mehmons' *Khoonchas* usually consist in the parents giving their daughter the pieces of furniture that will furnish her nuptial bedroom. The most important *Khooncha* ceremony is here called the *salamie*, where salutations expressing mutual respect are exchanged between the clans. The couple is given gold jewellery, valuables and money.

Once the gift-awarding ceremonies are over, the gifts are carefully recorded by both clans for future occasions. If both clans are reunited later on, through another marriage, reciprocity will then be easier to gauge. Gifts are an essential element of the social life of 'Indians', reaching paroxysm stage at births, engagements and weddings. In the case of weddings, gifts are a measure of mutual appreciation and of a willingness to forge ties. Much more than objects given to two individuals, gifts seal the union of two clans and the prestige that arises from the quality of the gifts is reflected on the entire fraternity.

Some of the Muslim marriage-related customs seem to be the vestiges of their links with Hindus. These customs are now rejected by a segment of the Muslim community because of their unorthodox nature and because they are still observed by Hindus.

The red *awdni* is either a muslin or an embroidered silk sash that the bride wears on the head during the *Nikah* ceremony. First she climbs the steps leading onto the stage where she will sit with her husband whilst the guests feast and take photographs. Once she is on the stage and in sight of everyone, the husband's clan representatives place the red sash on her head for a few minutes before removing it. The sash is a symbolic object meant to chase evil spirits away. Among Hindus, all or part of the bride's attire is red, red being the symbolic colour of a married woman. As far as Muslims are concerned, this custom is only observed within the Mehmon community.

The *garba* is a women's gathering that takes place on the eve of the *Nikah*. Women from the bride's clan and her entourage participate in the *garba*. The *garba* or *rasra* is a traditional dance still practised by

Gujarati Hindus and Mehmons. A woman stands in the centre of a ring formed by all other women and plays the tambourine. The others form a ring, dancing to the rhythm of the tambourine, beating time with colourful sticks. It is a very joyful occasion and women especially enjoy the privacy of the *garba*. The younger generation of Mehmons now refuses to celebrate the *garba* because it is becoming clear to them that it is a vestige of Hinduism.

Some of the Hindu purifying rituals that take place around weddings have also been transposed into Islam, although their original meaning was modified by Gujarati-speaking Muslims in South Africa. The *pithi* (in Gujarati) is a purifying paste made of turmeric, oil, sour milk and sandalwood. A few days prior to the wedding, a few women anoint the future bride's body and face with this paste. She will keep it on for one night and display a glowing complexion on her wedding day. That which assumed a cosmetic purpose among Muslims, for Hindus is a purifying rite performed on both future spouses.

The 'Indian' Muslim weddings, celebrated with such pomp and splendour, are now being criticised by the more orthodox segment of the Muslim community. Lately the orthodox consider the abundance of gifts and all the customs around the *Nikah* to be Indian, and therefore Hindu, practices. This sector of the community wishes weddings to conform to the precepts of Islam. They want discrete, intimate and solemn weddings. Whatever an orthodox Muslim wedding is supposed to be, there is little doubt that many of the current rituals are deeply influenced by Hindu rituals and traditions.

Even more interesting in terms of the influence of Hindu practices on Islam in South Africa is that a few Hindu practices have been transposed and modified with a few verses of the Quran. They are considered as Muslim practices by those who perform them, although they directly derive from Hinduism. All these practices have in common the fact that they refer to magical or superstitious events, depending on who looks at them.

When people experience recurrent pain or misfortune, it is suspected that they might be the victims of the evil eye, thanks to a curse or because of their own deeds. A *nazr* is then offered in order to counteract the evil eye or curse. *Nazr* means 'offering' in Urdu. The person in charge of the *nazr* could, for example, take a live chicken, preferably black, and stands before the victim. Starting at the feet of the patient, the officiating person twirls the chicken seven times, holding it by its wings, starting from the right hand side. During this operation, the *Durud Sharif*,[19] a verse of the Quran, is recited. Thereafter, the officiant must go back towards the patient's feet and walk straight on, without looking back, until the next crossroads. There, the chicken is released and must be allowed to go in the direction of its choice. The officiant then has to leave without looking back and without checking which direction the chicken took. The chicken takes the evil eye, the curse or the bad deed away from the patient.

Mithi nazr means 'sweet curse' in Urdu. It is not meant to harm a person but may influence his or her performance negatively. It too requires a form of exorcism and the officiant is a woman.

This curse is not intentional and actually expresses a good intention; even if the 'culprit' is revealed, it will not affect the relationship between cursed and curser. This curse is best understood as arising from compliments for tasks well done. If Mrs X is always praised for her samoosas, for example, and the samoosas that she makes become less good she will attribute this failure to a *mithi nazr*. To counteract this and recover her samoosa-making talents, she will offer a *sadaqa*. The *sadaqa* is a dole – the giving of charity[20] – and consists of varying quantities of seven items found in the kitchen. It includes packets of salt, sugar, rice and flour, some eggs, a tin of fish (and a bottle of oil). These offerings are given to the caretaker of the mosque, known as the *Bangi*.[21]

Mithi nazr can also affect babies. From birth, babies wear black cotton threads around their wrists and sometimes loosely around their necks. In some families a tiny penknife is pinned onto the infant's bib. In affluent families the black thread-bracelet has become a bracelet of onyx and gold beads. These bracelets are often given to the baby by an aunt. It is believed that the bracelets and penknife will protect the baby from *nazr*. Despite the baby's wearing of amulets to ward off even well-intentioned compliments, it is believed such praises can negatively affect her/him. The baby's crying, restlessness and loss of appetite are attributed to *nazr*. In this case a *sadaqa* and a burning ritual are performed to offset the curse. The burning ritual comes after the *sadaqa*. It consists of putting dry red chilies, some grass broom bristles and salt in a paper bag. This bag is circled around the infant followed by a chant. The bag is then burnt. In this way, the sweet curse the baby was inflicted with is burnt as well.

Two other areas where Hindu influence can be detected in Muslim practices are a particular form of prayer, the *nurnamah*, and funerary rites.

'Indian' Muslims practice several forms of imploring Allah through vows in ways that go beyond the precepts of Islam. When confronted with an important or difficult endeavour in life, people pray, promising Allah that should He grant success to the endeavour, money will be sent to a *Dargah*, the tomb of a Muslim saint in India or in South Africa, or a certain number of *nurnamah* will be recited. The *nurnamah* was written by Pir Mashaikh, a nizari missionary saint from Gujarat. He wrote thirteen works in verse in Hindi, Gujarati and Urdu.[22] The *nurnamah* contains a story about the Prophet Mohamed and other prophets as well as autobiographical details. It was written for the *nizari* in India and therefore for the Shiite Khojas. Some Sunni Muslims adopted it and it gradually became a sacred text because it tells about some periods of the Prophet's life.

After a burial, those Muslims who have retained Indian ancestral traits practice similar rites to those practised by Hindus. Hindus believe that as the soul leaves the body, it starts a period of migration during which it needs guidance from the living. Hindus pray for the soul on the third and the sixth day of its journey because these are supposed to be particularly trying for the errant soul.

Three days after the death and burial, some 'Indian' Muslims prepare a meal in the name of the deceased. This ceremonial meal is called the *Ziyarat*. Every subsequent Thursday afternoon, women from the village and environs come to the deceased's home and distribute chapters of the Quran among themselves. The reading of the Quran takes place every Thursday for forty days. On the fortieth day, friends and family are invited to a meal and prayers after which the period of mourning is officially over. The Muslims who practice the *zyarat* see it as fundamental because they believe that the soul can only find its rightful place after forty days. The reading of the Quran is meant to make the soul's journey lighter. Islam does not prescribe this practice. There is no such thing as mourning and migration of the soul in Islam. Those who practice the *zyarat* and other Indian practices do so in the name of their ancestral Muslim traditions, transmitted by their parents and grandparents, and defined as *Baap Dada Ka Islam* (lit. The Islam of the founding fathers).

Some elderly Imams still endorse these practices. This endorsement is to be seen in the larger context of a willingness to maintain ties with

India and with practices seen as originating from an Indian Islam in opposition to a growing movement towards the Arabisation of Islam. For some, the observation of funerary rites and practices seen as part of Indian Islam may be linked to a willingness to emphasise their attachment to the Islamic practices of their ancestors. On the other hand, for those who support the Arabisation of Islam, *Baap Dada Ka Islam*, so redolent of Hinduism, is rejected completely.

This chapter has taken a close look at the customs and traditions 'Indians' have maintained for over a century. The analysis of the process of settlement of, and differentiation within, the 'Indian' community suggests that caste did not disappear completely in South Africa. On the contrary, salient aspects of the social, cultural and religious heritage of 'Indians' are based on the perpetuation of communal endogamy and family structures underpinned by notions of purity and impurity that establish the frontiers between the prohibited and the allowed. Endogamy, family structure and purity/impurity are inseparable. These three elements belong to what has been called in this book the temporal axis that defines Indian identity.

A comparison between the socio-cultural and religious practices in India and those of the 'Indian' community suggests that the spiritual axis (composed of the *varna*s with the *Brahmins* at the top) disappeared during the emigration process. Similarly, the sub-caste's essential function, to determine hereditary specialisation, has also ceased in South Africa. What has survived of the Indian identity is its temporal definition. In other words, Indian migration to South Africa did not imply either a transposition or a transformation of the original caste structure but its reduction to an exclusive temporal dimension, as illustrated in the following graph:

CASTE SYSTEM : "INDIANS"

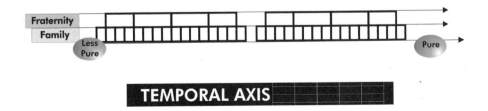

This analysis does not only apply to the Hindu members of the 'Indian' community, it also includes the 'Indian' Muslims. 'Indian' Muslims in South Africa not only reproduce patterns of communal endogamy and family structures, which are unmistakably Hindu. They also adhere to the Hindus' omnipresent notion of purity and impurity.

---

1. *South African Year Book 1987-1988*, p. 645.
2. The interval between the two celebrations could also be explained by the chronology of the event itself, where the gods first destroyed the demon and then went home. In the year 2000, in an unprecedented move towards homogeneity, rather than continuing with separate celebrations, the different Hindu associations of South Africa decided to celebrate the destruction of the Demon that imprisoned Sita – *Deepawali* – and the victory of light over darkness – *Diwali* – on the same day.
3. *Nelangu* in Tamil, *Pithi* in Gujarati and *Haldi* in Hindi.
4. One exception to the rule, though, is the Soni from Kathiawar, from the Gujarati group, who advocate marriage between cousins. The Kathiawar Soni are a sub-caste from India and even though it has not survived as a sub-caste in South Africa, endogamous practices have persisted.
5. We do not have sources on this, but it is quite possible that the colonial administration's influence in South Africa meant Indian emigrants needed to use a patronymic name for administrative purposes, notably to declare births. The use of a patronymic name was not that common in India at the time when migration to South Africa began. People would very often be known in their village as the son/daughter of so-and-so, of sub-caste X. The sub-caste or the first name of the father or the name of such or such a clan then naturally and understandably became surnames in South Africa. The South African administration being quite lax on this aspect, it is not rare to find several members of an Indian family, all siblings, carrying different surnames.
6. In addition to paragraph A, subsection 1, section 4 of the Immigration Law of

1913, amendment 43 of 1953 stipulated: 'No woman born outside South Africa who contracted a marriage with an Indian after 10 February 1953 would be allowed to enter or remain.' Bhadra Ranchod, professor and head of the department of private law at the University of Durban-Westville, contested this amendment in 1985 in these terms: 'South African Indian men marry overseas women mainly because of their parents' strong links with India. Some meet their wives while studying there. [...] There certainly won't be a flood of Indian brides to South Africa if the Act is repealed.' Speech by Bhadra Ranchod, extracts quoted in the *Daily News* newspaper, Durban, June 25 1985.

7. For more information, see G. C. Oosthuizen, 1979, *Religion, Intergroup Relations and Social Change in South Africa*, Greenwood, New York, pp. 523-525.

8. *South Africa 1987-1988, op. cit.*, p. 645 and A.J. Arkin, K.P. Magyar *et al* (eds), *The Indian South Africans, op. cit.*, pp. 146-147.

9. South Africa 1987-1988, *op. cit.*, p. 645-646.

10. The term *Ajlaf* (plural of *Julf*: 'vile' in Arabic-Persian) designates in South East Asia the Hindus who converted to Islam. They are the local converts.

11. The term *Ashraf* (plural of *Sharif*: 'noble' in Arabic-Persian) designates in South-East Asia the Muslims who claim direct descent from the Arab, Persian, Turk and Afghan immigrants. The *Ashraf* form the superior strata of Muslim society, above the local converts.

12. *Hafez-ul-Quran* (Lit. 'The one who has learnt the Kuran by heart') is a title obtained after having learnt the entire Quran by heart. This training is supervised by a religious authority.

13. We do not know the origin of this appellation. One can nevertheless advance the following hypothesis: '*Bhai*' means 'brother' and by extension can designate a fraternity. '*Mia*' is an affectionate suffix added to male Muslim first names (Hussein Mia, Mohammed Mia, etc.). The same suffix is also a mark of respect towards pious people in Northern India and Pakistan. The term '*Miabhai*' could have derived from the habit Urdu-speaking Muslim families had of adorning boys' and men's first names.

14. A.J. Arkin *et al* (eds), *op. cit.*, p. 147.

15. From Abdulla Ismail, *Mehmon Twariq* (in Gujarati), quoted in F. Meer, 1969, *Portrait of Indian South Africans*, Avon House, Durban, p. 188.

16. There are several interpretations of the term '*Vohra*'. According to Bhana and Brain, Vohra derives from *Vohuru* meaning 'to trade'. Misra says that the term Vohra is used in Northern Gujarat to designate the indigenous Muslims, in other words, the local converts. In India, Vohra is a suffix added to the name of a fraternity to indicate a certain type of Muslim. Vohra applies to various Muslim communities from Gujarat, the common denominator being to have been locally converted to Sunni Islam. S. Bhana and J. Brain, 1990, *Setting Down Roots. Indian Migrants in South Africa 1860-1911*, Witwatersrand University Press, Johannesburg, p. 40.

17. G. F. Schoombee and E. A. Mantzaris, 1985, 'Attitudes of South African Indians towards Interreligious and Arranged Marriages: A Preliminary Study', in *South African Journal of Sociology*, Vol. 16 No. 2, pp. 59-64, p. 63.

18. The Prophet's Hadith cites words attributed to the Prophet by sources other than the Quran.
19. This verse says: 'O, Allah, send blessings upon Prophet Mahomed (PBUH), and His posterity as You have sent blessings upon Ebrahim (AS) and His posterity.'
20. See glossary in *Lessons in Islam*, a translation of *Ta'limul Islam* (complete), p. 7. Originally written in Urdu by Al-Lama Mufti Muham-mad Kifayatul-lah (1872-1952), from 1912 the Grand Mufti of India. Translated into English by Sabihud-din Ahmad Ansari. This text formed/forms part of the core texts in teaching Islam to children. Published in India by Kutub Khana Azizia, in New Delhi, it bears no date of publication, making knowledge of its first publication pure speculation. Yet its importance in informing 'Indian' Muslims and especially children about the performance of rituals and customs in Islam is enormous. According to some of my informants, 'every Muslim home should have one'. Written in a question and answer form, it acts as a ready reference and as an introductory text to Islam. To paraphrase the translator, the *Lessons in Islam* is a sort of catechism on Islam (p. 1).
21. 'Indian' Muslims, we would argue, choose to give their *sadaqa* to the *Bangi* because he fulfils two roles: 1) as the caretaker of the mosque the alms are sure to go to a Muslim and 2) as the caretaker one is assured that the *sadaqa* will be given to a needy person as prescribed.
22. The *nurnamah* is the first of the thirteen works, dated 1688. Pir Mashaikh was concerned about the level of ignorance of his disciples and their unorthodox practices. He wrote his works in order to show converts the way of Islam. He wanted to rid converts' practices of Hinduism by informing them about Islam.

CHAPTER EIGHT

'Indian' identity: layered group identities

Indian immigrants in the 19th century were clearly a distinct community in South Africa. They were distinct through their origins, motivations, belief systems, customs and practices. South Africa was not a welcoming environment for either indentured or passenger Indians. The hostility encountered in the new society was the trigger for the formation of new groups around village of origin and language.

In the process of constructing group identities immigrant Indians operated within the principles and social behaviour that were known and familiar to them. Fundamental among these was the principle that society is based on the group and not on the individual. This, which in India has important consequences in the organisation of social hierarchy based on the idea of caste, was partially transformed in South Africa. However, the fundamental idea of the social value of the group was an active organising principle in the lives of 'Indians'.

The value attached to the group among 'Indians' fitted in an odd way with Apartheid ideology's obsession with ethnic groups. Apartheid was constructed to guarantee and safeguard the supremacy of the minority White population of South Africa. For this to be possible it was essential that all the local populations that could not be assimilated into the White group be classified, defined and given limited rights and restricted physical boundaries. As explained in chapter one, to achieve this, the state created a series of objective criteria that were used as instruments for the classification of individuals and therefore were tools in the constitution of groups. As part of the classificatory process the Apartheid state, aided by its team of sage Afrikaner anthropologists, defined the cultural specificity of each group. 'Indians' were in a sense easy to define because they had obvious phenotypical features and a common territorial origin. Despite the linguistic and cultural diversity within the 'Indian' group, the state did not further fragment it into ethnic subgroups based on language. In this context the main concern was not to be fair to the large number of linguistic communities by acknowledging them but rather to fragment and divide the African group in order to break the potential strength that resided in its size vis-à-vis the White group.

When Apartheid was being put in place, in the early 1950s, the Asiatic group consisted of a mere 366 664 people[1] and in 1960, when the 'Indians' were about to be recognised as a permanent South African population, they amounted to 477 125 people, or 3% of the entire South African population. This was indeed a tiny minority and the state did not look beyond the *Volkekundiges'* criteria of a common phenotype and foreign national home to classify them. In this sense Indians fitted rather neatly and easily into the architecture of Apartheid. Yet, as has been shown in chapter four, 'Indian' identity was far more complex than this.

At the time of their arrival in South Africa Indians grouped themselves around the *Madrassi*, *Calcuttie* and passenger categories; later on, language and village of origin, along with the two most prevalent religious faiths, became the elements of a classification accepted from within the 'Indian' community. Chapters six and seven looked into the stratification of the 'Indian' group and the variety of behaviours within each community that facilitated both the process of mutual recognition and the process of othering.

Among the circumstances that accentuate the process of othering, hostility and rejection are particularly powerful. The lives of indentured labourers in the colonial plantations and the experiences of passenger Indians as traders were marked by hostility, ill-treatment and anti-Indian laws, especially those directed at the shopowners. All 'Indians', without exception, experienced discrimination. In the 1950s, already under Apartheid, the Group Areas Act made many 'Indians' lose their businesses and properties.[2]

'Indians' registered huge losses as a result of the implementation of the Group Areas Act, but, as a matter of fact, very few formulated any opposition to the regrouping. Ironically, the legislated segregation introduced by the act allowed the 'Indian' community to reproduce family life within their extended families and fraternities. Isolated from other groups, 'Indians' resumed their community's life according to the accepted principles and social behaviours that defined their identity. Despite the internal stratification and the complex web of hierarchical relations within the community at large, most 'Indians' had the feeling of belonging to a distinct entity. The already existing boundaries between 'Indians' and the rest of the population were further reinforced by segregation and Apartheid. Compulsory classification and the creation of 'Indian' townships, together with the omnipresent threat of intergroup social conflict, helped sustain the boundaries between groups.

Identity is indubitably defined through the existence of the Other. Identity emerges and is reinforced through conflict or in the presence of a perceived threat. By clustering with their own a group can assert and strengthen, even crystallise, the components of their identity, very often via the reinforcement of stereotypes. In this sense 'Indians' – like other groups – found in South Africa favourable terrain for the elaboration of a specific identity. Apartheid gave each South African the means and even the obligation to differentiate from the Others. Ethnic differences, separate development along cultural criteria, and the need to belong to one ethnic group or the other were the tools with which Apartheid created or entrenched distinct identities.

While an 'Indian' supra-identity was developed in response to exterior conflict and threat, identities within the 'Indian' community developed around hierarchy and not conflict. In 140 years of 'Indian' history in South Africa both supra-identity and intra-communal identities have experienced re-arrangements, re-definitions and re-positioning which are related to both broader societal processes and the internal dynamics of the 'Indian' community.

In 1960, 94.5% of the 'Indian' population had been born in South Africa.[3] In 1995, the younger generation of 'Indians' (the thirty-year-olds and younger) was the product of at least three generations of 'Indians' born in South Africa. This generation is at least the fifth generation of 'Indians'. This is the first 'Indian' generation that will live the greater part of its life outside colonialism and Apartheid. The relationship of the younger generation with India is now quasi-mythical. Contact with the land of their ancestors is confined to exchanges with grandparents who still feel a strong link with India although they were not born there. The young generation is, however, aware of family, language and religious identity markers and often still has to comply with them.

Many things have changed in the social and political environment since the birth of the first generation of 'Indians' but change has been particularly rapid in the last decade. Apartheid ensured the restriction of the ethnic group to an ethnic space. The abolition of Apartheid meant the explosion of the ethnic space. 'Indians', like all other South Africans, can now live wherever they wish as long as they can afford it. Economic constraints, unemployment, free enterprise and the possibility of mixing socially with people from other groups are some of the aspects of the liberation from the ethnic yoke previously imposed by the state. Liberated as they are from the imposed *objective* 'Indian' identity and from the Apartheid group identity, disconnected from India, most young 'Indians' seem to be trying to redefine the constitutive elements of their own identity. The two essential factors of this are the quasi-total disappearance of the vernacular languages in favour of English and the prominent role played by religion, which has acquired a fundamental value in defining contemporary 'Indian' identity.

That the Indian vernacular languages are disappearing is an incontrovertible fact. They are still very often widely understood and, if spoken at all, are confined to communication with grandparents. The beginning of this gradual process can be traced back to the first decades of Indian settlement in South Africa. English in Natal and English and Afrikaans in the Transvaal and the Cape rapidly became the necessary instruments of communication on a daily basis. They were the media of instruction at school and the only means of social integration. Children spent around 25 hours a week at South African schools versus 10 hours at communal schools. Education in the vernacular was limited to a few years and did not allow them enough command of the language to communicate. English or Afrikaans fast became the language of communication among children. Moreover, a minimum education in English or Afrikaans was regarded as indispensable whilst the emphasis on education in the vernacular languages started declining from the 1960s.

'Indians' from different linguistic groups also started communicating in English or Afrikaans as early as the 19th century. Commerce and other professional activities naturally led 'Indians' to learn English or Afrikaans. As a matter of fact the state itself had a decisive role in the generalisation of the use of English among the 'Indian' community. The compulsory English test imposed as a condition to immigration to the Transvaal by the 1907 act and the European language aptitude test imposed by the 1913 Immigration Law, together with the Cape Agreement of 1927, strongly encouraged the Indian population to benefit from the 'uplift clause'.

The gradual disappearance of the vernacular languages has not meant the demise of the communities formed around linguistic criteria. 'Indians' still identify themselves as members of a linguistic community (Gujarati, Hindustani, Mehmon, Tamil, etc.) but the common vernacular language that gave the group its name is no longer the preferred language of communication of its members. Nevertheless, communication in English or Afrikaans within homes and with other community members is still peppered with vernacular terms and idioms, often literally translated.[4]

Vernacular terms are still widely used. They are idiomatic words or expressions that evoke Indian rites, traditions and practices. 'Indians' of all generations are still in touch with their vernacular languages via Indian music and films. Festive occasions still draw local musical groups playing Indian music. Popular songs in Indian languages are also quite widespread. However, religious education is now predominantly given in English.

The following figures on home languages among 'Indians', extracted from South Africa's official statistics for 1987-88, are self-explanatory:[5]

HOME LANGUAGE	NUMBER OF PEOPLE	%
English	600 565	73.3
Afrikaans	10 010	1.2
Tamil	13 020	1.6
Hindi	14 739	1.8
Telegu	1 875	0.2
Gujarati	17 757	2.2
Urdu	7 679	0.9
English + vernacular language, same proportion	1 598	0.2
English + vernacular language, English dominant	90 930	11.1
English + Tamil, Tamil dominant	8 105	1
English + Hindi, Hindi dominant	7 281	0.9
English + Telegu	1 134	0.1
English + Gujarati, Gujarati dominant	7 031	0.9
English + Urdu, Urdu dominant	4 303	0.5
Others (Mehmon, Konkani)	33 175	4

'Indian' identity markers are evolving and their hierarchical order is being altered. Religion is now supplanting Indianness as such. Until recently 'Indian' was the name of a boundary between one group of South Africans and others. From an emotional point of view to be 'Indian' has lost its previous charge because the ties with India have faded.

The demise of Apartheid has implied the lifting of all legislated boundaries between ethnic groups, thereby opening unexpected and unknown channels of communication between people. The 'Indian' community is still in its vast majority endogamous, although endogamy within each sub-group matters less. Endogamy seems to be evolving towards being confined to the larger 'Indian' religious communities. 'Indians' are still a small minority of approximately one million people. Most 'Indians' regard this minority status as a threat to the survival of the community. One response to such a threat is the hardening of religious positions. Each 'Indian' group is witnessing the diminishing relevance of their specific traditions among the youth. The youth is largely English-speaking, longs for a more Western and individualistic lifestyle, is more educated and has access to professions that were unthinkable for the previous generations, all of which constitute potential dangers for the preservation of tradition. In this context religion is regarded as the last bastion of actual 'Indian' identity, able to save both Muslims and Hindus from the loss of this identity.

With the intention of testing some of these observations on 'Indian' identity a field survey involving 70 'Indian' people was conducted.[6]

Age group distribution of the survey sample

AGE GROUP (YEARS)	% INTERVIEWED
18-29	20%
30-39	38%
40-49	22%
50-59	11%
60>	9%

The people interviewed do not constitute a true representative socio-logical sample of the 'Indian' community. Notwithstanding this, the results of the survey do corroborate the general argument of this book.

The answers to one of the open questions and to one of the closed questions are rather interesting. The questions deal with recent evolutions of 'Indian' identity on which no other documentary sources are available. The results indicate interesting new tendencies that need further research.

What place does religion occupy in your life? 69 out of 70 answered.

Out of 31 Hindus

Not so important	3	10%
Important	**25**	**80%**
Very important	3	10%

Out of 33 Muslims

Not so important	4	12%
Important	5	15%
Very important	**13**	**40%**
Extremely important	11	33%

Out of 2 Christians

Not so important	1
Very important	1

The number of individuals for whom religion has a minor importance in their lives represents a minority. Among Hindu interviewees and among Muslim interviewees 90% and 88% respectively thought that religion had an important to extremely important place in their lives. The Muslims were much more eloquent than the Hindus and the 33% who see religion as extremely important used superlatives like 'top priority', 'topmost' and 'first priority'. The percentage of Christians is absolutely no indication given the small number of people interviewed. Three persons indicated that they do not adhere to any religion.

Which of the following would you use to describe yourself? All 70 answered.

South African of Indian origin	9	13%
South African Indian	14	20%
South African	**24**	**34%**
South African Hindu	2	3%
South African Indian Muslim	5	7%
Indian of South African origin	0	0%
Indian South African	2	3%
South African Muslim	12	17%
Other	1	3%

Slightly more than one third (34%) see themselves as un-hyphenated South Africans. Even though this figure represents the responses of a relative majority, this is a weak score for the national sentiment. South African citizenship does not seem to mean enough and still has to be explained or qualified through the use of adjectives. This is probably a reflection of the weakness of a national feeling compared with the sense of belonging to a community. The fact that belonging to the nation does not carry great weight is hardly surprising; after all, the South African state rejected and threatened 'Indian' people long enough for them to feel defensive against it. Out of the nine available options, five contain the word 'Indian' and the word 'South African'. The 'Indian of South African origin' option did not appeal to any and no one therefore would claim Indian citizenship, even an imaginary one. However, the four options with the word 'Indian' obtain 43% of the poll, way over the percentage obtained by the 'South African' option. This seems to indicate the need to reduce the field of nationality to a community with which one can identify.

The three options containing a religious connotation obtained an aggregated total of 27% or one quarter of the responses. It is to be noted that some Muslims (7%) claim both their affiliation to Islam and India and that this might be in order to distance themselves from other South African Muslims. The 17% of Muslims who did not opt for 'Indian Muslims' obviously relate to the larger Muslim community of the Umma.

The survey raised a number of interesting questions and challenges, and vivid and enthusiastic reactions. Interviewees sometimes felt honoured that someone showed an interest in their community, others were worried about the consequences their answers might have or sorry that they could not answer some of the questions. The interviews with elderly people, who were particularly co-operative, were mostly conducted in Urdu and Gujarati.

A fifteen-year-old, who was not interviewed on account of her age, insisted on filling out a questionnaire. She returned the questionnaire having answered only one question: *'In a foreign country, how would you introduce yourself?'* She answered: 'I am a South African ANC.' Apart from the naivety of the response this answer illustrates the state of general confusion about belonging to the South African nation. The fact that the South African nation is not yet a reality among young 'Indian' people is reflected in the strength that other identities, including those of community, religion and politics, may have when it comes to expressing citizenship among the 'Indian' youth.

---

1. P. Brijlal, 'Demographic Profile', in A.J. Arkin *et al* (eds), *The Indian South Africans*, *op. cit*, p. 27.

2. One can of course argue that if they were one of the groups that most suffered under the Group Areas Act, it is because they had previously had the possibility of owning businesses and land through their use and misuse of the laws.

3. P. Brijlal, *op. cit.*, p. 27.

4. On Indian English particularities, see R. Mesthrie, 1993, 'South African Indian English', in *English Today*, Vol.9 No. 2, pp. 12-16, Cambridge.

5. Data extracted from a table entitled 'Home Languages: Asians, Coloureds and Whites, 1980' in *South African Year Book 1987-88*, p. 77. These figures are taken from the 1980 census and concern the so-called Asiatic group, which consisted of Indians, Chinese and Other Asiatics. The Chinese and Other Asiatics represented about 11 000 people. We do not know whether they were counted in the category Others with the Mehmon and Konkani speakers or in the category 'English + vernacular language, English dominant'.

6. The objective of the survey was to poll a small sample on some aspects of 'Indian' identity we had researched in order to establish whether our assertions would be corroborated. Each interview lasted between twenty and thirty minutes and every person was guaranteed confidentiality and anonymity.

Conclusion

'Did we ever have a hope?' he said. 'We rebelled
against an Empire that has shaped everything in our lives;
coloured everything in the world as we know it.
It is a huge, indelible stain which has tainted all of us.
We cannot destroy it without destroying ourselves.
And that, I suppose is where I am ...'

AMITAV GHOSH, *The Glass Palace*,[1]

Almost one and a half centuries ago Indian immigrants came to South Africa carrying with them the fundamental organising principles and accepted social behaviours of their country. These principles and behaviours were re-enacted in South Africa to help 'Indians' construct an identity that was different from both the rest of the South African population and from the people back in India. From the point of view of the internal dynamics of the 'Indian' community the purity/impurity continuum, which is the cornerstone of the caste system, allowed 'Indians' to establish distance and proximity among the different strands of Hindus and Muslims present in South Africa. The concerns that 'Indians' had with issues of purity and the practice of strict endogamy within the different subgroups, made it, at least in some senses, easier for them to grasp Apartheid's fear of miscegenation.

The demise of Apartheid has in many ways forced 'Indians' to rethink their place in South Africa. The certainties of Apartheid have disappeared and the comforts of living among one's own are challenged by the social mobility that democratic South Africa has accepted as the right of every citizen. The Group Areas Act, which had guaranteed strict measures of mutual control among the 'Indians', has disappeared. Today, more than ever before, 'Indian' people are faced with the challenge of maintaining, even protecting, their identity. The loss of physical control over possible contacts with the Other makes miscegenation very real and frightening. To many, the death of Apartheid signals the progressive destruction and disappearance of cherished communal values. The mutual surveillance between people living in the same designated area has vanished and the fear of not being able to hold back those who want to live elsewhere has grown. It seems that in post-Apartheid

South Africa 'Indian' identity will require mechanisms of protection that go beyond the external features of mutual recognition.

Despite the efforts to reintroduce objective parameters in order to establish differences with other South African communities, there is little consensus on how to relate to, or how to incorporate the memory of India. The memory of India has, in fact, become a point of tension and uneasiness within the community.

Religious faith has influenced the way in which the land of the ancestors is remembered. The memory of India is expressed in terms of religious orthodoxy. The distance or proximity to India expressed by many 'Indians' demonstrates their religiosity. To a range of Muslims and Hindus alike, India *is* the birthplace of Hinduism, yet their major contact with secular India is through films and music. 'Indian' Muslims who consider India as the holy land of Hindus are purging their Islam of all Indianness and are often of the opinion that their Indian origins are an accident of history, a fact that can be rectified by becoming 'truer' Muslims.

Religious faith aside, what mechanisms do 'Indians' use to become visible and stand out as a significant part of the diversity of South Africa? Dress and cuisine are perhaps the most obvious markers of 'Indian' identity, recognised as such by all South Africans. These parameters of identity have been used as markers of differentiation since the arrival of the first Indian immigrants in South Africa. The dress style of men, as breadwinners and persons who maintained contact with the outside world, changed considerably as they discarded ethnic dress in favour of a Western dress style. Women, similarly, modified their dress to include Western styles. The sari, punjabi or other Indian styles of dress were reserved for auspicious or religious occasions, this notwithstanding the fact that women, who within the community are regarded as 'traditional', continue to follow the Indian code of dress.

Among Muslims the issue of dress is especially complex. Initially, traditional dress was reserved for religious purposes and Muslims adhered to a dress sense that had its origins in India. Modesty was a fundamental criterion and the faithful covered their bodies to reflect a Muslim identity. The process of purging Muslim identity of any Indian influence has also had an impact on dress. Muslims who are overtly concerned with rejecting their Indianness have chosen a dress style to proclaim this. They have shifted their interest away from India towards Muslim countries that observe an Islamic way of life. The Muslim

South Africans' sense of dress derives from these countries; in this way dress has become a particularly important identity marker and sign of orthodoxy. In the case of women, the extent to which a woman conceals her body from the gaze of a stranger indicates the Islamic ideology to which she adheres.

While how much the body is covered is an obvious criterion to ascertain the degree of religiosity among Muslims in South Africa, external signs can be misleading. There are many Muslims who have rejected the Islam of their ancestors but who choose not to display it overtly. They oscillate comfortably between the worlds of Islam and Western modernity.

The ability to integrate modernity and religion can be found among Hindus and Muslims alike. Dressed in highly fashionable attire, they might express the principles of their religion in observing the dietary regulations. The consumption of *halaal* meat, or the interdiction against consuming any alcohol, pork or beef at all, demonstrates to a large extent the role of religion in their lives.[2] Likewise they might display their non-religiosity by expressing their like for forbidden foods.

It seems, however, that the Indian subcontinent might be the yardstick against which to measure the Indianness of 'Indian' identity. The images of India and Indianness received in South Africa come from typically modern sources: the media, including the internet. Apart from the latter or satellite television channels, 'Indians' have free access to programmes broadcast on national television, and to radio and print media.

The media reflected South Africa's identity politics during Apartheid and is still doing so after the installation of a democratic government. Under Apartheid Natal local newspapers in towns with a large number of 'Indian' inhabitants carried supplements with 'Indian' news. Since 1994 *The Sunday Times* and *The Sunday Tribune* have changed their format to become regional newspapers directed at all population groups. This, however, has created a gap in terms of publications directed to specific ethnic/cultural groups.

During the early 1990s, to fill this gap and also to respond to a renewed interest in 'Indian' identity, a series of new media products were launched. The print media launched *Indigo*, a magazine aimed at a middle-class readership, which started out as a monthly. Soon it began to be published only once every two months. A glossy magazine, it carries articles on 'Indians' in South Africa as well as features that allow readers to (re)connect with their Indian roots. Recipes and fashion are two important features that let readers experiment with 'new' elements in their repertoire of Indianness in South Africa. The horoscope is an interesting feature of the magazine because of the way in which it fuses the West and the East. The year is divided into segments that reflect Hindu astrology and the Western equivalent is indicated alongside.

The national television and radio programmes that reach the majority of 'Indians' are *Radio Lotus* and *Eastern Mosaic*. The latter is a weekly TV programme broadcast on Sunday mornings with a rebroadcast scheduled after prime time viewing on Monday evenings. It is a magazine programme concentrated on bringing news about India and about the Indian diaspora to viewers in South Africa. Fashion and food feature prominently and care is taken to screen programmes that reflect the diversity that is inherent among 'Indians'.

Though the programme is presented in English, the soap shows or recipes, both very important elements, are chosen to reflect the linguistic and religious diversity of 'Indians'. Newsworthy items from the subcontinent are also given airtime. Indian films and music, which for a long period were the dominant means of connecting to Indian roots, retain a prominent profile. Music videos and trailers of Indian films are shown and to this can be added gossip about Indian film stars.

The sense, and the reality, of being a minority, as well as the need to take pride in Indian roots were behind the launch of *Eastern Mosaic*. A striking example of this was an advertisement featuring a somewhat confused 'Indian' male wearing the feathered headdress of the Amerindians. Returning to his home and squaw he advises the viewers to watch the programme. *Eastern Mosaic* is the programme on national television that coaches 'Indians' on 'how to be a good Indian'. What is interesting about the advert is the way it emphasises the minority feeling of 'Indians', connecting it to the similar status of American Indians through a play on words.

Radio Lotus is broadcast from Durban in KwaZulu-Natal. The presenters are 'Indians' and the programmes are designed to reflect the interests of their community. The subjects of the talk shows are indicators of the concerns and dilemmas in the lives of ordinary 'Indians'. The entertainment side of the radio is a carefully balanced musical selection that represents the different Indian languages found in the community.

Accepting the linguistic stratification found among 'Indians', *Radio Lotus* organises special programmes in response. A noteworthy observation in this regard is the way in which such programmes are a mixture of Indian languages and English. A programme in Tamil and Urdu, for example, could teach basic language skills to the listener or explain in English the lyrics of a song about to be played.

A fundamental aspect of these programmes is the selection of the content. This has to be done observing the rules of distance practiced by the 'Indian' community. The producers of *Eastern Mosaic* and Radio Lotus need to be vigilant about not mixing religions or languages. A Tamil slot, for example, should be for Tamils only and should not contain anything that deals with the Gujarati.

These attempts by the media to attach the 'Indian' community to the larger diaspora are closely linked to the political environment in South Africa. The right to social mobility coupled with the recognition of cultural diversity in democratic South Africa has in many ways influenced 'Indians' to display their Indianness or their religiosity. Whether it is their Indianness or their religiosity, many now seek to integrate their community into a larger one, be it the Indian diaspora and or/the Umma.

The decades of discrimination experienced under the Apartheid regime have left a deep scar on all South Africans. 'Indians' also internalised the experience of having been second-class citizens who were denied the basic human rights that were the privilege of the minority White population. As individuals deprived of their political rights, Indianness for many became a rallying factor. The reality of the acquisition of full South African citizenship remains to be recognised and enjoyed by the majority of 'Indians', since South Africanness continues to be expressed in communal terms. They still consider themselves as South African 'Indians', but rarely as Indian South Africans and increasingly as Hindu South Africans or Muslim South Africans.

The task facing the country is to create a social and political space for all South Africans. Seven years after the first democratic elections citizens still prefer to use a label to claim or indicate their communal affiliation. Nation building, which requires the invention of symbols and rallying themes of solidarity and loyalty, is still in a project phase. It forms the crux of all reconstruction and development initiatives, which continually seek ways to involve all South Africans in redressing the imbalances of the past and in the construction of the nation. These ideas and sentiments were expressed in Nelson Mandela's address on May 10, 1994 to all South Africans:

> [...] The time for the healing of wounds has come. The moment to bridge the chasms that divide us has come. The time to build is upon us. We have achieved at last our political emancipation. We pledge ourselves to liberate our people from the continuing bondage of poverty, deprivation, suffering, gender and other discrimination. [...] We enter into a covenant that we shall build the society in which all South Africans, both black and white, will be able to walk tall, without any fear in their hearts, assured of their inalienable right to human dignity – a rainbow nation at peace with itself and the world. [...] We understand that there is no easy road to freedom. We know it well that none of us acting alone can achieve success. We must therefore act together as a united people, for national reconciliation, for nation building, for the birth of a new world.[3]

The birth of a new world as expressed in Nelson Mandela's inaugural address clearly depends on the degree of affinity that each individual feels towards the idea of a South African nation. Each South African has been liberated from the yoke of Apartheid. As emancipated South Africans, they have become independent and responsible individuals in relation to the political institutions.

The 'Indians', like their compatriots freed from obligatory ethnic affiliation, have become responsible for their actions and decisions as individuals. The choice of belonging to a community has theoretically become an individual concern. The collapsing of inter-communal boundaries has more than ever in the history of South Africa opened a repertoire of choice, of mobility, of transfer for each South African. The invention of the South African citizen today depends on the ability of the state to rally its citizens around the symbolic values of citizenry.

The 'Indians' adapted their culture to become South Africans. As a culturally distinct community who decided to settle in South Africa they embody the notion of a fusion of cultural paradigms. The perceptions they have of themselves are a combination of their experiences as subjects of the British Empire and second class citizens in Apartheid South Africa. Their future once again depends on how they respond to the challenge of reconciling in a creative way communal identity with citizenship, or, in other words, to be different yet one.

1. Ghosh, Amitav, 2000, *The Glass Palace*, Harper Collins, London, p. 518.
2. The consumption of prohibited foods is a complex issue. Some Muslims take alcohol and don't eat pork. Some Hindus, born vegetarian, include meat or fish but almost never beef, though in most cases this would be done outside the home and as far away as possible from the community. All would regard themselves as part of their respective religious communities but offer the explanation of not being practicing members, that is to say a person who strictly observes the rules and regulations laid down in the religion.
3. Extracts from 'Statement of the President of the African National Congress Nelson Rolihlahla Mandela at his Inauguration as President of the Democratic Republic of South Africa.' Union Buildings, Pretoria, 10 May 1994 in www.anc.org.za/ancdocs/history/mandela/1994/inaugupta.html

South African chronology

From pre-historic times until about 2000 BC, sporadic groups of hunters and gatherers formed the only population of the southern part of Africa. In about 300 BC, the first wave of human migration moves along the east coast of Africa, going towards southern Africa. Communities dating back to the Iron Age had already settled in north-eastern part of South Africa.

15th century Khoisan and other African peoples settle in various regions of South Africa. Many cultures, languages and lifestyles develop.

1488 Bartholomew Diaz lands on the shores of Cape Cross, north of Walvis Bay, today's Namibia.

1498 Vasco de Gama sails across the southern tip of Africa on his way to the Indias.

1552 Portuguese sailors shipwrecked on the south-eastern coast of South Africa meet Xhosa peoples.

1595 De Houtman is the first Dutch sailor to reach the Indias.

1602 The Dutch East India Company is founded.

1647 The Dutch ship *Haerlem* arrives at the Cape.

1652 Jan van Riebeeck of the Dutch East India Company arrives at Cape of Good Hope and establishes a supply station at Table Bay, intending to trade with Khoi herders for meat. The first permanent European settlement.

1657 First colonial farmers established on Khoi land. Slaves are imported from Angola, Madagascar, Ceylon and Malaya.

1658 War with the Khoi (First Hottentot War), who are beaten by superior Dutch firepower and then decimated by European diseases.

1688 French Huguenots settle. Dutch farmers search for grazing; northwards, they encounter San hunters who resist but are almost exterminated, surviving only in the Kalahari desert. Trekboers going east encroach on Xhosa land and meet resistance.

1690 Slave insurrection is repressed in Stellenbosch, Cape.

1779 First of a series of frontier wars between the Trekboers and the Xhosa, which carry on intermittently until the mid-19th century.

1795 After the French invasion of the Netherlands, the British annex Cape Town. In 1814, at the end of Napoleonic wars, the Cape is ceded to Britain.

1799-1802 Repression of Khoi-Khoin uprising in the east of the Cape Colony.

1815 Shaka becomes the Zulu King.

1819 King Shaka wins a decisive battle over his contenders which marks the emergence of Zulu power in Eastern Natal. Shaka is murdered in 1828.

1820   British settle in Eastern Cape: not allowed to import slaves. Economic recession in England.

1826   Missionary John Bennie publishes the first Xhosa glossary.

1828   Ordinance 50 introduces freedom of movement for Coloureds. They can own land and work where they want to.

1833   Slavery abolished from British Empire. White farmers lose labour force with little compensation. Labourers free to work for settlers.

1837   The Great Trek. 6 000 Boers leave Cape Colony, trek north and east to escape British rule, defeating Ndebele, who retreat over Limpopo river.

1838   Piet Retief leads a Trekker group over Drakensberg mountains into Natal, attempts to obtain land from Zulu leader, Dingaan, successor of Shaka. Dingaan has Retief murdered. On 16 December, Boer firepower defeats Zulu at Battle of Blood River. 3 000 Zulu die. This becomes a sacred day for the Boers – the Day of the Covenant.

1842   Xhosa unrest around Port Natal as Boer farmers take their land. The British intervene, fight the Boers, and annex Natal. The Boers trek back into the Transvaal.

1843   Natal becomes a British colony.

1847-49   British immigrants settle in Natal.

1851   First sugar-cane production in Natal.

1852   Britain recognises the independent Boer republic of the Transvaal.

1853   The Cape Colony gains its own elected government. The franchise is based on a property qualification.

1854   Britain recognises the independent Republic of the Orange Free State.

1855   Pretoria is founded.

1857   Diamonds are discovered at Kimberley in Griqualand West, an independent area between the Cape Colony and the Orange Free State.

1860   Labourers are imported from India to work in Natal sugar fields.

1868   Britain annexes Basutoland.

1871   Britain annexes Griqualand West. Kimberley has 50 000 inhabitants. The diamond mines are short of black labour. Africans buy guns with wages and go back to their farms.

1875   Formation in Paarl of the Genootskap van Regte Afrikaners, (Society of True Afrikaners). They start a campaign for the recognition of Afrikaans as a written language.

1876   *Die Afrikaanse Patriot*, first Afrikaans newspaper, published in Paarl.

1877   Britain annexes the Transvaal after the Pedi defeat Transvaal troops. British and Boers unite to defeat the Pedi. The British order Zulu King Cetshwayo to disband his army.

1879   Anglo-Zulu War. King Cetshwayo's army defeats British forces at Isandhlwana, but the reinforced British army defeats Zulu at Ulundi. The British gain control of Zululand, which becomes a crown colony in 1887 and is subsequently annexed to Natal.

1881 Transvaal forces win the battle of Majuba Hill against the British and regain their independence.

1883 The leader of the Boer rebellion, Paul Kruger, is elected President of the Transvaal the following year.

1884 Germany takes over South West Africa (now Namibia), offering military protection in exchange for sovereignty. British establish protectorates of Basutoland (Lesotho) and Bechuanaland (Botswana).

1885 After 20 years of war with the British, Xhosa resistance is extinguished. Xhosa land on both sides of the Kei river – Ciskei and Transkei – is annexed by Britain. Law 3 of 1885 in the Transvaal renders Asiatic registration compulsory.

1886 Large gold deposits found in the Transvaal. In the gold rush, Transvalers are outnumbered by prospectors, mostly British immigrants.

1887 Zululand is proclaimed British territory. King Dinizulu is deported to St Helena.

1890 Cecil Rhodes elected Prime Minister of Cape Colony and British South Africa Company army invades Mashonaland, which becomes Rhodesia (Zambia and Zimbabwe).

1891 Indian Immigration Law in the Natal Colony. The new law rules on all aspects of the new Indian segment of the population: access to hospitals, inheritance, debts, repatriation, marriages (polygamous marriages are now prohibited).

1893 Lawyer M.K. Gandhi arrives in South Africa and established the Natal Indian Congress to resist discrimination against Indians. The 3 pound tax comes into effect in the Transvaal. Any freed indentured labourer wanting to emigrate to the Transvaal has to pay the annual tax.

1896 Friction between Kruger and British miners. Rhodes resigns over the Jameson Raid, an attempt to engineer a miners' uprising. Pass laws introduced to control movement of black miners.

1897 Sir Alfred Milner is appointed governor of the Cape.

1898 Relations between Boers and British deteriorate as Kruger denies the franchise to miners. British troopships sail south. Kruger declares war. British burn Boer farms, herd women and children into concentration camps where 26 000 die.

1902 The Transvaal and Orange Free State annexed. British money flows into the former Boer colonies for economic reconstruction. British negotiate with Anglo-Boer War leaders Smuts and Botha to unite colonies.

1904 60 000 Chinese imported to work in goldmines, then repatriated.

1905 Abdullah Abdurahman becomes President of the African Political Organisation (APO) founded in 1902.

1907 Acts 2 and 15 passed in Transvaal. To reduce Indian immigration flux, any Indian is subject to an education test and to compulsory registration of finger prints.

1908 Gandhi leads Indian Passive Resistance to pass laws for Indians and other discriminatory legislation in the Transvaal. The Precious and Base Metal Act or Gold Law bars all non-whites from access to mining property and prospecting. The Township Act in the Transvaal restricts Asiatics to certain township streets. All Asiatic shops have to be grouped in one section of the township known as the 'Bazaar'.

1910 Act of Union. The four colonies are united as a self-governing colony within the British Commonwealth. The franchise is restricted to White people, except in the Cape, where existing property and educational qualifications exclude all but a few non-whites.

1911 The first election returns an alliance of pro-British Boers led by Louis Botha, Prime Minister. Jan Smuts becomes Botha's deputy. Labour legislation prohibits strikes by African contract labour and reserves certain categories of work for Whites.

1912 Formation of South African Native National Congress (ANC).

1913 Native Land Act restricts African land ownership to reserves, only 7.3% of the land. The legislation hopes to encourage Africans to work in the mines, short of labour. The Immigrants Regulation Act instates a compulsory European language test for all immigrants and aims at curbing Indian immigration in particular.

1914 Hertzog splits with Botha and forms the National Party. The Government offers to support Britain in WW1. Afrikaner nationalist forces revolt but are suppressed. At Britain's request, South African troops occupy German South West Africa. Indian Relief Act, Gandhi's victory over Smuts: the 3 pound tax is repealed, Indian priests can act as marriage officers, Indian wives can be brought over from India. Gandhi goes back to India.

1918 The Broederbond – a secret group of influential Afrikaners – is formed to promote cultural and economic welfare of Afrikaners. First major African strike of sanitation workers in Johannesburg.

1919 A black union, the Industrial and Commercial Union, is founded. Many strikes, especially by miners. The administration of South West Africa is transferred to South Africa under a League of Nations mandate. Louis Botha dies and is succeeded by Smuts.

1921 Communist Party of South Africa is founded, calls for a campaign against the pass laws.

1922 Army crushes strike by White miners wanting job reservation: 200 killed, 18 sentenced to death, four hung. Hertzog supports miners.

1923 Hertzog, champion of poor whites, workers and Afrikaner nationalism, combines with the South African Labour Party to defeat Smuts in Parliament. In 1924, Hertzog becomes Prime Minister. Natives (Urban Areas) Act restricts the rights of Africans to enter towns.

1925 Afrikaans replaces Dutch as the second official language.

1927 ANC President Archie Gumede visits Moscow. Sexual relations between Black and White are made illegal. Native Administration Act makes the Governor-General supreme over all Africans. The Cape Town Agreement is signed between India and the Union. Both governments recognise the right of the Union to try and maintain 'European values'. Union government agrees not to apply the Areas Reservation and Immigration and Registration Bill on Indians.

1929 Easy win for Hertzog during elections. Communists from the African League of Rights run for two seats in Parliament and are defeated.

1930   Native Service Contract Act increases farmers' control of workforce and in-cludes a 'whipping clause'. ANC launches a pass-burning campaign in Durban, which is ruthlessly suppressed.

1932   Feetham Commission allows for the amendment of the Transvaal Asiatic Land Tenure Act, making it possible for Indians to own property in certain areas, out of reach because of the Gold Law. The Feetham report also makes it com-pulsory for any Indian commercial license to be ratified by the Ministry.

1933   Economic problems force Hertzog's National Party to combine with Smuts' South Africa Party to form the United Party. Right-winger Dr D.F. Malan and other separatists leave National Party to form the Herstigte Nationale Party (HNP), which becomes the new National Party.

1936   Native Trust and Land Act transfers black people from Cape voters' roll to a separate list which can elect three White representatives. The Act also increases land allocated to native reserves to 13%. Hertzog hopes this will attract African support for the Act.

1938   United Party wins 111 seats against the Purified National Party's 27 in a gen-eral election. Re-enactment of Great Trek and centenary celebrations for the Battle of Blood River mark the revival of an Afrikaner culture. First stone laid for Voortrekker Monument.

1939   Hertzog and Smuts split over war with Germany. Smuts narrowly wins par-liamentary vote in favour of war. Hertzog resigns and is succeeded by Smuts. Extreme Afrikaner nationalists form the Ossewabrandwag and support Nazi policies. Members include future Prime Minister John Vorster. Hertzog dies.

1940   Presided over by the Mayor of Durban, the Lawrence Committee consisted of six Municipal Council Europeans and six Indians. Their task is to review property purchasing requests from Indians. The Broome Commission inves-tigates the reality and the extent of Indian penetration into European areas in Natal and the Transvaal. Their report shows that this infiltration is much less than thought or perceived: 512 cases in Natal, 339 in the Transvaal and 328 in other areas. The Broome Commission concludes that Indians do not wish to live among Europeans and that their purchasing properties in European areas stems from financial investment concerns.

1941   African Mineworkers' Union is founded.

1942   In the general election, Malan's National party wins 43 seats to Smuts' 49. ANC Women's League is formed. First boycott of buses succeeds in reversing an increase in fares. The Restriction of Trading and Occupation of Land Act or Pegging Act is promulgated. Severe restrictions are put to Indians' rights.

1943   ANC Youth League is formed. Leading figures include Robert Sobukwe, Nel-son Mandela, Walter Sisulu and Oliver Tambo.

1946   India wins a United Nations vote censuring South Africa for discrimination against Indians in Natal.

1948   Accusing Smuts of being soft on race, warning of a black threat, the National Party defeats the United Party. Malan becomes Prime Minister.

1949 Prohibition of Mixed Marriages Act bans marriage between Whites and non-Whites and nullifies mixed marriages by South Africans abroad. On 16 December, Malan inaugurates the Voortrekker Monument in Pretoria.

1950 Immorality Act extended to criminalise sexual relations between Whites and Cape Coloureds. Population Registration Act classifies adult population as: White, Coloured and Native. Coloured subgroups include Cape Malay, Indian, Chinese. Group Areas Act permits segregating the country by assigning separate areas to different groups. Police shoot 18 dead during a May Day general strike against discriminatory laws. Suppression of Communism Act enables Government to define as Communist, and ban, practically any person or organisation hostile to government policy. The South African Communist Party dissolves and many members join the ANC.

1951 Government legislation introduced to remove Cape Coloureds from voters' roll. Bantu Authorities Act establishes tribal and territorial authorities, first step in policy of retribalising the African population under government-appointed chiefs.

1952 Native Laws Amendment Act extends influx control to all urban areas and to black women. On Freedom Day, June 26, ANC and South African Indian Congress launch a defiance campaign against Apartheid laws. Repressive legislation increases protest, transforms the ANC into a mass organisation; thousands arrested, several killed. Chief Albert Luthuli is elected national president, Nelson Mandela, deputy president.

1953 Public Safety Act empowers the Governor-General to declare a state of emergency and rule by decree. Criminal Law Amendment Act makes passive resistance illegal. Separate Amenities Act segregates public amenities and transportation. Bantu Education Act sets out a compulsory inferior curriculum for black education. Native Labour Act makes strikes by black workers illegal.

1954 Native Resettlement Act provides for forced removal of black residents from Sophiatown, Johannesburg. This takes five years. Malan retires, aged 80, and is replaced by J.C. Strydom.

1955 South African Congress of Trade Unions, first non-racial trade union, is formed. 3 000 multi-racial Congress Alliance delegates meet at Kliptown and draw up the Freedom Charter.

1956 South Africa Amendment Act removes 45 000 Coloured voters from electoral roll. Industrial Coalition Act reserves certain skilled jobs for Whites and bans mixed trade unions. 156 Congress leaders charged with high treason: the Treason Trial.

1957 The Union Jack is removed as the dual official flag of South Africa. Ghana is the first African colony to become independent.

1958 In first all-White election, the National party wins 103 of 163 seats. Prime Minister Strydom dies and Hendrik Verwoerd replaces him. Nearly 2 000 women are arrested in major demonstrations against the extension of passbook regulations to black women.

1959 Verwoerd launches the black independent homelands project. The extension of the University Education Bill excludes all non-whites students from White universities and establishes separate universities for Blacks, Indians, and Coloureds. Robert Sobukwe and 300 members split from ANC and form the Pan-Africanist Congress (PAC), rejecting ANC policy of alliances with liberal White and Indian organisations. Albert Luthuli banned and banished. Progressive Party formed by 12 liberal United Party MPs. 1 000 black leaders meet in Durban to plan a passive resistance campaign. Natal rural women rise up against Apartheid laws.

1960 Harold MacMillan makes 'Winds of Change' speech to South African parliament. Police fire on a PAC-inspired anti-pass demonstration in Sharpeville, kill 69, wound 178. UN Security Council calls on South Africa to abandon Apartheid. Government declares a state of emergency and bans the ANC and PAC. Sobukwe is jailed. In a referendum, 52% of the White electorate votes 'Yes' to South Africa becoming a republic.

1961 Commonwealth Conference criticises South Africa and Verwoerd announces that South Africa will not apply to rejoin as a republic. UN General Assembly proclaims South West Africa's right to independence. South Africa is proclaimed a republic and 10 000 are detained to prevent disturbances. Albert Luthuli receives Nobel Peace Prize, launch of Umkhonto weSizwe (Spear of the Nation), military wing of the ANC. Radical Whites form the Afrikaner Resistance Movement and commit sabotage. Treason Trial ends after four years: all are found guilty. Indians are recognised as a permanent population of South Africa.

1962 Mandela addresses Pan-African conference in Addis-Ababa: sentenced to five years in prison for inciting a strike and travelling abroad. Sabotage Act provides death penalty for anyone convicted of sabotage. No right to appeal.

1963 General Law Amendment Act allows police to arrest and detain suspects for 90 days without trial and allows for indefinite detention of Sobukwe on Robben Island. Police capture ANC's underground leadership at Rivonia and eight, including Nelson Mandela, Govan Mbeki, Sisulu and Ahmed Kathrada are charged with sabotage and planning the violent overthrow of the state. UN calls for voluntary embargo on arms sales to South Africa. Transkei Self-Government Bill makes Transkei semi-autonomous.

1964 Chief Luthuli is banned for five more years. The 'Rivonia Eight' are sentenced to life. UN recommends complete economic sanctions as only feasible way to end Apartheid. South Africa is excluded from Tokyo Olympics after refusing to allow mixed-race teams.

1965 Bantu Laws Amendment Act strips seven million black people of rights inside South Africa, making them temporary dwellers, and establishes proscribed areas where black workers only are allowed. Rhodesia declares UDI, but South Africa refuses to embargo it.

1966 National Party wins 126 of 166 seats in general election. Progressive Party retains one MP, Helen Suzman. Verwoerd is stabbed to death. John Vorster suc-

ceeds him. Bechuanaland becomes independent Botswana and Basutoland becomes independent Lesotho. UN terminates South Africa's mandate over South
West Africa, placing it under UN responsibility, but Vorster ignores UN. Armed
struggle begins in Rhodesia and South West Africa.

1967   Defence Amendment Act makes military service compulsory for White males.
Terrorism Act widely defines terrorism as anything likely to threaten law and
order, confers unlimited powers of arrest, indefinite detention, trials without
jury, transfers burden of proof to the accused and equates terrorism with treason, therefore incurring death penalty. Luthuli dies. Oliver Tambo becomes
ANC president.

1968   Prohibition of Political Interference Bill prohibits one racial group from involve-
ment in political affairs of another. The Liberal Party disbands. The Progressive
Party becomes open to Whites only. Separate Representation of Voters Amendment Act transfers indirect representation of Coloured voters to a Representative Council. South African Students Organisation (SASO) is formed by black
students who embrace the ideas of the Black Consciousness Movement. Steve
Biko is the first president. Swaziland becomes independent.

1969   Bureau of State Security is established with wide investigative powers. Newspapers prohibited from reporting its activities. Sobukwe freed but restricted
to Kimberley. He dies in 1978. Winnie Mandela and 21 others are detained under Terrorism Act. She is held for 491 days. Vorster calls early election because
of a split with the right wing of his party. Albert Hertzog forms Herstigte National
Party and wins no seats.

1970   Bantu Homelands Citizenship Act makes all blacks citizens of a tribal homeland, irrespective of whether they have ever lived there. 19 out of 20 activists
are acquitted, including Winnie Mandela, who is banned for five years and
placed under house arrest.

1972   Bophuthatswana, Ciskei and Lebowa become self-governing homelands. Zululand becomes KwaZulu, a semi-autonomous homeland with Mangosuthu
Buthelezi as Chief Minister. The Black People's Convention is formed as a forum for black consciousness groups.

1973   Illegal strikes in Durban bring city to standstill as black workers demand higher
wages. Bantu Labour Relations Regulation Bill allows limited right to strike,
not in all industries, after strikes in Natal and Johannesburg. Rising student
agitation, SASO leaders banned. Homeland Chief Ministers dispute government's plans to allocate 14% of the country to homelands and leave them frag-
mented. Venda and Gazankulu become self-governing.

1974   Fresh strikes in Durban and the mines. Labour shortage forces South Africa
to depend upon workers from neighbouring countries. Job reservation relaxed,
black nurses allowed in White hospitals, black people allowed to work as motor
mechanics, Coloureds permitted to take office jobs and black recruits join
the army. Riotous Assemblies Act bans any gathering which might threaten law
and order. Any journalist quoting a banned person can be jailed. Eight out of
nine homelands reject plans for independence, demand land consolidation

and economic infrastructure. Transkei wants full independence. South African Defence Force (SADF) takes over from police in Namibia. South Africa expelled from UN General Assembly.

1975 Government reinstates right of black residents to buy leases on homes in segregated townships, forbidden in 1967. Chief Buthelezi re-activates Inkatha, a Zulu cultural movement, and becomes its president. Mozambique becomes independent. Portugal transfers sovereignty to the Angolan people.

1976 TV begins in South Africa, previously resisted as morally corrupting. Soweto Students' Representative Council calls for demonstration for June 16 to protest against use of Afrikaans language in black schools. Police open fire, months of protest follow. Trial of SASO leaders ends with nine found guilty. Transkei declared independent but only recognised by South Africa.

1977 Steve Biko is detained under Terrorism Act and dies of brain injuries. 18 anti-Apartheid and black consciousness organisations and two newspapers are banned.

1978 SADF forces in Angola kill hundreds of Namibian refugees. Guerilla war with South West African People's Organisation (SWAPO) intensifies. Azanian People's Organisation (AZAPO) founded. Azania is the name given to South Africa by black nationalist groups. P.W. Botha becomes Prime Minister.

1979 Wiehahn Commission recommends changes in labour laws, including recognition of black trade unions. Government lifts most restrictions on black employment. A peace treaty ends guerilla war in Rhodesia (Zimbabwe).

1980 Robert Mugabe's Patriotic Front wins Zimbabwe election with 57 of 80 seats. Umkhonto weSizwe attacks the Sasol oil complex.

1981 SADF commandos raid Maputo to attack the ANC. Botha's new President's Council, comprising government-appointed White, Coloured and Indian politicians, meets to advise on constitutional reforms. Botha rejects its advice. Ciskei is declared independent.

1982 National Party splits over Botha's proposal for limited power sharing for Coloured and Indian population groups. A.P. Treurnicht is expelled for refusing to support the reforms and founds the Conservative Party (CP). Gold plummets from $800 to $300 an ounce. Buthelezi rejects plan to make KwaZulu independent and proposes a single administration for Natal with multi-racial power sharing. National Forum created by black consciousness to resist constitutional reforms.

1983 ANC raids intensify. United Democratic Front (UDF) is formed to co-ordinate resistance to the new power sharing constitution that excludes black people. UDF calls for boycott by Coloureds and Indians of coming elections.

1984 Tricameral Parliament opens and P.W. Botha is elected president unopposed. UDF calls for boycott of elections for local councils in the townships. SADF moves into townships. Bishop Desmond Tutu is awarded the Nobel Peace Prize.

1985 Nelson Mandela rejects an offer to release him from prison in return for his renunciation of the armed struggle. At Langa, on the 25th anniversary of

Sharpeville, police fire upon a funeral procession for black activist, killing 21. Townships erupt and Tambo calls on them to 'make the townships ungovernable'. 35 000 troops are deployed. More than 1 000 killed. Indefinite state of emergency is declared. Congress of South African Trade Unions (COSATU) is launched, representing 36 unions, including mineworkers. The rand plunges and South Africa freezes debt repayment. South African business leaders defy Botha and travel to Zambia to talk to the ANC. Botha's 'Crossing the Rubicon' reform speech offers nothing new, only defiance. Immorality Act abolished.

1986   Commonwealth Eminent Persons Group (EPG) visits South Africa to seek a peaceful resolution but SADF attacks the capitals of Botswana, Zambia and Zimbabwe, supposedly aiming at the ANC, but intending to sabotage the visit. EPG report calls for sanctions, opposed by Margaret Thatcher. Government-sponsored vigilantes burn large sections of the Cape squatter camps. Nation-wide state of emergency declared. More than 8 000, mainly UDF members, are detained. US Senate overrides President Reagan's veto and imposes strong sanctions on trade and investment. More than 500 foreign companies withdraw from South Africa. President Samora Machel of Mozambique is killed in a plane crash inside South African airspace. Prohibition of Political Interference Act and Prohibition of Mixed Marriages Act abolished. Pass laws abolished.

1987   White railway workers' strike turns violent. Mineworkers' Union strikes. In general elections, CP emerges as main opposition, with more than a quarter of the vote. 60 Afrikaner dissidents, led by former opposition leader Frederick van Zyl Slabbert, meet the ANC for talks in Senegal. Former ANC chairman Govan Mbeki is released, but placed under restrictions. Fighting between Inkatha and UDF supporters in Natal intensifies.

1988   18 anti-Apartheid organisations are banned. COSATU banned from political activities. Church leaders take over as spokesmen for the resistance movement. 143 conscripts refuse to serve the SADF. End Conscription Campaign (ECC) placed under restrictions. Delmas Trial ends: four UDF leaders convicted of treason, seven of terrorist offences and eight acquitted. Botha reprieves the 'Sharpeville Six' sentenced to death for being in a crowd that killed a black councillor. Mandela is moved to a house in Victor Verster Prison. SADF and Cuban forces agree to withdraw from Angola and Namibia.

1989   Botha is sick and resigns as National Party leader and later as President. F.W. de Klerk succeeds him. Botha meets Mandela. Mass Democratic Movement begins defiance campaign against segregation. National Party's majority is reduced in elections. De Klerk claims a mandate for his reforms and begins talks with black leaders, including Mandela. Transkei leader Bantu Holomisa appears with ANC leaders and denounces Transkei's independence. Sisulu and remaining Rivonia Trial prisoners are released. SWAPO wins Namibia elections with less than two-thirds majority.

1990   De Klerk unbans political organisations including ANC, South African Communist Party (SACP) and PAC, announces release of Mandela, end of news censorship and suspension of executions. Mandela released nine days later.

Separate Amenities Act repealed, state of emergency lifted. Talks in Cape Town between ANC and government. Violence between ANC and Inkatha worsens. 'Pretoria Minute' is signed in August. ANC agrees to suspension of armed struggle in return for political prisoners, end of political trials and executions. Oliver Tambo returns after more than 30 years in exile.

1991   10 300 prisoners released. UDF disbands to concentrate on building ANC as mass political party. Government strikes down the pillars of Apartheid: Population Registration Act, Land and Group Areas Acts. Convention for Democratic South Africa (CODESA) talks. Government and ANC sign declaration of intent towards non-racial, democratic South Africa. Inkatha will not sign, PAC opposes CODESA.

1992   Referendum for Whites to vote on his proposals to abolish Apartheid. 85% turnout, 68% 'yes'.

1993   Successor to CODESA, the Multi-Party Negotiating Forum, convenes with 26 delegations. Riots erupt after SACP leader Chris Hani is assassinated by White extremists on April 10. 4 000 die in township violence. Government relinquishes control over state broadcasting. Mandela calls for an end to remaining sanctions against South Africa. Mandela and De Klerk are jointly awarded the Nobel Peace Prize 'for their work for the peaceful termination of the Apartheid regime, and for laying the foundations for a new democratic South Africa'. ANC and government agree on final terms for new constitution. New interim constitution is approved by parliament.

1994   PAC president Clarence Makwetu announces suspension of armed struggle to contest the election. Talks between ANC and right-wing Freedom Alliance on an Afrikaner homeland break down. The constitution is altered to encourage the White right and Inkatha to register for election. In March, Freedom Alliance Bophuthatswana leader Mangope is overthrown. The right-wing alliance splits as Constand Viljoen announces Freedom Front will participate in election. The first free and democratic elections take place on 27 April 1994. Nelson Mandela is elected President of the Republic of South Africa.

Selected bibliography

Abdul, Karrim, 1990, '"The Indian People" and the National Democratic Movements in South Africa', in *African Communist*, No. 122, pp. 29-41, London.

Adam, H. and Gilliomee, H., 1979, *The Rise and Crisis of Afrikaner Power*, David Philip, Cape Town.

Adam, Heribert (ed.), 1971, *South Africa. Sociological Perspectives*, Oxford University Press, London.

– October 1985, 'Variations of ethnicity. Afrikaner and Black Nationalism in South Africa', in *Journal of Asian and African Studies*, Vol. 20, No. 3-4, pp. 169-180.

Afrique du Sud Ambiguë – Politique Africaine, March 1987, No. 25, Karthala (ed.), Paris.

African Chronicle, The, June 1908-July 1930, edited by P. S. Aiyar, Documentation Centre of the University of Durban-Westville, Durban.

Ahmad, Imtiaz (ed.), 1973, *Caste and Social Stratification among the Muslims*, Manohar Book Services, New Delhi.

– February 1984, 'The Islamic Tradition in India', in *Islam and the Modern Age*, Vol 1, No. 1, pp. 44-62.

Ahmed, Akbar S., 1992, *Postmodernism and Islam*, Routledge, London and New York.

Aiyar, P. S., 1925, *The Indian Problem in South Africa*, African Chronicle Printing Works, Durban.

Alexander, Neville, December 1985, 'An Approach to the National Question in South Africa', in *Azania Worker*, Vol. 2, No. 2.

Amselle, J.-L., 1990, *Logiques Métisses. Anthropologie de l'Identité en Afrique and Ailleurs*, Payot, Paris.

– and M'Bokolo, E. (eds), 1985, *Au Coeur de l'Ethnie. Ethnies, Tribalisme et État en Afrique*, La Découverte/Textes à l'Appui, Paris.

Apffel-Marglin, F., 1985, 'Types of Oppositions in Hindu Culture', in *Journal of Developing Societies*, Vol. 1, pp. 65-84.

Argyle, W. J., 1986, 'Migration of Indian Muslims to East and South Africa', in *Islam et Société en Afrique du Sud, Etudes Réunies par Marc Gaborieau*, Collection Purusartha, Edition de l'Ecole des Hautes Etudes en Sciences Sociales, Paris.

– 1982, 'Muslims in South Africa. Origins, Development and Present Economic Status', in *Journal: Institute of Muslim Minority Affairs*, Vol. 3, No. 2, pp. 222-255.

Arkin, A. J. *et al* (eds), 1989, 'Symposium: Facing the Future', in *The Indian South Africans*, Owen Burgess Publishers, Pinetown.

Magyar, K.P. and Pillay, G.J. (eds), 1989, *The Indian South Africans*, Owen Burgess Publishers, Pinetown.

Austin, D., 1966, *Britain and South Africa*, Oxford University Press, London, New York and Toronto.

Bailey, F.G., 1957, *Caste and the Economic Frontier*, Manchester University Press, Manchester.

Balandier, Georges, 1985 (1974, PUF, Paris), *Anthropo-logiques*, Le Livre de Poche, Paris.

Barbier, Jean-Claude,1991, *L'Afrique du Sud Après l'Apartheid*, Editions Kimé, Paris.

Bekker, Simon, 1993, 'Ethnicity in Focus. The South African Case', in *The Indicator South Africa*, University of Natal, Pietermaritzburg, 1993.

Bell, D., 1975, 'Ethnicity and Social Change', in *Ethnicity, Theory and Experience*, Cambridge, USA.

Benedict, R., 1935, *Patterns of Culture*, Routlege and Sons, London.

Berger, Peter, 1969, *The Social Reality of Religion*, Penguin, Harmondsworth.

Bhana, Surendra, 1991, *Indentured Indian Emigrants to Natal 1860-1902. A Study Based on Ships' Lists*, Promilla & Co. Publishers, New Delhi.

– and Brain, Joy B (eds), 1990, *Setting Down Roots. Indian Migrants in South Africa 1860-1911*, Witwatersrand University Press, Johannesburg.

– and Pachai, Bridglal (eds), 1984, *A Documentary History of Indian South Africans*, David Philip, Cape Town.

Biardeau, Madeleine, 1967, *Le Sacrifice dans l'Inde Ancienne*, PUF, Paris.

Boberg, P.Q.R., 1977, *The Laws of Persons and the Family*, Juta, Cape Town.

Boonzaier, Emile and Sharp, John (eds), 1988, *South African Keywords. The Uses & Abuses of Political Concepts*, David Philip, Cape Town.

Bouglé, Célestin, 1971, *Essays on the Caste System*, Cambridge University Press, Cambridge.

Branford, J., 1980, *Dictionary of South African English*, Oxford University Press, Cape Town.

Brass, P., 1974, *Religion, Language and Politics in North India*, Cambridge University Press, Cambridge.

Brewer, J. D., August 1982, 'Racial Politics and Nationalism: The Case of South Africa', in *Sociology*, Vol. 16, No. 3, pp. 390-405.

Buijs, Gina, September 1992, 'The Influence of Migration on Ethnic Identity. A Historical Analysis of the Disappearance of Caste among Indian South Africans', article delivered at the *Ethnicity, Society and Conflict in Natal* conference, University of Natal-Pietermaritzburg.

Bunting, B., 1969, *The Rise of the South African Reich*, Penguin, Harmondsworth.

Bullier, Antoine Jean, 1982, *Géopolitique de l'Apartheid. Stratégie Ethnique de Pretoria*, PUF, Paris.

Burger, John, 1943, *The Black Man's Burden*, Victor Gollancz, London.

Buss, Andreas, 1985, 'Max Weber's Contributions to Questions of Development in Modern India', in *Journal of Developing Societies, Max Weber in Asian Studies*, Vol. 1, pp. 130-150.

Cachalia, Firoz, 1993, 'Citizenship, Muslim Family Law and a Future South African Constitution: Preliminary Enquiry', in *Tydskrif vir Hedendaagse Romeins-Hollandse Reg/ Journal of Contemporary Roman-Dutch Law*, Vol. 56, No. 3, pp. 392-413.

Calpin, G.H., 1949, *Indians in South Africa*, Shuter and Shooter, Pietermaritzburg.

Carman, John B. and Marglin, Frédérique A., 1985, *Purity and Auspiciousness in Indian Society*, E.J. Brill, Leiden,.

Centenary of Indians, Cavalier Publishers, Durban, 1960.

Chenu, B., 1989, 'L'Apartheid comme Théologie Chrétienne', in *Mondes en Développement*, Vol. 17, No. 65, pp. 239-249.

Chetty, Dhianaraj R., February 1991, '"Sammy" and "Mary" go to Gaol: Indian Women and South African Politics in the 1940s', article delivered at the *Women and Gender in Southern Africa* conference, University of Natal.

– September 1992, 'Identity and "Indianness": Reading and Writing Ethnic Discourses', article delivered at the *Ethnicity, Society and Conflict in Natal* conference, University of Natal-Pietermaritzburg.

– September 1992, '"Indianness", Identity and Interpretation: Stories from the Natal Cane Fields', article delivered at the *Ethnicity, Society and Conflict in Natal* conference, University of Natal-Pietermaritzburg.

Cillié, Piet, Spring 1988, 'Bestek van Apartheid: Wat is (was) Apartheid?', in *Die Suid-Afrikaan*, p. 18.

Clarke, C. *et al*, 1984, *Geography and Ethnic Pluralism*, Allen & Unwin, London.

Clay, Jason W., October 1989, 'Epilogue: The Ethnic Future of Nations', in *Third World Quarterly. Special Issue on 'Ethnicity in World Politics'*, Vol. 11, No. 4, pp. 223-233.

Cloete, Stuart, 1968, *South Africa. The Lands, Its People and Achievements*, Da Gama Publishers, Johannesburg.

Coertze, P.J., 1973, *Inleiding tot die Algemene Volkekunde*, Voortrekker Pers, Johannesburg.

– 1968, 'Akkulturasie', in *Kultuurbeïnvloeding Tussen Blankes en Bantoes in Suid-Afrika*, Pretoria.

Coetzee, H.J., 1982, 'Veranderende Menseverhoudinge in Suid-Afrika', in *Die Suid-Afrikaanse Tydskrif vir Sosiologie*, Vol. 13, No. 1.

Cohen, A. P., 1985, *The Symbolic Construction of Community. The Poetics and Politics of Ethnography*, University of California Press, Berkeley and Los Angeles.

Cohn, B.S., 1971, *India. The Social Anthropology of a Civilization*, Prentice Hall Inc., Englewood Cliffs, New Jersey.

– and Singer, M., 1968, 'Structure and Change in Indian Society', in *Anthropology*, Vol. 47, Wenner Gren Foundation for Anthropological Research, Viking Fund Publications.

Colas, Dominique, 1994, *Sociologie Politique*, Collection Premier Cycle/PUF, Paris.

Connor, W., 1978, 'A Nation is a Nation, is a State, is an Ethnic Group, is a . . .', in *Ethnic and Racial Studies*, Vol. 1, pp. 377-400.

- 1990, 'When is a Nation?', in *Ethnic and Racial Studies*, Vol. 13, No. 1, pp. 92-103.

Martin, Denis-Constant, April 1993, 'The choices of identity', article delivered at the *Ethnicity, Identity and Nationalism in South Africa. Comparative Perspectives* conference, University of Rhodes, Grahamstown.

Coopan, S. and Lazarus, A. D., 1956, 'The Indian as an Integral Part of South African Society', article delivered at the South African Institute for Race relations Symposium on *The Indian as a South African*, Johannesburg.

Coquerel, Jean-Paul, June 1989, 'Noirs et Blancs en Afrique du Sud', in *L'Histoire*, 123, pp. 36-41.

Cox, Oliver C., 1948, *Caste, Class and Race in Social Dynamics*, Doubleday & Co., New York.

Cronjé, G., 1946, *Afrika Sonder die Asiaat. Die Blywende Oplossing van Suid-Afrika se Asiaatvraagstuk*, Publicité Handelsreklamediens, Johannesburg.

- 1946, *'n Tuiste vir die Nageslag*, Publicité Handelsreklamediens, Johannesburg.

Dangor, Suleman, 1992, 'The Muslims of South Africa: Problems and Concerns of a Minority Community', in *Journal: Institute of Muslim Minority Affairs*, Vol. 13, No. 2, pp. 375-381.

Darbon, Dominique, November 1992, 'The Purple Shall Govern!: Réflexions Critiques de l'Identité Ethnique à Travers Quelques-uns de ses Significations et Enjeux Sud-Africains', CEAN Conference, Bordeaux.

Das, Veena, 1977, *Structure and Cognition. Aspects of Hindu Caste and Ritual*, Oxford University Press, Delhi.

Dasgupta, Satadal, 1986, *Caste, Kinship and Community*, Madras University Press, Madras.

Davey, A.G., 1981, 'Prejudice and Group Conflict', in *Patterns of Prejudice*, Vol. 15, No. 1, pp. 3-14.

Davie, Ferguson, January 1946, 'The Indian Situation', in *South African Institute of Race Relations*.

Degenaar, Johan, n.d. 'Nations and Nationalism. The Myth of a South African Nation', in *Occasional Papers*, No. 40.

Dekker, G., 1947, *Afrikaanse Litteratuurgeskiedenis*, Nasionale Pers, Cape Town and Bloemfontein.

Deleury, Guy, 1979, *Le Modèle Indou: Essai sur les Structures de la Civilisation de l'Inde d'Hier et d'Aujourd'hui*, Hachette, Paris.

- August 1992 ,'Des Identités en Politique (I)', in *Revue Française de Science Politique*, Presses de la Fondation Nationale des Sciences Politiques, Paris.

- October 1992, 'Des Identités en Politique (II)', in *Revue Française de Science Politique*, Presses de la Fondation Nationale des Sciences Politiques, Paris.

– January 1956 'Die Asiaat en Afrika', in *SABRA Report. Racial Affairs,* Vol. 12, No. 6.

Douglas, Mary, 1966, *Purity and Danger,* Routledge & Kegan Paul, London.

Du Toit, B. M., December 1970, 'Afrikaner Nationalists and Apartheid', in *Journal of Modern African Studies,* Vol. 8, No. 4, pp. 531-551.

– 1978, *Ethnicity in Modern Africa,* Boulder, Colorado.

Dubow, S., March 1986, 'Race, Civilization and Culture: The Elaboration of Segregationist Discourse in the Inter-War Years', in *African Studies Institute,* University of Witwatersrand, Johannesburg.

Dugard, J., 1979, 'Independent Homelands, Failure of a Fiction', in *South African Institute for Race Relations,* Johannesburg.

Dumont, Louis, 1966, *Homo Hierarchicus. Le Système des Castes et ses Implications,* Bibliothèque des Sciences Humaines, Gallimard, Paris.

– 1970, *Religion, Politics and History in India. Collected Papers in Indian Sociology,* Ecole Pratique des Hautes Etudes, Sorbonne et Mouton & Co., The Hague and Paris.

– 1975, *Dravidien et Kariera. L'Alliance de Mariage Dans l'Inde du Sud et en Australie,* Textes de Sciences Cociales, 14, Editions de l'Ecole des Hautes Etudes de Sciences Sociales et Mouton & Co., The Hague and Paris.

– 1992, *Une Sous-Caste de l'Inde du Sud. Organisation Sociale et Religion des Pramalai Kallar,* Editions de l'Ecole des Hautes Etudes de Sciences Sociales, Paris.

Dhupelia-Mesthrie, Uma, 2000, *From Cane Fields to Freedom. A Chronicle of Indian South African Life,* Kwela Books, Cape Town.

Durand, J.P., 1992, 'Radcliffe-Brown, Structure et Fonction dans la Société Primitive', in Van Meeter, K.M. (ed.), *La Sociologie, Textes Essentiels,* Larousse, Paris, p. 396.

Du Pre, Roy.H., 1990, *The Making of Racial Conflict in South Africa. A Historical Perspective, History for the Layman Series,* No. 1, Johannesburg.

Edwards, John, 1985, *Language, Society and Identity,* Basil Blackwell, Oxford.

Encyclopédie Universalis, 1985, Paris.

Esack, Farid, April 1988, 'Three Islamic Strands in the South African Struggle for Justice', in *Third World Quarterly,* Vol. 10, No. 2, pp. 473-498.

February, Vernon, 1991, *The Afrikaners of South Africa,* Kegan Paul, London and New York.

Ferguson-Davie, C.J., 1977, *The Early History of Indians in Natal,* South African Institute of Race Relations, Johannesburg.

Filatova, Irina, July 1991, 'One, Two, or Many? Aspects of the South African Debate on the Concept of Nation', unpublished. Article included in the *Southern Africa Research Program,* University of Durban-Westville.

Finkielkraut, A., 1987, *La Défaite de la Pensée*, Gallimard, Paris.

Freund, Bill, 'Indian Women and the Changing Character of the Working Class Indian Household in Natal 1860-1990', in *Journal of Southern African Studies*, Vol. 17, No.3, Johannesburg.

Gaboriau, Marc, January-March 1994, 'Le Culte des Saints Musulmans en Tant que Rituel: Controverses Juridiques', in *Archives de Sciences Sociales des Religions*, No. 85, Paris, pp. 85-98.

Gandhi, M.K., 1928, *Satyagraha in South Africa*, S. Ganeson, Madras.

Gangal, S.C., April-June 1992, 'Gandhi in South Africa', in *International Studies*, Vol. 9, No. 2, New Delhi, pp. 187-197.

Gans, H., 1979, 'Symbolic Ethnicity', in *Ethnic and Racial Studies*, Vol. 2, No. 1, pp. 1-20.

Giliomee, H. and Schlemmer, L., 1989, *From Apartheid to Nation-Building*, Oxford University Press, Cape Town.

Ginwala, Frene N., October 1974, *Class, Consciousness and Control. Indian South Africans 1860-1946*, unpublished PhD, Philosophy, Oxford University.

– 1977 , 'Indian South Africans', in *Minority Rights Group, MRG Report*, No. 34, London.

Glock, C.Y. and Stark, R., 1965, *Religion and Society in Tension*, Rand McNally, Chicago.

Goldin, I., 1987, 'The Reconstitution of Coloured Identity in the Western Cape', in Marks, S. and Trapido, S. (eds), *The Politics of Race, Class and Nationalism in Twentieth Century South Africa*, Longman Group, United Kingdom, pp. 156-182.

Gopal, Sarvepalli, 1965, *British Policy in India 1858-1905*, Cambridge University Press, Cambridge.

Gould, H.A., 1987, *The Hindu Caste System. The Sacralization of a Social Order*, Chanakya Publications, New Dehli.

Guelke, A., October 1992, 'Ethnic Rights and Majority Rules: The Case of South Africa', in *International Political Science Review*, Vol. 13, No. 4, pp. 415-432.

Gupta, Dhruba, September 1992, 'Indians in Future South Africa', article delivered at *Ethnicity, Society and Conflict in Natal*, conference, University of Natal-Pietermaritzburg.

Gupta, Dipankar, 1991, *Social Stratification*, Oxford University Press, Delhi.

Gupta, Raghuraj, January 1984, 'Changing Role and Status of the Muslim Minority in India: A Point of View', in *Journal: Institute of Muslim Minority Affairs*, Vol. 5.

Hall, Edward, 1969, *The Hidden Dimension. Man's Use of Space in Public and Private*, The Bodley Head, Great Britain.

Hancock, W.K., 1968, *Smuts. The Fields of Force 1919-1950*, Cambridge University Press.

Hasan, Mushirul, November 1988, 'In Search of Integration and Identity. Indian Muslims since Independence', in *Islam and the Modern Age*, Vol. 19, No. 4, pp. 217-250.

Hick, John and Hempel, Lamont C., (eds), 1989, *Gandhi's Significance for Today*, The Macmillan Press, London.

Hirson, Baruch, 1990, 'The struggle for a Post-Apartheid Society in South Africa', in *Third World Quarterly*, Vol. 12, No. 2, pp. 159-164.

Hobsbawm, Eric and Ranger, Terence (eds), 1992 (1983), *The Invention of Tradition*, Canto Edition, Cambridge.

Hofmeyr, Jan Hendrik, 1931, *South Africa*, E. Benn, London.

Horrell, Muriel, June 1969, 'The Distribution of the Indian People in the Transvaal', article delivered at the *Social Work among Indians in the Transvaal* conference, the Johannesburg Indian Social Welfare Association, Johannesburg.

Houtart, François, 1981, *Religion et Castes. l'Inde du Sud*, Centre de Recherches Socio-Religieuses, Louvain, France.

Husain, Asad, Summer 1985, 'Muslim Minorities with Special Reference to Muslims in India', in *Journal of South Asian and the Middle Eastern Studies*, Vol. 8, No. 4, pp. 85-114.

Hussain, Monirul, October 1988, 'Caste Among Non-Hindu Indians. An Eploratory Study of Assamese Muslims', in *The Eastern Anthropologist*, Vol. 41, No. 4, pp. 273-285.

Huteau, J., February 1968, 'La Communauté Indienne en République Sud-Africaine', in *Revue Française d'Etudes Politiques Africaines*, pp. 72-84.

Hutton, J., 1963 (1946), *Caste in India. Its Nature, Function and Origin*, 4th Edition, Oxford University Press.

– 1946, *Caste in India. Beyond Organic Solidarity*, Benjamin Cummings, Menlo Park, CA.

Indian People of South Africa, The, Natal Region/South African Institute of Race Relations, Information Sheet No. 1/1967, 2 January 1967.

Ireland, R.R., January 1970, 'Some Effects of Apartheid on Indian Education in the Republic of South Africa', in *The Indian Journal of Economics*, Vol. 50, No. 198, pp. 267-275.

Jelen, Ted G., 1991, *The Political Mobilization of Religious Beliefs*, Praeger Publishers, New York.

Joosub, H.E., 1958, *Bitterness towards the Indians*, The Pretoria Indian Commercial Association, Anchor Printing Co., Johannesburg.

Joshi, P.S., 1973 (1942), *The Tyranny of Colour. A Study of the Indian Problem in South Africa*, Kennikat Press, Port Washington, New York.

Joyce, Peter (comp.), 1990, *The Rise and Fall of Apartheid. The Chronicle of a Divided Society as Told Through South Africa's Newspapers*, Struik, Cape Town.

Khare, R.S., 1984, *The Untouchable as Himself. Ideology, Identity and Pragmatism among the Lucknow ChaMarch*, Cambridge University Press, Cambridge.

– 1985, *Culture and Democracy. Anthropological Reflections on Modern India*, University Press of America, Lanham, New York and London.

– and Rao, M.S. (eds), 1986, *Food, Society and Culture. Aspects in South Asian Food Systems*, Carolina Academic Press, Durham, North Carolina.

Kolenda, Pauline, 1983, *Caste, Culture and Hierarchy. Essays on the Culture of India*, Vedprakash Vatuk, Folklore Institute, New Delhi.

Krishna, Gopal, December 1972, 'Piety and Politics in Indian Islam', in *Contributions to Indian Sociology*, New Series, No. 6, London.

Kuper, H., July 1956, 'Indian Elites in Natal, South Africa', article delivered at the *Social Science* conference, Durban.

– 1960, *Indian People in Natal*, University of Natal Press, Pietermaritzburg.

Kuper, Leo, 1957, *Passive Resistance in South Africa*, Yale University Press, New Haven.

Kuppusami, C., 1983, *Religions, Customs and Practices of South African Indians*, Sunray Publishers, Durban.

Lal, Barbara, 1983, 'Perrspectives on Ethnicity. Old Urine in New Bottles', in *Ethnic and Racial Studies*, Vol. 6, pp. 154-173.

Lazarus, A.D., January 1958, 'Some Observations on the Group Areas Act', in *Institute Council Meetings 1958*, South African Institute for Race Relations, Cape Town.

– January 1961, 'Indians and Local Government', in *Institute Council Meetings 1961*, South African Institute for Race Relations, Cape Town.

Leach, Edmund Ronald, 1969, *Aspects of Caste in South India, Ceylon and North West Pakistan*, Cambridge University Press, Cambridge.

Lewis, G., 1987, *Between the Wire and the Wall. A History of South African 'Coloured' Politics*, Citadel Press, Landsdowne, Cape Town.

Lötter, J.M. and Schutte, C.D., 1980, 'Enkele Politieke Oriëntasies van Indiër-Suid-Afrikaners', in *RGN. Navorsingbevinding SW 191*, Pretoria.

Lugan, Bernard, 1986, *Histoire de l'Afrique du Sud de l'Antiquité a nos Jours*, Collection Vérités et Légendes, Perrin, Paris.

Mafeje, A., 1971, 'The Ideology of Tribalism', in *Journal of Modern African Studies*.

Maharaj, Brij, September 1992, 'Ethnicity, Class and Conflict. The Indian Question in Natal', article delivered at the *Ethnicity, Society and Conflict in Natal* conference, University of Natal-Pietermaritzburg.

Mantzaris, E.A., 1988, 'Religion as a Factor Affecting the Attitudes of South African Indians towards Family Solidarity and Older Persons', in *South African Journal of Sociology*, Vol. 19, No. 3, pp. 111-116.

Marais, J.S., 1957 (1939), *The Cape Coloured People 1652-1937*, Wits University Press, Johannesburg.

Maré, Gerhard, 1992, *Brothers Born of Warrior Blood*, Ravan Press, Johannesburg.

– 1993, *Ethnicity and Politics in South Africa*, Zed Books, London.

Maree, W.A., 1962, *Policy Statement on the Position of Indians in South Africa*, The Government Printer, Cape Town.

– 1963-64, *A Representative Indian Council*, The Government Printer, Pretoria.

Marks, S. and Trapido, S. (eds), 1987, *The Politics of Race, Class and Nationalism in Twentieth-Century South Africa*, Longman, London.

Marquard, L., 1952, *The Peoples and Policies of South Africa*, Oxford University Press, London.

Martin, Denis-Constant, (ed.), 1992, *Sortir de l'Apartheid*, Collection Espace International, Editions Complexe, Paris.

– (ed.), 1994, *Cartes d'Identité. Comment dit-on 'Nous' en Politique?*, Presses de la Fondation Nationale des Sciences Politiques, Paris.

Mayer, Adrian, 1973, *Peasants in the Pacific*, University of California Press, Berkeley.

Meer, Fatima, 1969, *Portrait of Indian South Africans*, Avon House, Durban.

– 1987, 'Indians within Apartheid. Indentured Labour and Group Formation in South Africa', in *Studies in Third World Societies*, Vol. 39, Williamsburg, South Africa, pp. 49-68.

Meer, Y.S., 1980, *Documents of Indentured Labour. Natal 1851-1917*, The Institute of Black Research, Durban.

Meillassoux, Claude (ed.), 1988, *Verrouillage Ethnique en Afrique du Sud*, Etude Préparée pour la Division des Droits de l'Homme et de la Paix de l'Unesco, Unesco/OUA, Paris.

– et Messiant, Christine (eds), 1991, *Génie Social et Manipulations Culturelles en Afrique du Sud*, Arcantère Editions, Paris.

Mesthrie, Rajend, Autumn-Winter 1990, 'The Linguistic Reflex of Social Change. Caste and Kinship Terms among People of Indian Descent in Natal, South Africa', in *Anthropological Linguistics*, Vol. 32, Nos 3 & 4.

Mesthrie, Uma Shashikant, 1989, 'Indian National Honour Versus Trader Ideology. Three Unsuccessful Attempts at Passive Resistance in the Transvaal 1932, 1939 & 1941', in *South African Historical Journal*, Vol. 21, pp. 39-54.

Misra, S. C., 1964, *Muslim Communities in Gujarat. Preliminary Studies in their History and Social Organisation*, Asia Publishing House, London.

Moodie, T. Dunbar, 1974, *The Rise of Afrikanerdom*, University of California Press, Berkeley and London.

Moodley, K., 1989, 'Cultural Politics', in *The Indian South Africans*, Pinetown, Natal.

Müller, A.L., June 1969, 'The Socio-Economics of the Indian Community', in *Johannesburg Indian Social Welfare Association* conference, Johannesburg.

Naidoo, Jay, 1990, 'Clio and the Mahatma', in *Journal of Southern African Studies*, Vol. 16, No. 4, pp. 741-750.

Naipaul, V.S., 1978, *A House for Mr Biswas*, Penguin, Harmondsworth.

Naudé, J.A., 1992, 'South Africa. The Role of a Muslim Minority in a Situation of Change', in *Journal: Institute of Muslim Minority Affairs*, Vol. 13, No. 1, London, pp. 17-32.

Nkrumah, Gorkeh Gramal, 1989, 'Islam. A Self-Assertive Political Factor in Contemporary South Africa', in *Journal: Institute of Muslim Minority Affairs*, Vol. 10, No. 2, London, pp. 520-526.

No Sizwe (Neville Alexander), 1979, *One Azania One Nation. The National Question in South Africa*, Zed Publications, London.

Offisiële Jaarboek van die Unie en van Basoetoland, Betsjoeanaland-Protektoraat en Swaziland 1956-1957, Nr. 29, Die Staatsdrukker, Pretoria.

Oosthuizen, G.C., 1979, *Religion, Intergroup Relations and Social Change in South Africa*, Greenwood, New York.

Pachai, B., 1971, *The International Aspects of the South African Indian Question*, C.T. Struik, Cape Town.

– (ed.), 1979, *South Africa's Indians. The Evolution of a Minority*, University Press of America, Washington D.C.

Padayachee, M., January 1984, 'A Comparative Analysis of the Economic Status of Muslim and Non-Muslim Indians in the Durban Municipal Area, in *Journal: Institute of Muslim Minority Affairs*, Vol. 5.

Padayachee, Vishnu and Morrell, Robert, 1991, 'Indian Merchants and Dukanwallahs in the Natal Economy 1875-1914', in *Journal of Southern African Studies*, Vol. 17, 1, pp. 71-102.

– and Vawda, Shahid *et al*, August 1985, *Indian Workers and Trade Unions in Durban 1930-1950*, Institute for Social and Economic Research, University of Durban-Westville.

Pahad, E., 1972,'The Development of Indian Political Movements in South Africa, 1924-1946', unpublished PhD thesis, University of Sussex.

Palmer, M., 1957, 'The History of Indians in Natal', in *Natal Regional Survey*, Vol. 10, Oxford University Press, Cape Town.

Pienaar, E.C., *Die Triomf van Afrikaans*, Cape Town, 1943.

Pienaar, S.W., 1964, *Glo in U Volk. D.F. Malan as Redenaar, 1908-1954*, Tafelberg, Cape Town.

Pillay, B., 1976, *British Indians in the Transvaal. Trade, Politics and Imperial Relations, 1885-1906*, Longman Group, London.

Pillay, Naidoo and Tillayvel, Dangor, 1989, 'Religious Profile', in *The Indian South Africans*, Pinetown, Natal.

Polak, H.S.L., 1909, *The Indians of South Africa. Helots within the Empire and How They are Treated*, G.A. Natesan & Co., Durban.

Poovalingam, Pat, 1979, 'The Indians of South Africa. A Century on the Defensive', in *Optima*, Johannesburg.

Pyrah, G.B., 1955, *Imperial Policy and South Africa 1902-1910*, Clarendon Press.

Radakrishnan, 1991, 'The Hindu View of Life', in Sen, K.M., *Hinduism*, Penguin Books.

Radcliffe-Brown, A.R., (1952), *Structure and Function in Primitive Society*, Cohen and West, London.

Ramamurthi, T.G., July-September 1989, 'Apartheid and Indian Rebels', in *Indian Journal of Ethnic Studies*, Vol. 2, No. 3, pp. 287-300.

Rambiritch, Birbal and Van den Berghe, Pierre L., 1961, 'Caste in a Natal Hindu Community', in *African Studies*, Vol. 20, No. 4, pp. 217-225.

Ramphal, Rita, 1989, 'Social Transition', in *The Indian South Africans*, Pinetown, Natal.

– 1993, 'Changes in the Religious Views and Practices of a Minority Group in South Africa', in *South African Journal of Sociology/Suid-Afrikaanse Tydskrif vir Sosiologie*, Vol. 24, No. 2, pp. 58-61.

Rex, John, 1986, *Race and Ethnicity*, Open University Press, Milton Keynes.

Rich, Paul, July 1983, 'Landscape, Social Darwinism and the Cultural Roots of South African Racial Ideology', in *Patterns of Prejudice*, Vol. 17, No. 3, pp. 9-16.

Riley, Eileen, 1991, 'Major Political Events in South Africa 1948-1990', in Arms, Thomas S., *Facts on File*, Oxford and New York.

Robert (Le), 1984, *Dictionnaire Alphabétique et Analogique de la Langue Française*.

Schapera, Isaac, 1990, 'The Appointment of Radcliffe Brown to the Chair of Social Anthropology at the University of Cape Town', in *African Studies*, Vol. 49, No. 1, pp. 1-13.

Schoombee, G.F. and Mantzaris, E.A., 1985, 'Attitudes of South African Indians Towards Interreligious and Arranged Marriages. A Preliminary Study', in *South African Journal of Sociology*, Vol. 16, No. 2.

Schutte, C.D., 1985, 'Politieke Deelname onder Indiërs en Kleurlinge in Sekere Stedelike Gebiede in Suid-Afrika met Spesiale Verwysing na die Eerste Verkiesings onder die Nuwe Grondwetlike Bedeling', in *Verslag S-125,* Instituut vir Sosiologiese en Demografiese Navorsing, Pretoria.

Sen, K., 1991 (1961, Pelican Books, London), *Hinduism*, Penguin Books, Harmondsworth.

Sharma, K.N., 1975, 'On the word "Varna" ', in *Contributions to Indian Sociology (NS)*, Vol. 9, No. 2, pp. 293-297.

Sharp, J., 1980, 'Volkekunde. Roots and Development in South Africa', in *Journal of Southern African Studies*, Vol. 8, No. 1.

Singer, Milton, 1985, 'Max Weber and the Modernization of India', in *Journal of Developing Societies, Max Weber in Asian Studies*, Vol. 1, pp. 150-168.

Singh, Ratnamala, March 1986, 'Apartheid and Resistance. An Axiological Analysis', paper delivered at the Professors World Peace Academy Conference on *Ideas have Consequences: An Examination of the Concept of Apartheid*, Johannesburg.

– and Vawda, Shahid, 1988, 'What's in a Name? Some Reflections on the Natal Indian Congress', in *Transformation*, Vol. 6, pp. 1-21.

Sinha, Sachidanand, 1982, *Caste System. Myths, Reality, Challenge*, Intellectual Publishing House, New Delhi.

Smith, A.D., 1986, *The Ethnic Origins of Nations*, Basil Blackwell, Oxford.

Sookdeo, Anil, Winter 1988, 'The Transformation of Ethnic Identities. The Case of "Coloured" and Indian Africans', in *The Journal of Ethnic Studies*, Vol. 15, No. 4, pp. 69-83.

South Africa 1974, Official Yearbook of the Republic of South Africa, Government Printer, Pretoria.

South Africa 1976, Official Yearbook of the Republic of South Africa, Government Printer, Pretoria.

South Africa 1987-1988, Thirteenth, Condensed Edition, Official Yearbook of the Republic of South Africa, Government Printer, Pretoria.

South Africa 1991-1992, Official Yearbook of the Republic of South Africa, Seventeenth and First Condensed English Edition, Government Printer, Cape Town.

South Africa Official Yearbook 1994, Directorate of Publications of the South African Communication Service, Pretoria.

Srinivas, M.N., 1962, *Caste in Modern India and Other Essays*, Asia Publishing House, Bombay, Calcutta and New Delhi.

Stern, Henri, 1969, 'Hindouisme et Bouddhisme de Max Weber. Analyse Critique', unpublished PhD, E.P.H.E., Paris.

Steyn, J.C., 1980, *Tuiste in Eie Taal*, Tafelberg, Cape Town.

Strauss, J., September-October 1975, 'Identity and Social Changes in South Africa', in *Patterns of Prejudice*, Vol. 9, No. 5, pp. 1-10.

Swan, Maureen, April 1984, 'The 1913 Natal Indian Strike' in *Journal of Southern African Studies*, Vol. 10, No. 2, pp. 239-258.

– 1985, *Gandhi. The South African Experience*, New History of Southern Africa Series, Ravan Press, Johannesburg.

Swanson, Maynard W., 1983, 'The "Asiatic Menace". Creating Segregation in Durban, 1870-1900', in *International Journal of African Historical Studies*, Vol. 16, No. 3, pp. 401-421.

Taguieff, Pierre-André, 1989, *La Force du Préjuge. Essai sur le Racisme et ses Doubles*, Editions La Découverte, Paris.

Thompson, L.M., *Indian Immigration into Natal 1860-1872*, *Archives Year Book of South African History*, Vol. 2, Government Printer, Cape Town, 1952.

Vail, Leroy (ed.), 1989, *The Creation of Tribalism in Southern Africa*, James Currey, London.

Van Diepen, Maria (ed.), 1988, *The National Question in South Africa*, Zed Press, London.

Van Jaarsveld, F.A., 1958, 'Die Afrikaner se Geskiedbeeld', in *Communications of UNISA*, B 6.

– 1961, *The Awakening of Afrikaner Nationalism 1868-1881*, Human & Rousseau, Cape Town.

Vanhanen, Tatu, 1992, *Politics of Ethnic Nepotism. India as an Example*, Sterling Publishers, New Delhi.

Watson, Graham, 1970, *Passing for White. A Study of Racial Assimilation in a South African School*, Travistock, London.

Weber, Max, 1958, *The Religion of India. The Sociology of Hinduism and Buddhism* (translated by Hans H. Gerth and Don Martingale), The Free Press, Glencoe, Illinois.

– 1964, *The Sociology of Religion* (translated by Ephraïm Fischoff with an Introduction by Talcott Parsons), Beacon Paperback, Boston.

Weeraperuma, Susunaga, 1979, *So You Are Going to Emigrate to England, Mohandas. Letter to a Coloured Emigrant*, Lake House Printers & Publishers, Colombo, Sri Lanka.

Wetherell, Violet, 1946, *The Indian Question in South Africa*, Unie-Volkspers Bpk., Cape Town.

Wieviorka, Michel, 1991, *L'Espace du Racisme*, Editions du Seuil, Paris.

Wilkins, Ivor and Strydom, Hans, 1978, *The Super-Afrikaners. Inside the Afrikaner Broederbond*, Jonathan Ball, Johannesburg.

Wilson, M. and Thompson, L.M. (eds), 1982, *A History of South Africa to 1870*, Croon Helm, London and Camberra.

Zainuddin, S., February 1990, 'Status Groups among Muslims in India', in *Islam and the Modern Age*, Vol. 21, No. 1, pp. 36-52.

Subject index

Name index